Having worked for many years in both conventional and alternative education, Lindsay Clarke is a freelance writer living in Somerset, whose work has been widely translated. His novel *The Chymical Wedding* won the Whitbread Fiction Award in 1989 and more recently *The Water Theatre* was long-listed for the IMPAC Dublin International Literary Award. He is an Associate of the MA Creative Writing Programme at Cardiff University and Creative Consultant to the educational work of the Pushkin Trust in Northern Ireland.

# Green Man Dreaming

Reflections on Imagination, Myth, and Memory

## LINDSAY CLARKE

AWEN
Stroud

First published in 2018 by Awen Publications
12 Belle Vue Close, Stroud GL5 1ND, England
www.awenpublications.co.uk

Cover design: Kirsty Hartsiotis
Editing: Anthony Nanson
Proofreading: Richard Selby

ISBN 978-1-906900-56-4

For more information about Lindsay Clarke visit:
www.lindsayclarkeauthor.com

Dedicated to S.H.

'Who would have thought my shrivel'd heart
Could have recover'd greennesse?'

*George Herbert*

And for my family and friends, living and dead

'In dreams begins responsibility'

*Ascribed to an 'Old Play' by W.B. Yeats*

# Contents

# Introduction

Over the thirty years of my career as a freelance writer I've written many occasional pieces and given a number of talks on a variety of themes, some of them literary, others touching on wider preoccupations, but all of them seeking to make a contribution to what I believe to be a vital evolution in consciousness that is taking place in these difficult transitional times. This book is an edited selection of those essays and talks, along with some newly written pieces designed to serve that same increasingly urgent purpose.

In his essay *The Style of the Mythical*, written shortly after the Second World War, the novelist Hermann Broch said, 'Every true artist, aware that he must form his own universe, is in some ways a rebel, willing to shatter the closed system into which he is born. But he should realise that revolution is not enough, that he must also build anew the essential framework of the world.' Broch's exclusive use of the masculine pronoun reveals the relatively unevolved state of consciousness in his time, but the promethean duty he assigned to the artist remains a matter of pressing need. We are living in an era when much of the old order has begun to feel threadbare and dysfunctional in increasingly destructive ways, and yet a newly creative vision, one adequate to the formidable demands now facing us, has not emerged into clear enough solution to gain general assent. In such times the attempt to revision the framework of the world is a task that falls not just to artists but to all who care for the decent survival of our species and the wider welfare of life on this planet.

In that respect it may be helpful to recall that the word 'world' derives from two Anglo-Saxon roots – 'wer' meaning 'man' and 'eld' meaning 'age', suggesting that a world is best understood as 'an age of man'; which is to say that it is a man-age-ment system that can be expected to hold good only for a time. The framework of a world is always endowed with coherence by a prevailing mythology, and when that myth loses its vitality in the imagination of the people they must begin to imagine otherwise.

A new myth, whether of a life or of a world, has to be imagined into being, and the words 'myth' and 'imagination', sometimes combined as 'mythic imagination', will appear frequently in the following pages, somewhat like motifs from a recurring dream. My hope is that, as with a symphonic piece of music, the way in which certain themes resonate between pieces may furnish an armature for the book as a whole.

In pulling these pieces together, it occurred to me that the addition of anecdotal reflections of the kind more commonly found in a memoir would provide a more immediate and personal context for ideas that are explored elsewhere in more general terms. By also including a selection of the verse I've written, I hope to stress the importance of staying in touch with what the archetypal psychologist James Hillman has helped us to recognise as the 'poetic basis of mind'. I take that to be a term that speaks to the deep formative activity of the unconscious but also to that of the imagination as the wellspring of both our inventive vitality and our capacity for compassion.

Though I occasionally quote from other writers who have influenced my thinking, all the essays included here are reflective, speculative, and subjective rather than scholarly, and so go unaccompanied by the customary apparatus of referential footnotes. However, I provide a bibliography of quoted works for those who may care to read those authors for themselves. Publications in which earlier versions of some of these pieces have already appeared are gratefully acknowledged in the text, as are the names of organisations and groups which kindly invited me to give otherwise unpublished talks.

# Daimon

Though I'm too deeply in love with the incarnate world to be much of a Platonist, I've long been intrigued by Plato's myth of Er and its insistence that we come into this life with a specific calling that it is our duty and – if we are fortunate and diligent enough – our destiny to fulfil. According to the myth, each of us is attended by a personal daimon, an inward escort whose voice is the guardian of that calling and the most reliable guide to its fulfilment. However, this arrangement is less simple and comforting than it may sound, because the particular nature of our allotted task is delivered under sealed orders – orders of which the daimon remains aware but which we have already begun to forget by the time we arrive in the world. Thus, the course of our life becomes a more or less conscious process of trying to remember what that calling might be, and then, perhaps, to answer it.

Looked at in another, more conventional way, our mortal lives can appear to be an entirely arbitrary matter – the random consequence of the fertilisation of a receptive egg by one among millions of eager spermatozoa released at a particular moment during one of possibly many acts of love between two people whose first meeting may only have occurred as the result of merely coincidental events. Yet out of such apparently chance encounters an order swiftly begins to form – the genetically informed, biological order of the body, yes, but also the invisible unfolding of a unique human soul preparing to encounter the blessings and vicissitudes of the world, and of a mind eager to make sense of them – a mind that can at moments (and I'm far from alone in having this experience) feel startlingly precognitive. Perhaps that too is a function of the attendant daimon's larger knowledge.

In *The Soul's Code* the archetypal psychologist James Hillman offers a provocative study of the implications of the myth of the daimon for the way we live our lives. His exploration of a number of well-documented case histories shows how some of us – Mozart and Menuhin are notable examples – attain an early understanding of their life purpose and quickly set about realising it with precocious confidence. Though few of us may be gifted with such immediate genius, for the ancient Greeks eudaimonia, the state of being calmly at one with the daimon, was also the hallmark of simple contentment. Perhaps most of us, therefore, pursue less dramatic lives in which the daimon quietly shapes our sense of character and an unassuming sense of purpose; yet, for others, the relationship with the daimon can prove difficult and more demanding.

'Man and daimon feed the hunger in each other's hearts,' wrote W.B. Yeats in his *Mythologies*, and elsewhere he saw the daimon as antithetical to the soul. In the chapter on the daimon in his provocatively titled *A Complete Guide to the Soul*, Patrick Harpur asserts that the daimon will certainly guide you – 'but only the "you" who serves its plan for yourself. Who knows what sojourn in the wilderness this might entail? And, because the personal daimon is, finally, grounded in the impersonal Ground of Being itself,' he warns, 'you will inevitably be led way, way out of your depth.'

Whatever the case, we now live in a time largely, and often impatiently, disinclined to give serious consideration to such mythologies of the soul. Instead we are conventionally taught that the course of each life is shaped not by mysterious preternatural forces but by a combination of specific genetic inheritance, efforts of the personal will, and the pressure of various environmental factors. Offered impressive scientific evidence for this pragmatic view of existence, we are confidently assured that this is simply how things are.

And yet, and yet ...

I remember an afternoon, during a break at school – I must have been about fourteen – when, thinking about my future, I wondered whether I would rather become a teacher or a writer. The former possibility must have been inspired by some heartening exchange with one of the more engaging masters at the grammar school to which, like many other working-class boys, I had been consigned by the Butler Education Act. I can't recall what was said in that talk, only its effect on me, and it must have been heady stuff if it could call the latter ambition into question, for the desire to be a storyteller had been strongly seeded in me years earlier by my reading of *Grimms' Fairy Tales*.

I'll have more to say about that early awakening elsewhere in this book, but for now what interests me is the premonitory way in which that afternoon of self-questioning anticipated a dilemma that would confront me, much later, at two critical moments in my adult life.

The first came on graduation when I was faced with the challenge of earning a living. Like many young aspirants before me, I felt driven to the doleful conclusion that my writing would never be strong enough to claim serious attention, and so resigned myself instead to a career as a teacher of literature. The second – an urgently compelling dream – came much later when I realised that, if I was not to end my days as an unhappy corpse, the time had come to step out of the relative security of the teacher's life and answer the claims of that earlier, more challenging aspiration.

It may be an unfashionable and, in these sceptical times, a risky confession to make, but I'm pretty sure that something that might reasonably be called my daimon played an active role in both decisions: the first to forestall a hasty and premature attempt at publication; the second to pick me up by the scruff of my neck and tell me to get on with it.

As things turned out, the choice I posed to my juvenile self on that afternoon at school was not as clear as it then seemed. Once I became a full-time teacher, I continued to try to write (though not to publish), and throughout my career as a freelance writer I have given a considerable amount of time to teaching in a variety of different modes.

As the following pieces try to show, Imagination (which I here capitalise in Shelleyan manner to indicate a larger source of creative energy than just our human share in it) has been the element common to both kinds of work. I believe that related values underpin my writing and my teaching, and in its insistence that those values are what finally matter my daimon seems to have known what was happening all along.

So, perhaps, like the plot of a well-constructed novel, a life may unfold unpredictably but come in retrospect to seem inevitable?

Minds exclusively committed to the sceptical tradition of rational positivism may find such reflections meaningless, yet as the accelerating processes of cultural and technological change daily demonstrate, we are living in transitional times, and such times seem ever more urgently to demand a radical evolution of consciousness. But how best to meet that demand?

I've long been impressed by the wise manner in which that great novelist, John Cowper Powys, insisted that the Shakespearean sense of life combines the maximum of scepticism about everything with the maximum of openness towards everything. Perhaps it is through such a creative tension of apparent contraries that consciousness may evolve. If so, might it not be in a way that recognises and respects the many life-changing gains that have accrued from the procedures of objective rational analysis, yet is also willing to recall what is of timeless value in ancient and traditional wisdom and thus remain, like them, open to subjective, transrational modes of apprehending experience?

As I have indicated in the Introduction to this book, my own principal concerns have always lain beyond the literary, and it's in service to the current difficult evolution of consciousness in these transitional times that I write and teach. After ten years of working in conventional schools and colleges I moved into more exploratory places of learning and found there that the educational mode that most excited me and produced the most substantial results is experiential and transformative rather than prescriptive and didactic.

Meanwhile, in my work as a writer I have tried to examine and articulate in fictional form what have felt to be significant, sometimes elusive, often confusing, and occasionally contradictory aspects of my own experience in a manner that I hope may be both imaginatively entertaining and personally affirmative for others engaged in their own quest for larger consciousness.

For as William Blake once wrote (upside down) in the notebook to his *Everlasting Gospel*:

> Do what you will this life's a fiction
> And is made up of contradiction.

# Green Man

However thorough the search, there are some books that will never be found on the shelves of either public or private libraries; and, no, I'm not thinking of ebooks which inhabit only the immaterial recesses of cyberspace, for to those of us who grew up loving not only the secret-door feel of the books we owned, but also their palpable texture and even their smell, such electronic texts don't really qualify as books at all. What I have in mind are those rather rare volumes that, apart from their titles and perhaps a briefly quoted extract or two, have no readable existence because they are the fictional work of fictional authors, and therefore merely epiphenomena of other, more substantial books that have found their way into publication.

A number of such books figure in my novel *The Chymical Wedding*, and one of them has haunted my imagination for a long time. Its title is *The Green Man's Dream*, and the author of that slim volume of verse is the fictional narrator of the novel, Alex Darken. An early page of the novel lets us know that he has already published a collection titled *Shadowgraphs*, and it soon becomes clear that, though he may be restlessly incubating a second volume, *The Green Man's Dream* will not be written until sometime after the end of the story that Alex is telling. But the title indicates that its theme will be strongly influenced by the events and preoccupations of that transformative time in his life, for already, at the opening of the novel, shortly after his arrival in rural Norfolk, Alex is imaginatively engaged with the figure of the Green Man:

'And it was not that I expected to encounter him *out there*,' he says, 'this clumsy, feral creature sired sometime in the dark between the Fifth Day and the Sixth, and neither man nor beast. But this, if ever, was the season of the Green Man, and this almost medieval wood was Green Man country. If I looked long and quietly enough he might shiver into focus, print himself across the page, and I would know then what kin he was to me, and whether he was likeliest to injure me or aid. Such, anyway, was the dream in which I lived those days.'

Readers of the book won't be surprised to learn that its author shared Alex's fascination with the image, and it seems we were not alone in that obsession. Just a year after the publication of *The Chymical Wedding*, William Anderson's detailed study *Green Man: The Archetype of Our Oneness with the Earth* appeared. It opens with an account of how in May of the same year, to the lively accompaniment of a band of morris men, the leafy figure of a Jack-in-the-Green danced beside the sea at Hastings in what has subsequently become an annual festival of death and resurrection.

Both Anderson's book and my novel were relatively late explorations of an image that, having been active and vital in the folk culture of rural people for many centuries, resurged into consciousness in the heady days of the 1960s. In 1967 Ted Hughes published a volume of verse and prose titled *Wodwo* – a Middle English noun cognate with the word 'woodwose', meaning a woodland-dweller who is both a wild man and a vegetation spirit. Fascination with the Green Man figure intensified around that time with the increasing ecological awareness of the harm we were doing to the natural environment.

My attention was seized by the image when I first consciously encountered it as an undergraduate studying medieval literature. Reading the Arthurian verse romances of the Middle Ages felt like opening up a half-forgotten gallery in the house of my own imagination. Their dreamlike narratives struck me as at once familiar and strange, as though those heraldic adventures into the realms of the otherworld were also inward journeys into a terrain where knights and ladies, hermits and enchanters, marvellous beasts and other daimonic figures dramatised and illuminated what had previously been only dimly perceived as impersonal energies active in the theatre of the soul.

The feelings excited inside me by the romances resonated with those of childhood days when my imagination had quickened into life under the spell of the folktales collected by the brothers Grimm. At six or seven years old, to open that treasured book was to enter a realm of magic palaces and dark tangled forests, of cruelties and kindnesses, terrors and transformations, through which some – mostly the apparent simpletons, often aided by helpful animals – made their way, ordeal by arduous ordeal, to their happy endings. And so strikingly did that world ignite my imagination it felt as real as – and sometimes more real than – the soot-black buildings and busy streets of the northern town around me. Industrial Halifax may have been my place of birth, but each time I returned to the pages of that book I recognised my deeper homeland in its luminous realm of stories.

Twelve years later, at Cambridge, my first reading of the poem *Sir Gawayne and the Grene Knyghte* impacted on me with a similar shock of recognition. Though the Middle English language of the verse was so archaic that I needed a glossary to translate many passages, its dialect was identifiably of the north. To the ears and tongue of a lad who had grown up in a county where – as if to rhyme with the clatter of its fall – the word 'water' was still often pronounced as 'watter', those alliterative consonants and flattened vowels had a rough, familiar ring. They contrasted sharply with the polished tones heard in seminar rooms and dining halls where the chatter was largely dominated by privately educated 'southron' voices. Conveyed in such stark, provincial language, the image of a barbarous green figure gatecrashing the civilised court of King Arthur, brandishing an axe and offering to have his head chopped off by any knight who dared to suffer the same fate a year later, held a satisfying appeal for a class-conscious young northerner who knew he would never be quite at ease in the sophisticated, overly cerebral culture of Cambridge.

Yet the disturbing images of that poem reached deeper still, and in ways that would only come clearer to me ten years after I had left the university. At that time a major life crisis shocked me into the belated understanding that the Green Knight's beheading game at the heart of the poem was rather more than just a game. In its forgotten origins, it was far too serious to be a game at all, for – symbolically understood – it enacted a transforming rite of initiation.

In secular cultures such as England's, cultures that take pride in rational freedom from superstition, few traces remain of initiatory rites of passage. Stag nights, and similarly boozy masculine rituals, can still prove edgy and unnerving; and the young, with their instinctive need to test their courage against life, can be worryingly wild in their invention of unguided ordeals (such as 'tombstoning' leaps from cliffs into uncertain waters) to mark their passage out of childhood. But the formal, public rites of graduation and marriage ceremonies, for example, though earnest and moving in their significance, are, by and large, relatively tame, polite, and well-behaved affairs rather than deeply transformative experiences.

Thus, by the time I was thirty I had graduated through formal education, had passed each exam that was put before me, had travelled and worked abroad, got married, bought property, and won promotion in my work; yet, with the possible exception of being heart-stirringly present at the birth of my daughter, I had experienced no convincingly profound sense of having undergone any existentially transforming initiation into adult manhood. On the contrary, my identity had begun to feel little more than a socially compromised, flimsily constructed, and increasingly false self.

Gradually, the gap between the voluble, opinionated persona I presented to the world and any well-founded sense of personal authenticity had become so wide that, even to my own ears, I sometimes sounded less like a man than a talking ghost. That was when life found me out. Time had been called on falsity, and I began to learn what it feels like to have one's head lopped off. For against the ego's will, but with the daimon insisting that change was overdue, the bewildered, slightly schizoid simulacrum of an adult male into which I'd dwindled found himself in emotionally devastating circumstances against which all the sharply honed powers of a lonely, self-righteously assertive intellect raged in vain. Only then did he begin to glimpse the Green Knight's secret: that once the head is chopped off one can begin to think through the senses and with the heart.

This happened to me in the spring of 1970. I was thirty years old. Ten years later the renewed sense of life arising from that initiatory turning point would open the ground in which *The Chymical Wedding* would slowly grow into its final form. By then, I had some inkling that when the Green Man appears it's always as consort to a powerful female figure – Morgan Le Fay in the *Gawayne* poem, the Sheela-na-gig Gypsy May, in my novel – and that it's when the two come together that a transformative initiation can happen.

I'll have more to say about this in the next piece, though it's not easy to speak of such matters without sounding cryptic or delusory, because the words never quite seem to fit – which is perhaps why one of the poems in Alex Darken's unavailable slim volume, *The Green Man's Dream*, might have read like this:

# Green Man

Leaf-mould, tree-bark, lithe by wood-light
on the spongy earth, he steals from shade
to denser shade wherever trees pack deep.

On hunkers he observes the acorn's fall,
the badgers' sett, the owl's eye blinking
in the dusk, the ivy's stranglehold.

Ears catch wing's touch on twig, trekkings
of ant and beetle, bracken's stir at footfall,
and every heralding of air and rain. Not tree,

not ape, nor yet quite man, his habitat
the dark between the fifth day and the sixth,
his senses and his thought are one, and silent

as the forest glades at noon; for if
he strains for language, look – his tongue unfurls
and yet his opened mouth breaks only into leaf.

# Imagining Otherwise

In 2003 I was invited as guest speaker to the annual gathering of GreenSpirit. What follows is a slightly revised text of the talk I gave on that occasion. It was published by GreenSpirit Press as GreenSpirit Pamphlet No. 6 in 2004.

Imagination, change, and the reconciliation of opposing principles – these are big themes – themes that can soon turn abstract and sententious if they are not kept in close touch with the immediacy of lived experience. So I hope you will bear with me if I begin this talk on a personal note by sharing with you some aspects of my own experience on which such understanding as I have of these themes is founded. It's very likely that each of you here has been drawn to this conference not only out of a serious intellectual, moral, and spiritual engagement with its global concerns but also as part of your own adventure into meaning. In that respect, I'm no different from anyone else here, so I hope this personal approach will open up the general themes in an earthed and engaging way.

Looking around the room, I would guess that I'm probably among the oldest people here. I was born in August 1939, just a month before the Second World War began, and that makes me older than the Holocaust, older than the atom bomb, older even – and this makes me feel really old – than rock 'n' roll. In the many years I've lived since then I've observed some extraordinary changes – most obviously in the technological realm. For example, there were so few cars on the street when I was a child that each year we used to collect sightings of the new registration numbers, and I can remember the boyish excitement of seeing my first vapour trail scarring the sky. Few houses had telephones in those days, and central heating was a rare luxury. (I sometimes wonder if today's kids ever see the patterns of crystalline magic with which Jack Frost used to dazzle our window panes.) Computers, of course, were almost unheard of. But before you start shifting in your seats let me say that I've no intention of playing the old fogey by romanticising what was in many ways a hard, uncomfortable, and colourless past, or by bewailing the obvious evils of overpopulation, environmental degradation, and social, political, and economic injustice that crowd around our lives these days. For the changes that most impress me are changes in the philosophical attitudes of thousands of people – changes that carry, I believe, such hopes as we can legitimately entertain for the decent survival of our troubled and troublesome species. I'll come to those in a moment, but let me first say more about the formative influences on my thinking.

I grew up in the northern industrial town of Halifax and can vividly remember how, in the years before the mills were electrified, on most days the town used to lie scarcely visible within its valley under a thick sulphurous pall of smoke. As the stoker in a cotton mill, my dad was a vigorous contributor to that yellowish-grey smog and he no more than the rest of us had any idea how it would drift across the moors and crags and out across the North Sea to fall on the spruce forests of Norway as acid rain. One simply took the smoke for granted, just as we kids assumed that the buildings of the town were made out of black stone – not the creamy yellow sandstone that was eventually revealed when their grimy faces were cleaned.

I would probably still be living somewhere in those northern streets if the Butler Education Act hadn't sent me to the local grammar school, from where, as an unwitting part of a well-intentioned programme of social engineering, I was eventually admitted as a student to King's College, Cambridge. By that time, I already knew that I wanted to be a writer. I'd known it since I was about six, when I began to read the stories in a copy of *Grimms' Fairy Tales* that my mother bought for me from Woolworth's. I had been excited by the way the book opened like a magic door on to a landscape utterly different from that of the grimy industrial world around me, a landscape that was at once alien and strangely familiar, as though it mirrored back to me, and helped me to recognise, hitherto unfocused aspects of my inner world.

11

That's one of the most important things a book can do for us, and it left me wanting to tell stories as well as to read them. So throughout my teens I wrote pages and pages of what I am now sure was quite dreadful stuff and then, in my innocence, went up to Cambridge to read English literature, imagining that such a course of study would provide a kind of apprenticeship that would help me to become a writer. What I didn't know was that the English Faculty wasn't turning out writers: it was turning out literary critics – and critics of such ferocious intellectuality that I was quickly robbed of any conviction that I could ever be a writer myself. It took me the best part of twenty years to recover the confidence to try to write seriously again.

In the meantime I had done what many other disheartened would-be writers had done before me: I became a schoolteacher. As a student I had come alive to the terrible injustices prevailing across the planet and believed that education was an effective means of beginning to right them. Excited by the exuberance with which the newly independent African nations seemed to be offering real possibilities for change, I went to work for three years as a teacher in a school in Ghana – a coeducational boarding school two hundred miles upcountry from Accra, six miles from the nearest town, and completely surrounded by dense rainforest; a forest that, I learned to my grief quite recently, has now almost disappeared. That time taught me a great deal about the endemic racism of the manner in which English assumptions underpinned the curriculum of study in African schools. It also taught me a great deal more about the limitations of my own naïve idealism.

When I eventually returned to England it was to work in further education, with students on day and block release from industry, in the hope of refunding to kids from the working class something of the privileges that had been afforded to me. In addition to teaching English, I worked on a programme of general studies with apprentice builders, gas-fitters, car mechanics, hairdressers, engineers, and others. At that time I was a member of a sort of unofficial lay clerisy – the gallant band of left-wing intellectuals who believed they were transforming society by working within the state education system and spreading the word of humanist rationality throughout the land.

You've probably met the kind of young man I was. I still run into him every now and then, and he usually gives me a healthily hard time. In my day I was pretty good at convincing both myself and others that there was no meaning to life other than that imposed on it by the sceptical, largely masculine exercise of human reason. For a time, I thought it was working. Suffice it to say that under a growing awareness of the contradictions in my work, the pressures of early marriage and fatherhood, and an abiding sense of personal failure, I was retreating into an ever falser, more withdrawn condition, when, aged thirty, my embattled ego suffered the massive insult of discovering that my wife was in love with a friend and my marriage was over.

As my brittle world collapsed I went through a brief but intense episode of breakdown. It lasted for two days and three sleepless nights, during which time I was possessed by a frenzy of violent emotions such as no reasonable man likes to own as his. Long-exiled feelings flooded back with a vengeance and – beyond whatever words were spoken – I felt up against a cold, lunar principle, impervious to all but its own laws, against which my proprietorial ego raged in vain. At that point, as Joseph Campbell would say, I dropped into the unconscious, which is another way of saying that I made a journey into the otherworld. For the mythical fact is that, while still dimly aware of my external circumstances, I was elsewhere, in the interior, traversing an arduous terrain, and encountering some fearsome figures on the way. There are passages in my novels where I've tried to dramatise through fictional events something of the quality of that journey; but truth, being less credible than fiction, is largely unpublishable. Let me just say that, in exhausted acceptance of a kind of defeat, I eventually fell asleep, and when I woke I found the world changed.

I walked out of the house into lanes, bright with morning sunlight, that were rife with campion and vetch and ragged robin, and it felt as if frequencies of information I had jammed for years were beaming freely around me. Filled with the exhilarating sense that the unfolding flow of life was not only larger but richer in meaning and interest than my tightly managed model of it had been, I realised that the change was not out there in the world, for which I now felt an almost virgin taste, but inside me. It turned out that the alteration was radical and lasting. Something overdetermined and exhausted had died, my perceptions were cleansed, and with my rational head lopped off I was learning to think with the heart. My collapsed ego would build back quickly enough, but the terms on which I lived my life were irrevocably altered.

Out of the need to recognise more of the nature of that transforming journey for myself, and in the hope that doing so might help others to similar recognitions of their own, I had to find both a context for it and a language. It began as a quest for meaningful images. The first that came was the image of the tarot Fool with its jaunty reminder of what an untutored fool I'd been and its promise of a wiser fool figure in the offing. From the tarot I found my way into the rich vocabulary of images through which alchemy speaks of transformation, and for guidance there I turned to Jung – not in therapy or analysis, just free-ranging reading following my nose. I found other teachers too: Mircea Eliade on shamanism, Esther Harding on the goddesses, Campbell on the hero's quest, Blake and the romantic poets reread in a different light. And out of this intuitive casting about – it was more dream-quest than research – came a growing conviction that I might be a writer after all, for I was now beginning to feel my way towards the kind of story I had to tell.

It would be the kind of novel that, in a phrase used by John Fowles in his introduction to *The Magus*, 'offers an experience beyond the literary'. Interestingly, Fowles seems to turn his back on the phrase, dismissing it as a merely adolescent longing, so I hope I'm not being regressive if I see no reason why such a longing should die with adolescence. For me, it's a phrase that conjures the initiatory power of writing, its scope for offering a fictional correlative to a rite of passage. The novels that have always most deeply engaged me are those which act on the reader's imagination with something of the force of an initiatory ordeal, stories that draw us into deep vicarious involvement in a process of transformation, attended by ambiguous tutelary figures offering what Gaston Bachelard once called 'a homoeopathy of anguish', and from which the reader emerges with heightened recognition of comparable moments in their own past lives; and perhaps also with an enlarged sense of the possibility for change and renewal in the future. That was the kind of writing I now hoped to do – though there's a danger, of course, that such an abbreviated, retrospective account of how I came to this point suggests a more orderly and deliberate process of choice than was truly the case.

Having said that, it occurs to me that there is no reason at all why you should believe that anything of what I have just told you is true. After all, you have only my word for it, along with, I suppose, a general tolerant assumption that anyone making such a public admission is likely to be sincere. But let's be strict about this, for isn't there a sense in which what I've just said can't possibly be true? How could a ten-minute account even begin to offer a realistic picture of more than thirty years of complicated experience? I for one don't believe that it can. So, no, what I have just told you can't be the truth as an empirical positivist might understand it. But it does carry, I believe, the truth of myth – of my personal myth, the myth by which I make sense of the kind of person I've become and the kind of work I do. And as such it's a work of the imagination. I have, in fact, been telling you a story.

It won't surprise you to learn that, as a novelist, I assign a very high value to the role of story in human affairs, but I think I do so with good reason. Those of you already familiar with my work will know how preoccupied it is with myths, and one of my favourite creation myths is very brief indeed. It comes from the Jewish rabbinical tradition and it says simply, 'God invented people because he likes to hear stories.' What I like about it is that a person of sceptical inclination might turn it round to make it say, 'People invented gods because they like to hear stories,' and it could still make good sense. In thinking about the issues it raises, I like to put that story alongside some words once uttered by an Apache Indian called Benton Lewis, words that still make the hairs stand up at the back of my neck each time I read them. What he said was this: 'Stories go through you like arrows. Stories make you live right. Stories make you replace yourself.'

Think about those words for a moment. Isn't it the case that if you are told a good story, or read one, you know that something powerful has struck and entered you? Isn't it also the case that, while avoiding the perils of didacticism, a good story carries a moral dimension that has ethical consequences for the imagination? And if those implications are seriously considered might they not have a transformative effect on the way you live your life?

What matters to me most about both those quotations is the way they place storytelling at the very centre of human experience. They seem to identify the capacity to tell stories as the characteristic that makes us truly human. Perhaps it's possible that the telling of stories is what most distinguishes us from the other species. The animals have their own languages, some of them use simple tools capably, and they all have their own social arrangements; but, as far as we know, they live only inside the received world of the natural order except in so far as we distort it. We live inside that order too, of course, and – though we too often forget it – our human life is finally dependent on it; but we also live inside a universe of stories, and those stories to a large extent define our character and our experience.

We tell our lives in stories – the story of our day, of our journey, of our accidents, adventures, joys, griefs, and tribulations. I sometimes think the seeds of my own life as a novelist were sown through listening to my mother talking to her friends, telling them about some recent event in a more or less orderly narrative form, amply illustrated by the use of dialogue – 'I said such-and-such, then she said, so and so. So I said to her …' – in such a way that, if it were written out, might provide a lively contribution to a script for *Coronation Street*. We live in a time that lays great stress on the value of information, but when we communicate intimately with one another about the most important things in our lives we don't do it by imparting information – we do it by telling stories. Story is the means by which we convert the raw events of our lives into recognised experiences that make sense to us; and it's by telling such stories that we open up a way through from dumb feeling into shared meaning.

Nor is it just the stories that we tell about ourselves, for we are born into a world of stories. Each of us is born into a family that already cherishes a story about what kind of family it is, and much of our struggle into a sense of personal identity is shaped, for good or ill, by the pressures of that story and the degree to which we are prepared – or not – to acquiesce in the role it assigns to us. Beyond that, our lives are conditioned by the wider stories of our tribe, of our clan, of our regional culture, of the nation to which we belong – its history – and of the larger stories our culture tells about the nature of the universe and our place within it.

These last are the big stories or myths through which people try to cope meaningfully with the big, otherwise unanswerable questions: Where do we come from? Why are we here? Where are we going? The comparatively recent insights offered by relativity theory, anthropological research, and the critical acumen of feminist thinkers have shown us that our very sense of reality is shaped by the stories we choose to believe. Though it may be easy for us to recognise that the life of an alien culture such as that of the Aztecs of Mexico was shaped by belief in myths that strike us as frankly incredible; in a scientistic and literal-minded culture such as our own – one that is convinced that its systematic method of scientific enquiry gives access to the demonstrably real nature of things – it's less easy to recognise the degree to which we too live inside our myths. Yet a moment's thought will tell us that, for example, the Pope and Richard Dawkins inhabit entirely different universes of story. For the one, life is a spiritual drama of life and death in which the fate of the immortal soul is at stake. For the other, such considerations are absurd in a morally neutral universe where evolution is driven by the curiously human selfishness of genes. Both would claim their version of the universe is real – yet if adherence to different mythical stories creates different realities, then doesn't the idea of reality itself become problematic?

In my experience, people who pride themselves on being realists have all too often settled for one of the meaner fictions of the age. Once we recognise that we live inside our myths – that as Jules Cashford says in *The Moon: Myth and Image*, 'the world is not given as fact but inhabited through interpretation'– we begin to see that reality is not simply out there, obdurate and impervious, but changes according to the stories we tell about it. Which is to say that it is always porous to the imagination.

And what is true of the big mythic stories of the culture is also true of our personal myths – the stories we tell about ourselves. In *Healing Fiction*, James Hillman says that 'the way we imagine our lives is the way we are going to go on living our lives'. But the implication is that once we have begun to understand the mythic underpinning of our experience, we begin to realise that we don't have to carry on telling the same story in the same way. So the story I'm encouraging you to work with now is one that recognises that there is a sense in which we are all creatures of fiction and that the stories we tell that shape the course of our lives can be changed through the active power of the imagination.

Such a story offers a larger take on the power of the imagination than the prevailing conventional view of its nature. It puts us back in touch with a tradition of thinking about the imagination which has always been alive and vital among the poets. Wasn't it something along these lines that Coleridge was thinking and feeling when he wrote in his *Biographia Literaria* that 'the imagination is the prime agent of human perception'? Wasn't William Blake rejoicing in this world-endowing aspect of the imagination when he declared that 'to me this whole world is one continuous vision of fancy and imagination' and claimed elsewhere that 'The Imagination is not a State: it is the Human Existence itself'?

But this tradition is much older than the romantic poets. It can be traced back through the hermetic philosophy of the alchemists, one of whom, Ruland the Lexicographer, beautifully declared that 'the Imagination is the star in man', suggesting a deep visionary link between human nature and the nature of the cosmos. Beyond the alchemists, variants of it can be found among the Gnostics and the Platonists and in the Hindu concept of the sensory world as 'maya', which is usually translated as 'illusion' but may be more fruitfully translated by a word stemming from the same root '*ima*gination'. Take this world-creating view of the imagination back far enough and its roots may be found in the animistic vision experienced by traditional societies since the dawn of time.

It will already be clear that my own view of the imagination is more closely associated with this ancient tradition than with currently prevailing assumptions. I regard the imagination as the means by which, with more or less psychic energy, we shape our vision of the world and our place within it, and also as the primary means by which we can transform it. What matters, of course, is the degree to which we are conscious of what we are doing.

When working with students in my writing classes, I encourage them to think about the imagination through a kind of thought experiment that tries to *imagine* the imagination. I ask them to visualise two circles, one of which represents the outer world (everything outside themselves which is not them) and the other their inner world (everything that is *only* them – their thoughts, feelings, hopes, fears, intuitions, dreams, the entire realm of their private experience). Then I ask them to bring the two circles together so that the circumference of each passes through the centre of the other as in a Venn diagram –

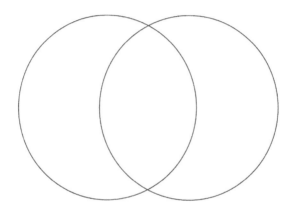

– and to visualise the almond-shaped area of overlap between the two circles as the place where they actually live – that region where their inner world is in a permanent state of negotiation with all the intelligence reaching them from the outside world about what is real and true. I think of that area of overlap – which is known as the 'mandorla' (from the Italian word for 'almond') – as the house of Imagination.

The mandorla is a very ancient symbol for the mysterious reconciliation of opposing principles through which something new enters into life. Originally it symbolised the meeting of Heaven and Earth through which life itself was first generated, and as such it forms the ground plan of many sacred sites. A notable example is Glastonbury, where the abbey was built to this plan and where the symbol appears on the lid of the chalybeate spring that was sacred there long before the Christian era. Christians recognise the symbol as the Vesica Piscis – the sign of the fish's belly – because the Fish – 'Icthus' in Greek, a word composed of the initial letters of a Greek phrase meaning 'Jesus Christ Son of God Saviour' – was a secret signifier of one's Christian faith in the early days of the church. But long before Christ the mandorla was seen as the vulva of the Great Mother Goddess, the gateway between worlds through the passages of birth and death, as displayed by the Sheela-na-gig in my novel *The Chymical Wedding*. The symbol is also found in Egyptian hieroglyphics, where its name is 'Ru' and the glyph has several meanings. These all have to do with the passage between worlds and include the idea of a secret entrance in a temple and of the female organ of generation through which life enters the world. It can also be related to the eye, through which the outer world enters inner consciousness and the inward world looks out.

As an emblem of the imagination, the 'mandorla' is a value-free term representing the place where, all the time, our inner world merges with the outer world to shape the experience from which each of us builds our personal myth. For we don't just live in the public world around us, or only in the private world within. We live in the mandorla where those two worlds meet and negotiate about reality with one another as a more or less vigorous exercise of the imagination. The mandorla is our gateway to meaning, and the problem is to keep it open so that the claims of both outer and inner worlds are honoured.

We all know people who live in a narrow mandorla by over-rating external quantifiable 'facts' at the expense of inner values such as the feeling dimension of a situation. Conversely, there are people so lost inside their private myths that they shut out the evidence trying to reach them from the outside which might call their myth into question. Nor are these things constant, for the scope of our mandorla fluctuates all the time. But the greater the area of overlap then the larger and more inclusive the embrace of our imaginative vision. If the two circles were to overlap completely then I imagine one would have a single circle which would then represent total knowledge and be reminiscent of the medieval image of God as a circle whose centre is everywhere and circumference nowhere. But we are only human, betwixt and between creatures, caught up in contradictions. For us the challenge is to keep the mandorla as open as possible.

The nature of that challenge was brilliantly defined by Ted Hughes in an essay in *Winter Pollen*, titled Myth and Education. 'The real problem', he says, 'comes from the fact that outer world and inner world are interdependent at every moment. We are simply the locus of their collision and whether we like it or not our life is what we are able to make of that collision ... So what we need is a faculty that embraces both worlds simultaneously'... a vision 'which pays equal respect to both sides. This really is imagination. This is the faculty we mean when we talk about the imagination of great artists. The character of great works is exactly this – that in them the full presence of the inner world combines with and is reconciled to the full presence of the outer world. And in them we see that the laws of these two worlds are not contradictory at all: they are all one inclusive system.'

So the proper exercise of the imagination is an energetic process of negotiation between outer world and inner world through which we strive to hold together their often contradictory pulls. By engaging in that effort we can begin to work extraordinary changes because it's through the meeting and reconciliation of opposites that something new gets made for life. In that respect, the I*ma*gination is related to a word stemming from the same root – *ma*gic – the power to bring about changes in the world which seem to defy the normal laws of causality. In its powers of conjuring something out of nothing and working its astonishing transformations, magic can be viewed as an active principle of the Imagination.

Before you start imagining me as a member of some occult coven, however, let me add to what has already been said the importance of recognising two different aspects of the imagination. Firstly, its inventive aspect, by which we are free to make up the story of our life and world; and, secondly, its ethical aspect, by which it acknowledges the right of others to do the same. For it is through the empathic aspect of the imagination that we try to perceive the world as others experience it, so that we feel how things are for them in the world that they inhabit, and can relate to their sense of reality in a spirit of compassionate understanding. It seems to me absolutely vital that, in all aspects of our creativity, we strive to hold these two aspects of the imagination together, for when the inventive aspect loses touch with the empathic the results can be calamitous, and when the ethical aspect loses touch with the poetic then the work soon becomes dry, abstract, theoretical, and dogmatic.

Imagined in this way, as the mandorla linking all our lives, the imagination becomes an instrument of liberation, one to which we all have equal access and which, by its own intrinsic standards, serves to celebrate and enlarge our common humanity. It may only be a fiction but, as Benton Lewis suggests, it very much matters what kind of stories we tell each other, because it is through them that we shape our world. In my experience, as novelist and teacher, this story has proved to be a fruitful one, both in liberating my own creativity and in encouraging creativity in others.

You will remember me saying that after the breakdown and transformation of my values when I was thirty, I began to see what kind of books I might write, but it took me a long time to begin to pull together anything publishable. In the meantime I began to work for an unusual exercise in experimental education that had been inspired by a dream that came to an American Quaker, a member of the New York Yearly Meeting, in the 1960s. The dream was of founding a world college that would be based entirely on the practice of learning through cross-cultural experience, while its curriculum would be work towards non-violent social change and the understanding of what it might mean to become a world citizen.

The dream was made real. The headquarters of Friends World College were on Long Island and regional study centres were set up in Cuernavaca, Mexico, Machakos in Kenya, Bangalore in India, and Kyoto in Japan; the European Centre, for which I worked, was based in Norwich. To graduate from this college with a first degree, students had to design a learning programme with the advice of faculty members, and then pursue their studies through placements on experiential learning projects in at least two cultural regions other than the one in which they were born, acquiring at least one new language along the way. The record of their experience was kept in journals submitted for evaluation, and a final thesis on their special-ist area of study was submitted to oral examination by an expert in the field who was not a member of the college. So for several years I was busy placing students under the supervision of experts working on extraordinary projects right across Europe. Among the fields in which they were engaged were community development, alternative methods of education and psychotherapy, peace studies, the estab-lishing of law centre services for the young, organic farming, experi-ential developments in archaeology, and practical research into a field that was still very much in its infancy – ecology and environ-mental science. Much of my work consisted of guiding the students in the writing of the journals through which their learning would be evaluated. These contained not only detailed accounts of the project and related reading, but also a self-evaluative account of subjective changes in their own growth and perspectives as a result of the ex-perience they were acquiring. Thus the focus of their study was al-ways on both the inward and outward worlds – all of this happening in places and cultures far from home.

It was a demanding, innovative programme and, as such, not al-ways entirely successful; but when it worked, it worked brilliantly, and the college turned out some truly remarkable graduates. There can be few radical organisations in the United States that haven't had one or more of its graduates working hard among their ranks. For me, it was deeply satisfying work – an imaginative form of education that was directly linked to social action in a manner that was con-sistent with my own spiritual values. Yet a time came when I recog-nised that I was keeping myself busy helping other people to do what they wanted to do while evading the central challenge of my own creativity. So, eventually, encouraged by a new wife and in-spired both by a powerful dream and by the example of my stu-dents, I gave up the work in order to concentrate on becoming a writer.

It took me a long time to sort out my ideas into any sort of form, but eventually I found inspiration in a mode of writing that I'd first met through one of the few sensible decisions I made at Cam-bridge. Pushed by a saving intuition, while my friends seized the chance to study modern writers, I had decided to explore the period from 1066 to 1385. Looking back from this new perspective, I found in the medieval romances a rich trove of initiatory stories actively concerned with the high adventure of the human soul.

In their imaginative approach to the general problem of how one becomes a whole person in a violent, complicated world, those stories were seeking to renegotiate the balance between many of the apparently contradictory forces that rack our lives. Most evidently they were looking for a new relation between the masculine and feminine principles, both in the erotic relations between the sexes and as an inward dilemma of the individual life. In particular they were questing for ways to convert the male talent for aggression into energy available for the cultivation of the feelings. In examining that problem, they took seriously those dynamic aspects of the unconscious which feel as though they belong to the otherworld yet which are lively guides to the complexities of this one – the encounters with imperious summoners, with unexpected helpers, with demanding mentors, with coldly daemonic shadow figures, and with those in whom ambiguously characterised contrasexual aspects of the psyche incarnate both the perils of the quest and the rewards of completion. I found myself intrigued by the traffic between civilisation and wilderness in those stories, and by the way their landscapes elided fluently with the dream landscapes of the symbolic imagination. Similarly, there was a generative tension between Christianity and paganism in their vision, and between what was inherited from Celtic culture and the standards set by Rome. Above all, in its preference for the vision-quest form, the genre of the romance seemed to be an appropriate instrument for exploring the difficulties and wonders encountered when a person begins to feel their centre of consciousness shifting from ego to soul, from a sense of wounded isolation into a renewed, feeling relationship with the deep ground of our being. It is for that reason that I think of them as adventures of the metaphysical imagination, and in the best of those stories, such as Wolfram von Eschenbach's *Parzival*, the unfolding poetic energy seems to insist that this can only be done through the scarcely tolerable pain of holding opposing powers in tension together until they are reconciled and a renewing evolutionary way opens between them.

Now all of these seemed to me to be urgent contemporary issues

– they were urgent anyway to me, and I began to see that when I found the confidence to tell my own stories they would be contemporary romances in that ancient tradition. In her lively study of *The Romance*, Gillian Beer points out how the genre has always flourished in periods of rapid change. We live in such a time if ever there was one, and it will be clear from my work that, in both the structure and thematic preoccupations of the form, I see the romance as an apt mode of public storytelling for an age characterised, as I believe ours to be, by an unprecedented reach for individuation.

My novels are concerned throughout with the difficult problem of bringing contradictory aspects of our experience into some degree of creative reconciliation. It is, as far as I can see, the only way that something new gets made for life. We can see it obviously enough in the biological process by which a child emerges from the intimately reconciled meeting of a man and woman. Less visibly, we are slowly becoming aware that a fuller sense of what it means to be human can arise from the reconciliation of male and female principles inside ourselves, whatever our gender. In the social and political domain, the examples of South Africa and Northern Ireland should encourage the Israelis and Arabs and other warring factions to recognise that something new and better can only begin to happen when the difficult process of reconciliation is begun. Such reconciliation of the opposites is the very meaning of the emblem of the Chymical Wedding which provided the title for my best-known work. And in particular I've been concerned with renegotiating the balance between the conscious and unconscious minds by telling stories that illustrate the degree to which our lives are driven by the archetypal forces that shape much of our experience and can overwhelm us if we fail to integrate them into consciousness and thus avoid falling into their grip.

However, the deeper I got into writing novels, the more I became aware that the landscapes in which they were set were playing such an important part in the evolution of the stories that there was a sense in which the landscape was itself the most important character. At the same time, through my association with the work of Schumacher College, I was becoming more aware of the evolution of what was called 'deep ecology' by such thinkers as Arne Næss and

Theodore Roszak, whose book *The Voice of the Earth* provided me with an intellectual underpinning for what had remained until then an unfocused intuitive and imaginative awareness. Roszak writes of what he calls the 'ecological unconscious' – a dimension that reaches deeper than the human realm of Jung's collective unconscious into a lively awareness that our physical being has its roots in the order of natural processes and that just as mind and body are a single, indivisible, interactive system, so there is a living hotline between the human mind and the natural world, for the two are of one substance and in constant communication with each other (see pages 232–4).

That hotline is, in my view, the Imagination, and, again, etymologically we are returned to the same root 'ma', for the Imagination has a connection not only with *maya* and *magic* but with *matter* itself, the very stuff of which the world is made. This connection is eloquently established by my friend Richard Tarnas in *The Passion of the Western Mind*, where he says,

> Nature becomes intelligible to itself through the human mind … And it is only when the human mind actively brings forth from within itself the full powers of a disciplined imagination and saturates its empirical observation with archetypal insight that the deeper reality of the world emerges. A developed inner life is therefore indispensable for cognition. In its most profound and authentic expression, the intellectual imagination does not merely project its ideas into nature from its isolated brain corner. Rather, from within its own depths, the imagination directly contacts the creative process within nature, realized that process within itself, and brings nature's reality to conscious expression.

Tarnas goes on to conclude that 'The human spirit does not merely prescribe nature's phenomenal order: rather, the spirit of nature brings forth its own order through the human mind when that mind is employing its full complement of faculties – intellectual, volitional, sensory, imaginative.'

Another way of putting this would be to speak of a two-way process of communication between the human soul and the Soul of the

World – the Anima Mundi – or Gaia, to give it the mythological title that the novelist William Golding recommended to James Lovelock as an appropriate name for his concept of the earth as a self-regulating, intelligent pattern of living activity. This is where I come from in my own view of imaginative activity. I feel that we are all filaments of the planet's intelligence and that, if we only open our senses clearly enough to listen, it can speak to us through the active imagination in the language of the soul.

I know that my own best work as a writer is done when I get myself out of the way, forget my ego with its ambitions, anxieties, and craving for attention, and become something that more resembles a pipeline than an engineer. The sensation then is that of channelling what one is writing from an impersonal source other and wiser than one's self. I don't mean to pretend that things always happen that way, or that it's ever easy. Often enough, the opening up of oneself is the hardest part. But once we find the means to do so, then that receptivity to frequencies of imaginative intelligence from sources deeper than one's own ingenuity can offer new perspectives on our endeavours in astonishing ways.

At the start of this talk I spoke of recent changes I've observed that give me heart and hope when I contemplate what can often seem a darksome future. I was referring to the more or less simultaneous emergence of ecological understanding, by which we are coming to recognise that everything is indissolubly connected and that what we do to the planet we do also to ourselves, along with the drive towards psychological individuation which has developed on an utterly unprecedented scale in recent years. Never before, in the recorded history of the planet, have so many individuals consciously devoted their lives to a conscious quest for self-knowledge and the wider understanding that it brings. If there is hope for the future it must lie, I believe, in the convergence of those two aspects of our imaginative activity and in the further evolution of both consciousness and action that it may generate.

In *The True Story of the Novel*, Margaret Anne Doody shows how the novel is not, as some have academics suggested, a largely English invention of the eighteenth century, but has its roots in the prose romances written two centuries either side of the birth of Christ. She argues that those ancient stories sought to make the esoteric wisdom of the mystery rites of Isis available in entertaining public form, and that because the whole thrust of their narratives was towards a rite of initiation (in which a recurrent key word was 'tharsei', meaning 'take heart, be of good cheer'), the reading of those romances was in the nature of a religious experience for their first readers. 'So the novel turns out to be a Mystery Story indeed ... and it is no different from other ancient genres in having a religious wellspring.'

The ancient mystery rites demanded a process of going under, a guided passage through the darkness of the underworld and a suffering of an ego-death, so that a newly ensouled self could emerge reborn. If Doody is right, then the imaginative telling of stories by which the nature of such transforming experiences might be recognised is where the long history of prose fiction begins. Two thousand years later, the need for new stories consciously invested with kindred energy and value has, I think, never been more urgent. Nor is it without significance that the archetype of the Goddess has emerged with fresh vigour in our time, looking for a new relation with the lost and once again dismembered God.

But we are not ancients, we live in exile from a sacral culture, and as we cast about, trying to make sense of such things, there is a risk of substituting rhetoric for earned experience, of rejecting irony and cold dissociation as the fashionable voice of fiction only to fall into didacticism, or an inflation that might prove as dangerous in its way as the spirit of negation. As a guard against that, I try to stay in touch with an injunction laid by that wise old writer, John Cowper Powys, who encouraged us towards what he calls 'the great Shakespearean sense of life', one that combines the maximum of openness towards everything with the maximum of scepticism. Such an attitude keeps our interior poet in lively debate with our inward critic and insists that the real issues are never only literary. While nourishing the imagination and checking fantasy, it warns against blind enthusiasm and shallow rationality. It reminds us that, though our culture may have dethroned God and cast itself loose into empty spaces, even the slickest nihilist among us may also be a child of earth and the starry heavens. It counsels us that there may still be larger and richer stories to be told about the universe, while keeping us alert to the trials and delusions of this incarnate world and wakening us daily to its wonders. It tells us that we are as capable of love as of cold, ironical detachment; that we are the case for hope as well as the authors of our own despair; and that as we make the effort to imagine otherwise each of us is a makeweight in the balance. These are the kind of marvels that truly life-enhancing fiction can still encourage us to credit.

As my friend Patrick Harpur puts it in *The Philosopher's Secret Fire: A History of the Imagination*: 'If we wish to reinstate the Soul of the World in her original glory, we will have to do more than introduce environmental remedies … We have to cultivate a new perspective, or seeing through: and a sense of metaphor, a seeing double. We may even, if we are to shift our obdurate literalism, have to let in a bit of madness, give ourselves up to a spot of ecstasy. We can always make a start,' he suggests, 'by trying to develop a better aesthetic sense, an appreciation of beauty, which is the first attribute of soul. For the way we see the world can restore its soul, and the way the world is ensouled can restore our vision.'

In a world far too freely driven by greed and the lust for power and control, and where the degradations consequent upon the loss of soul proliferate around us with devastating effect, there is, I believe, no more urgent and important enterprise of the imagination.

# A Defence of Poetry

I write against forgetfulness. I write
so that as little as is possible of what
has mattered to the heart should be
forgot. I write because I know no cure
more sovereign against amnesia
than words, which can become
a life-support machine for memory.

And so I write this way because I want
to hear it said again how in the days before
TV when she was young – a barmaid
working in the tap-room of a crowded pub –
the long skirt of my mother's dress hung stiff
as cardboard from the swill of beer behind the bar.

# Halifax in the 1940s

Sometimes these things return: the sound
of barrels rolling from the brewer's dray
into the vaults; the leather-aproned men;
the yeasty smell of ale above the reek
of dung and tar where brown shire horses
jingled as they shook their massive heads;
hot days when sky was made of smoke, and how
the winter light would lean across the town
like a pale widow kneeling in the street
to scrape her doorstep with a scouring stone.

# Climbing Beacon Hill

## 1 *Lily Bridge*

A span of girders fenced with wire and slung
above the railway line, the bridge led down
to where a paint-works fouled the weir
beside a bleak canal; but for our gang
it marked a crossing into magical terrain.
We'd loiter high above the tracks and hear
the shunted wagons clattering their chains
and buffers in the station-yard; then stare
and stare until the wire mesh seemed to fall
away before our eyes. And when a train
went by, the smoke gasped from its funnel
shuddered round us; and we'd disappear
inside that cloud, come back, and only then
Resume our summit bid for Beacon Pan.

## 2 *The Brow*

Then halfway up the hill we found the Brow –
a scruffy recreation ground with swings,
a see-saw and a roundabout, but when you
picked a swing and grabbed its iron chains
and kicked your heels, you saw the whole town lurch
beneath your feet – the mills, the steeples,
gasworks, terraces, and parks, the stone lanes
tilting from the nearby Parish Church
to distant Highroad Well; cars, lorries, people
caught up in the sway, and toppled back and forth
for our delight, as though the sky had sprung
its hinges and the glad wind shouted as it swung.

### 3 Beacon Pan

The high horizon pushing at the sky; a last
elated canter brought us panting
up a slope to where the iron brazier
of Beacon Pan stood rusting on its post.
There at the summit of the hill, wind
tugged our breath and pulled our hair;
the clouds moved on; the grass around
us quailed. We faltered, wondering
in silence at a world that reached beyond
the hill to Shibden and High Sunderland,
and bigger skies disclosed to us, who were
town children on the edge of everything.

# Harvest

One still June Saturday we caught the bus
to Mytholmroyd and walked out to Cragg Vale
where my dad's brother, Uncle Jim,
had called for help to mow the hay
that stood waist deep in summer on
the rough slope of his tenant farm.

Hot sun; the adults swaying with their scythes
among the poppies and bright buttercups;
the beck heard talking to the stones at noon
down at the valley foot; the hay-stooks
glinting in the field, while we kids ran
and larked inside a dark byre rank with dung.
Then Aunty Edna fetched in water from
the trough to brew the tea, and with a deft
flick of her cloth she'd sweep the brown hens
from her kitchen table, slice the loaves
she'd baked, and fill the jug with milk
that tasted warm still from the patient cow.

And at day's end, the slow walk back
beneath Scout Rock, across the river-bridge;
the bus-ride into dusk; the shadowed town
that turned things into smoke and memory
when time declared that stony crag too poor
to yield a life; and one day they were gone,
Australia-bound. For years the farm stood empty
to the Pennine wind until – I guess – someone
with money and a four-by-four drove up the track
and left it gentrified. I've not been back:
the past reproaches us unless it's harvested –
as once that meadow by my strong remembered dead.

# Ancestry

Perhaps in some primordial era of human consciousness, when time was experienced as a continuous present rarely afflicted by significant change, and each soul may have known itself intrinsically part of the Great Soul, reverence for the ancestors and respect for the wisdom of the elders were established as the foundational values of culture. For millennia afterwards, those values remained vital to the stability of most societies across the earth. Not so, of course, today. In a world where time is money, families are easily dispersed, and people's lives are constantly hurried along by the consequences of rapid technological change, those duties of respect have largely become obsolete.

These days, in a discomfiting reversal of roles, elderly people are frequently forced to draw on their grandchildren's expertise to help keep their mobiles, laptops, and remote controls obedient. They may also find that much of their accumulated experience is of no more use than their wartime ration-books. Meanwhile, reverence for the ancestors commonly amounts to little more than a more or less vague desire to know something about the family tree.

Yet the past still has its hold on us. DNA testing of one's origins has become an increasingly popular fad, and TV schedules indicate an insatiable appetite for greater knowledge of archaeological discoveries, the events of dramatic historical eras, and the affairs, sexual and otherwise, of royal dynasties. But millions also watch the provocatively titled show *Who Do You Think You Are?* and their keen, if vicarious, engagement with the quest for forgotten forebears of carefully chosen celebrities suggests that the show's appeal may reach deeper than that of an evening's entertainment.

It could be argued that such programmes are popular because they offer a comforting retreat from the unsettling stresses of the complicated world we presently inhabit. But the fact that many people are now making use of online registers and other specialised websites to pursue their own genealogical trails may indicate that something more interesting is happening. Might it be the case that some atavistic urge to know and care about our ancestral lineage still lingers in our genetic code and our unconscious mind? Or could it be a stirring in the long-neglected soul? Certainly, my own desire for greater knowledge about my ancestry felt like more than mere curiosity. But that desire quickly ran into an obstacle. It turned out that, where others have identifiable ancestors they can name in the male line of descent, I have only a story.

*

Some time before I was born, an undistinguished oil painting was relegated to the dusty cellar of the terraced house my parents shared with one of my father's married sisters. My guess is that it was hung there, not out of any lack of respect for its subject, but because that portrait of a shovel-bearded man wearing a buttoned merchant seaman's coat and a peaked hat looked out of place in a modest 1930s sitting room. He was, I was told, my grandfather, and the story I was told about him ended in a mystery. What I learned in later life about the consequences of *that* mystery opened on yet another.

The story begins simply enough. His name was William Job Clarke. Born in 1872 of Liverpool-Irish Protestant stock, he met my Scottish grandmother, Donaldeina Cameron, while working as a crane driver on the Merseyside waterfront. They were married in 1894 and raised a family of seven children in a small Seaforth house. Bill Clarke might have remained a dock worker all his days if he hadn't gone to the aid of a friend who fell into a dispute with the port authority after getting involved in a scuffle. Both men were branded as troublemakers. Both lost their jobs.

With a large family to feed, and work scarce in Liverpool at the turn of the century, Bill decided to try his luck at sea. Knocking three years off his age to better his chances of getting a berth, he signed as a deckhand on a merchant vessel bound for Australia. On arrival in that energetic young country, he saw that work was not hard to find and his prospects would be brighter there. Soon he wrote to his wife that he had signed with the Adelaide Steamship Company and intended to stay on, working the coastal shipping trade until he had put by enough money to bring his family around the world to join him. His children and theirs would grow up as Australians.

Bill was given a berth on the SS *Koombana*. A modern passenger and cargo liner, the pride of the company's fleet, she was plying the west coast routes from port to port as one of the few vessels in southern waters equipped with a Marconi wireless. On 7 March 1912 the steamship docked at Fremantle, where Bill signed off from Captain Allen's command and went ashore. He had already stashed into his canvas money-belt almost all the cash needed to bring his family across the globe, so maybe he was thinking of settling in that city. But then he changed his mind and rejoined the ship before she sailed.

On the morning of 19 March the *Koombana* put to sea from Port Hedland in dirty weather, heading north for Broome and Derby. Aboard the liner were 75 other seamen and 63 passengers, including two army captains, a corporal, several businessmen, two lawyers, a land surveyor, an American tourist, seven women (among them two unmarried sisters named Skamp), and an author. Three prisoners – 'a Japanese, a Malay and an Aboriginal' – had been shackled in steerage before the other passengers were allowed to board.

The barometer was dropping as the *Koombana* butted into heavy seas driven by a stiff northeasterly wind. With much of her cargo already unloaded, she was riding high enough in the water for her propellers to be spotted breaking the surface by her southbound sister-ship the *Bullara*, which left the harbour around the same time. As the skies blackened above them, her passengers would have taken comfort from the knowledge that their experienced skipper was confident of his ship's ability to ride out a squall.

Captain Allen was aware that, sooner or later in most years, people living along the perilously shoaled reach of coastline between Broome and Onslow in northwest Australia expect to be hit by a hurricane. The storms brew up in the Arafura Sea south of Timor and can drive westwards with appalling force. These days meteorologists see them coming, but by tide-turn on that Tuesday morning no warning had reached Port Hedland that a cyclone later described in a report as 'a willy-willy without parallel in its extraordinary characteristics of violence and destruction' was bearing down on that coast.

The *Koombana* was last seen, occasionally flashing her propellers in the murky afternoon light, by the captain of the *Bullarra*. Three days later the *Bullarra* would limp into Cossack Roads smoking like an ashcan. Though she had stood out to sea when the scale of the storm became apparent, anchoring well away from the shoals with her head to the wind and all hatches battened down, the hurricane had blasted into her with such terrifying force that, along with other severe damage, her smokestack had been wrenched off its bolts.

For thirty-six hours one of Australia's most devastating cyclones had raged across La Grange Bay, south of Broome, before scouring the Eighty Mile Beach and ransacking the coast as far west as Roebourne. A Norwegian liner, the *Crown of England*, was utterly wrecked; the *Concordia* lay stranded on a reef; and three sailing barges and nine luggers were smashed or sunk.

The *Koombana* had been in wireless contact with the German liner *Gneisenau* on her first afternoon out, but no word had been heard from her since then. On Sunday 24 March, attempting to allay anxiety among the Fremantle public, a Steamship Company manager offered the reassurance that 'Captain Allen was a very careful and cautious master and no doubt would have kept well out to sea when the cyclone struck'. By the next day, the *Koombana*, which should have docked in Broome twenty-four hours after leaving Port Hedland, was five days overdue, and no amount of optimistic speculation could dispute the fact that nothing was known about her whereabouts or condition.

By the end of the month, although a scattered flotilla of vessels was out looking for her as far afield as Rowley Shoal, there was still no sign of the missing liner. Among the searchers was the steamship *Moira*, which had run before the hurricane for nearly 150 miles, and the federal government's fishery research trawler *Endeavour*. Even the battered *Bullarra*, sailing with a jury-rigged funnel, joined the search for her sister-ship, but could signal no news to the Broome lighthouse on her return.

On 3 April, a fortnight after the *Koombana* had put out from Port Hedland, the SS *Gorgon* spotted a floating litter of wreckage to the north of Bedout Island. Only a single object was immediately identifiable: a white panelled door of state-room quality, sporting the design of a Grecian urn. On one side of the door the handle was smashed, and on the other it had vanished completely, so the door must have been thrust from its frame under tremendous pressure. There was only one liner plying the coast that could boast staterooms

Other ships converged on the area, The mast of a ship's boat and other flotsam were found; and then a lifeboat bearing the crest of the Adelaide Steamship Company was spotted. No one was aboard. A few days later, a party of Aborigines walking on a beach north of the Amphinome Shoal discovered three copper buoyancy tanks that had drifted loose from another lifeboat. Nothing much else was ever salvaged.

A court of enquiry convened at Perth later that year to hear evidence about the loss of the *Koombana*. The prevailing weather conditions were described, the seaworthiness of the ship was well attested, and not a word of criticism was uttered about her captain. So what had become of her? From the irregular surfacing of the flotsam he had found, the master of the search vessel *Una* believed it must have risen from somewhere deep within the forty fathoms of water under his keel. But if the stricken ship had indeed gone down, no one knew where she lay. So the court of enquiry into the last voyage of the *Koombana* was driven to the unconsoling conclusion that 'her fate passes beyond human knowledge, and remains a mystery of the sea'.

Not a single body had been recovered, and for that reason – such was the law at the time – none of the passengers, prisoners, or crew could be officially registered as dead. For practical purposes, such as the proving of wills, the custody of children, and the recognition of marriages, courts were free to make the obvious presumption; but otherwise the 139 souls lost at sea with the SS *Koombana* – absent from whatever form of funeral their grieving relatives might devise, no longer alive yet not numbered among the dead – went missing from this life, having wrested from the storm a ghostly, bureaucratic kind of immortality. Among them, by dint of an unlucky change of mind that day in Fremantle, was William Job Clarke.

That Perth court of enquiry might have assigned his fate to a mystery of the sea but, for me, neither the story nor the mystery ended there.

In 1972, sixty years after the *Koombana* vanished, I was present at the death of my father, Victor Metcalfe Clarke, in the bedroom of the house where he lived with his dearly loved wife Clara in Halifax. He had been seriously ill for some time, and my mother was already exhausted and distraught. But she was also strangely flustered when, some days later, she handed me his birth certificate, which was needed for official business. Looking at the flimsy form, I saw that his mother, Donaldeina, who was described as a flax-drawer, had registered his birthdate as 21 June 1914, but the column reserved for the name and surname of his father had been marked by the registrar with a dash as blank.

Such was my mother's Edwardian sense of shame that she was embarrassed to reveal a secret she'd kept from me for 33 years. Nor could she understand why I didn't seem at all upset by the news. She had lived through times when a birth out of wedlock was a public disgrace; I'd grown up in a more permissive culture largely untroubled by such matters, so my dad's illegitimacy didn't bother me. On the contrary, I was amused that his certificate of birth officially confirmed that he was in actuality the bastard I had secretly judged him to be in my younger days, when he and I were often at odds and not at all the deeply affectionate father and son we became in the years before he died.

But if his illegitimacy was no problem to me, its discovery gave birth to a different issue. I had learned something new and enlightening about my father but I now had no idea who my grandfather was. Certainly not William Job Clarke, the shovel-bearded man in the seaman's cap and coat whose portrait I'd seen in the cellar when I was a boy. No, he had gone down with the *Koombana* somewhere off Australia in March 1912 – two whole years before my own father smuggled himself into life.

If not him, then who? The only clue offered by the birth certificate was my dad's unusual middle name, which was shared by no one else in the family. Had the mystery man's surname been Metcalfe? Might he too have been a Scot? A resident of Halifax or a visitor? Perhaps someone from the Royal Oak across the street, or even one of the performers from the nearby Palace of Varieties? None of my immediate relatives knew. When I contacted my father's oldest brother, also called Bill, who had emigrated to Australia many years earlier, he remained tight-lipped. So my grandfather's identity remains a mystery of my grandmother's bed; one that no amount of online searching will solve.

Sadly, I never knew Donaldeina, who died before I was born. But, given her distinctively Scottish forename, it proved easy to trace her forebears through seamen and ship's carpenters, all the way back to the Cameron of Lochiel who was killed at Culloden. She was well loved by my aunts and uncles and must have been a doughty lady to have raised, almost single-handed, eight children (including my dad) into a family of good-humoured, honest, hard-working, and adventurous individuals, while her husband was away on the high seas across the world and, at the early age of thirty-nine, already (if not officially) dead.

Because I have no share in that seaman's genes, I can't blame the 'willy-willy' that ravaged the northwest coast of Australia for cutting short my male ancestral line. On the contrary, I have to thank it for my existence. Had William Job not changed his mind in Fremantle, or had he proved to be the disaster's sole survivor, his family might have joined him in Australia, and my father would never have been part of it. He would not have been born, and neither, later, would I. But he lived out his fifty-eight years and turned merchant seaman himself during the war, before working as the stoker and, later, the warehouse manager of a Halifax cotton mill. By the time of his death I was already the father of his granddaughter, and I would eventually become – like one of the passengers who went down with the *Koombana* – an author.

That being the case, it makes a kind of daimonic sense that I was born into a sea story that is also a mystery story; and though I can know nothing about my male-line ancestors, I cherish a novelist's – and a fantasist's – freedom to invent stories about who and what they may have been.

So what then about the story that I've just told? If it has a place in this book, perhaps it's as a reminder of something we too easily forget: that every life is mysterious in its beginning and its end and, though our daimon may understand the secret nature of that mystery, it remains a secret that has to be kept, even from ourselves.

# Stoker

The scrape of steel on coal:
down more than half a century
I hear my father's shovel
in the dark grime of the boiler-house,
and watch him banking heat
against the start of work next day.

It's Sunday morning; I am
nine years old; he's brought me here
for company, to try to make me talk;
and my glum shying from his questions
troubles him, while all around us,
empty of its staff, the mill is filled
with ghost-ship silence, from
the shiny smell of oil and drive-belts
in the idle engine house, up
into the dusty halls where skips
of varnished bobbins wait beside
the stunned ranks of machines.

Tomorrow will be loud with shouts
and din of work, but right now
we are speechless and uneasy, as if
some strict, annihilating force
has cancelled everybody else,
and only he and I – two strangers
baffled by each other's love –
are left to feed this fire, to send
this silent plume across the hill
and moors, across the more than
fifty years in which the sadness
of our mutual defeat undoes me still.

# Wind

This piece was commissioned for a volume of essays celebrating the work of Ted Hughes and its widespread influence on other writers. Sadly, the poet's death in 1998 meant that the collection would be published as a tribute honouring his memory. Edited under the title *The Epic Poise* by Nick Gammage, the book was published by Faber & Faber in 1999.

Sometimes, in a culture bereft of other meaningful rites of passage, a book encountered at the right moment can act on the imagination with the force of an initiatory ordeal. Certainly something of the sort was true for me when I was a moody sixth-form student at Heath Grammar School in Halifax, in the 1950s.

My weekly timetable of English, History, and Art left plenty of gaps for private study, and I spent a lot of time mooching about in the school library. Its windows looked out to where Beacon Hill loomed over the town with its restless-making reminder that, beyond the valley's blackened congregation of mills and factories and spires, wilder horizons were unfolding across a raw landscape of high moorland and introverted crags, of ling and blowing cotton grass, of water, rock, and wind.

Meanwhile, inside the library a desultory collection of books lolled in their cases. Most of them were heirlooms from the time when the Elizabethan Free School was rebuilt in 1878, but a few more recent acquisitions were of particular interest to me. Among them were Yeats's edition of *The Oxford Book of Modern Verse* and a black-bound volume of T.S. Eliot's *Collected Poems*, for around that time I'd begun to fancy myself a poet.

Enthused by the delusion, and for shamelessly selfish reasons, I put pressure on our English teacher, 'Biddy', to respond to a leaflet from the Poetry Book Society which offered what sounded to me

43

like a good deal. In return for a modest annual subscription, the library's stock would be enlivened by the work of two contemporary poets each year. Eventually Biddy agreed that it wouldn't wreck his department's budget for 1957 if we gave the thing a try.

I got to unpack the first book when it came. It turned out to be the first volume of verse by a young writer called Ted Hughes. It's title was *A Hawk in the Rain* and I'd turned only a few pages when a big wind came blowing out at me. The poem titled 'Wind' buffeted me back on my heels, picked me up, tossed me about for a time, then blew me clear away. Watching all the known world pitch and roll beneath me, I was gone from the library, up across the smoky town, down the dark cleft of the Calder Valley, and out towards Mytholmroyd, where one of my uncles had been a tenant farmer, and from whence the voice of this breathtaking wind had first blown.

Its accent was recognisably local. I heard it gusting in vowels flat as the rainwater in a moorland reservoir. Its tongue clattered out a palate-dance of consonants that strummed with Pennine energy. For this was a local gale, straight off Top Withens, blowing the whole West Riding into shape, then out of it again, snatching up ships and horses, tents and iron bars in its frenzy, yet trembling with a kind of nervous awe at all it stumbled on.

I stood in the silence of the school library, blinking in the teeth of the gale, and knew that poetry was alive, immediate, and here.

As Ted Hughes wrote later, 'Almost every poet, when he mentions the wind, touches one of his good moments of poetry.' Long before he published his own first collection of verse, he well knew how high the standard had been set by Shelley and others, and he was truly on his mettle in this poem. In retrospect one wonders whether he also might have sensed its oracular air of prophecy, that a whole life would have to be lived in the hard eye of that wind?

I came to realise much later that this extraordinary man from Mytholmroyd was also venturing across the weird, metamorphic landscape of the alchemical imagination, but far ahead of me. It gave a strange kind of comfort, at once heartening and gruelling, to watch him pass through the bleak nigredo of *Crow*, over the grim terrain of *Elmet*, down among the *Cave Birds*, and on to the creatures of light in the radiance of *River*'s end.

Sadly, that lifetime's journey has ended, but the commitment to its rigours that took him ever further into the interpenetrating realms of myth and memory has proved so deep-searching that the perspectives he opened on the poetics of the soul will continue to unfold as long as there are readers.

When I look back at 'Wind' now it makes me think of the robust emblem in Michael Maier's alchemical document *Atalanta Fugiens*, where a vortex of wind whirls from the head of a naked man to spin the Philosopher's Stone from air. But I knew nothing of such hermetic images in 1957. Nor could I have guessed then how widely Ted Hughes's important essay on 'Myth and Education' would later enlarge my understanding, both as teacher and as writer, of the role of the Imagination as mediator between the contending realities of inner and outer worlds. One day, much later, I would find a shape for my novel *Alice's Masque* around what he had taught me there, but all that mattered to me at seventeen when I first read 'Wind' was that I shared my natal landscape with a prodigious new poet who had proved that poetry was still able to breathe visionary fire.

I took this poem personally. It filled me with a quickening sense of exhilaration and dread. In its appetite for language, its generation and consumption of metaphor, its attention to colour, scale, and stress, and the ardour with which its power of hyperbolic invention stilled itself at last to a steady, unflinching gaze, it seemed to demonstrate exactly why writing mattered.

Like the people in the poem, I felt the wind had gripped my heart. It began to answer passionate questions that I hardly dared to put, while posing others that I wasn't ready yet to answer. In doing so, it joined the converging forces that were blowing me through to a risky place where, in the long run at least, no other life than a writer's life would do.

With the rough affection of the elder brother that I never had and always wanted, it stretched and dared and bullied me. For a book, as I say, can offer a kind of initiation. It may not even take a whole book: at the right time just a single, hard-earned poem will serve; and I think this poem astonished my young imagination into consciousness.

# Into the World of Light

This review of *The Laughter of Foxes: A Study of Ted Hughes* by Keith Sagar (Liverpool University Press, 2000) was originally published in *Resurgence*.

At a time when so much of our experience is oppressed by impersonal forces that appear almost impervious to the resistance of the individual human spirit, more and more people are writing poetry. The proliferation of magazines, small presses, and poetry competitions – all of them receiving far more material than they could possibly publish – seems to speak to something indomitable in our need to utter the kind of language that, as Ingmar Bergman once memorably suggested, is 'spoken from soul to soul, in phrases which escape the control of the intellect in an almost voluptuous way'. Yet, when so much is urgently and disastrously wrong with our relations to the world, can poetry finally matter? Was Auden right in insisting that poetry makes nothing happen, or was Shelley closer to the truth in declaring poets to be the unacknowledged legislators of the world?

Much will depend on what kind of poetry one's talking about, and on the degree of imaginative commitment brought to the task by the poet. It's also a matter of courage, of whether the writer is cosily content to play word games round the fire (as D.H. Lawrence once put it), or there is an acceptance of the daunting responsibility to stride into the dark and see what lies out there. By which I also mean, of course, to see what lies *in here*.

In our own time, there has been no more impressive exemplar of the courage required by that kind of exploration than Ted Hughes. For him there was no doubt about the evolutionary importance of poetry. In an interview given in 1989 he declared his conviction that

'One of the great problems that poetry works at is to renew life, renew the poet's own life, and, by implication, renew the life of the people, if they respond to the way he has done it for himself'.

Taken seriously – and the timeline of Hughes's life and work provided in the volume under review indicates just how seriously we have to take him – the scale of these simply expressed demands is immense and terrifying. It makes of the poet's own quest for articulated consciousness a spiritual agon that is at once personal and public. Far from the comfort of an ivory tower, the poet's career is elevated to a kind of shamanic rite, fraught with all the risks of hubris, by means of which something visionary and evolutionary may be won for the public good. The lacerating stress of living with the contradictory tensions of such an ordeal may also (vide Delmore Schwartz, John Berryman, et al.) kill the poet. Yet, in this view of the poet's task, if those tensions are sustained and converted into creative energy, then something powerfully transformative can happen. For Hughes it was as if such a prophetic order of poetry was 'a biological healing process', one that 'seizes on what is depressing and destructive, and lifts it into a realm where it becomes healing and energizing'.

In championing this ambitiously vigorous myth of poetic activity, Hughes places it near the heart of our deepest human need. But, as he himself insisted, responsibility for the wider implications of this process does not stop with the poet. For whether or not the words make any difference in the world will depend on our capacity to bring to the reading a degree of imaginative energy commensurate with the demands of the ordeal that has been undergone on our behalf. In Keith Sagar, a scholar who shares both his faith in the visionary imagination and his passionate concern for the natural environment, Hughes found one of his most conscientious and sensitive readers – the kind of reader Hughes himself was for Wyatt, Shakespeare, Coleridge, Eliot, and many others, one who brings to bear 'the co-operative, imaginative attitude of a co-author'.

Everything in *The Laughter of Foxes* will be of abiding interest to those who already love and admire the poetry of Ted Hughes. The chapter on the evolution of one of Hughes's poems, 'The Dove Came', offers illuminating insights into the process by which the crucible of his imagination transformed and reduced the teeming prima materia of the poem until what remained was a phenomenal simplicity of the kind to be found only on the far side of complexity. The Appendix in which Sagar reconstructs 'The Story of Crow', the 'epic-folk tale' that provides the mythological underpinning for the life and songs of *Crow*, will be invaluable to future scholars – not least because the materials were assembled with Hughes's guidance and permission. The chapter titled 'From Prospero to Orpheus' traces in a maturely critical and imaginatively profitable spirit the difficult and tragic issues of Hughes's evolving relationship with Sylvia Plath, while those titled 'The Mythic Imagination' and 'From World of Blood to World of Light' may have the strongest resonance for anyone seriously engaged with the grave public issues of our time.

In reviewing Hughes's achievement, Sagar starts from two fundamental premises: firstly, that 'the history of Western Civilization has been the history of man's increasingly devastating crimes against Nature'; and, secondly, that 'the most important role for the poet is to challenge the false myths we all live by and offer true myths which involve the inward journey and the painful acquisition of self-knowledge'. Sagar also makes a case for the imagination as the voice of nature – 'the voice of human nature, of course, but not a human nature that defines itself in contradistinction to the rest of life'. Writing in a humane, accessible language throughout, he associates Hughes's life and work with the value and force of living myth in a cultural context where 'art, science, philosophy, religion, are converging towards a common centre which we are now in a position to recognize as holistic, sacramental'.

As its title suggests, the chapter called 'From World of Blood to World of Light' traces Hughes poetic journey from an unflinching confrontation with the apparent brutality and savagery of existence to the visionary moment at the end of *River* where both men and bears, fishing for salmon together, are experienced as 'creatures of light'. The journey has taken the poet across a burning-ground of personal suffering, and if, after the psychic dismembering dramatised in the earlier works, the hero-poet has emerged at last to recognise and celebrate the creative power of what he names the Goddess of Complete Being, it is a triumph won not by rhetoric, Sagar lucidly argues, but through a language honestly forged out of knowledge, grief, and silence.

In an age when most literary criticism is of interest to no one but initiates of its own scarcely penetrable codes, this book reminds us what an enlarging joy, privilege, and challenge it is to read the work of a master poet. In so doing, it performs a valuable service both to its subject and to the wider evolution of consciousness in our time. Yet the problems confronting us on a planetary scale are not, of course, soluble through the endeavours of a single poet, however embracing and rigorous their scope may be. Whether poetry matters to us or not, in critical times such as these the responsibility remains with each of us to bring to our lives the highest degree of conscious ethical commitment and imaginative energy of which we are capable. In that always difficult struggle, as the life and work of Ted Hughes so magnificently demonstrate, poetry can be far more than the consolation of an idle hour: it becomes a vital source of transforming energy.

# Scabby Donkeys

In 1994 I was invited to join a small group gathering at Sharpham House, the Devon home of the environmentalist Maurice Ash, to explore the personal and cultural relevance of myth in a secular age. Eight of us were present for that lively colloquium, each with an informed interest in the theme – interests that were creatively and spiritually engaged rather than academic. We soon found ourselves so engrossed by the issues it raised that one of our members, Satish Kumar, proposed the running of a week-long course on the subject at the recently founded Schumacher College, of which he was director. Sharing his enthusiasm, John Lane, the founder of the Beaford Arts Centre, who had succeeded Maurice Ash as Chairman of the Dartington Trust, suggested that the end of the course should coincide with a public conference at Dartington Hall on the theme of 'Myth in Our Time'. I was asked if I would act as resident scholar on the course and direct the weekend conference. Wen it became clear that I would have a more or less free hand on the selection of speakers, the first name that came to mind was that of Ted Hughes.

In part, I suppose, because I had never met him, Ted had himself been a mythological figure for me since the day when, as a seventeen-year-old would be poet living a few miles down the Calder Valley from the place where he was born, I first encountered his work. Unlike Ted, who was unshakeably confident of his own daimonic calling, I had felt my adolescent belief in myself as a poet quickly shrivel in the austere critical light of Cambridge intellectuality. But I'd followed his career closely, revering and envying him as a champion of the poetic imagination – a writer whose work, like that of William Blake, Emily Brontë, and D.H. Lawrence before him, reached into life with a passional energy that was lit with a unique visionary radiance.

I was impressed by his resolve to stay loyal to what Lawrence once called a 'stark, bare, rocky directness of statement [which] alone makes poetry today'. For Ted, the litmus test of poetic truth was the conviction it brings that 'the observer has paid in full for what he records, and that has earned him a superior stake in reality'. Such strict, self-interrogative resolution made each fresh volume of his verse like a timely injection of steroids into a literary culture that had cut itself off from its mythic ground and was too ready to keep the heart at bay with apotropaic dosages of irony, scepticism, and wit.

Ted was nine years older than me, tougher minded, yet with a tenderness of the senses that left him more open and responsive to what, in his essay 'The Hanged Man and the Dragonfly', he called '*mana* as the goddess of the source of terrible life, the real substance of any life that has substance, in spite of what we might prefer'. To me, in my still tentative and unformed condition, he came across as a mature, fiercely antlered, dominant alpha male; I found the thought of him as daunting as it was compelling. He seemed like the elder brother I never had, and would never meet, the kind who, out of sheer vigorous exuberance, might be just as likely to bully me into shape as to protect and assist. Perhaps that was why, though I often thought of doing so, I never got around to writing to him to say how deeply I admired his work and how important it had been in the development of my imagination. Instead I told myself that the man must be deluged with fan-mail and had better uses for his time than to listen to my adulation, let alone respond to it.

Then came the disasters that beset his life, making unconscionable the thought of penning such a letter. Even some years later, having undergone a calamity of my own which – though nowhere near as devastating as the savage ordeals of the heart and mind that he endured and survived – gave me some measure of insight into the anguish he must have suffered – even then, I couldn't bring myself to write to him. What could possibly be the point?

That feeling was confirmed in 1975 when I travelled from Norfolk to Cambridge, where Ted was booked to give a reading at the Poetry Festival. A large, excited audience was packed into – was it the Senate House or the Corn Exchange? – I can't remember – but I was sitting close enough to the podium to study the gaunt figure of a man who, in another context, might have passed for a Yorkshire fast bowler. Such was the nervous intensity of the reading as his distinctively Pennine voice read from the poems, and told us stories hidden behind 'the Life and Songs of the Crow', that his whole body seemed to quiver. Watching the pages tremble in his fingers, I knew, even more emphatically than when I'd first opened that copy of *The Hawk in the Rain* back in 1957, that poetry was alive, vital, and here.

But now, after another twenty years had gone by, this unexpected invitation to call a conference at Dartington gave me both incentive and occasion to approach him. After all, I knew of no one with a deeper, more eloquent experience and understanding of the living power of myth in our own desacralised age.

By that time, I had published work of my own. Keith Sagar, an old friend of Ted's and an early champion of his work, and now a new friend of mine, had told me that he and Ted had spoken of it. I also now knew that for some years, though with no conscious intention, I had been following the trail the poet had already blazed into the sometimes luminous, often bewildering terrain of alchemical symbolism, and that it had proved meaningful to him in his quest for self-understanding, as it had also proved for me in mine. Perhaps, after all, there were matters about which he and I might correspond.

So I gathered my wits and sat down to write a letter. It told him of the moment, almost forty years earlier, when I'd first read his work, and of the way it had instantly ignited my imagination. I spoke of how much each successive volume of his verse had meant to me across the years, and how, when I was working as a lecturer in further education, I had read an article he had published in the *Times Educational Supplement* which carried the title 'Myth and Education'. It had, I told him, utterly transformed my understanding of the nature of the Imagination in ways that still inspired both my writing and my teaching. The letter concluded by saying that, as I'd been asked to direct a conference on myth at Dartington, it was now my eager hope that he would join us there.

When, after much rewording, I had a draft that might work, I placed it inside a signed copy of *The Chymical Wedding* and posted it off to Court Green.

At that time, I couldn't have known the extent to which, in addition to all his other duties, Ted had been wearied and depleted by three exacting years of writing prose. Since completing his revelatory interpretation of the Complete Works in *Shakespeare and the Goddess of Complete Being,* he had felt compelled to write first a major essay on 'Myths, Metres and Rhymes' and then an intense visionary study of Coleridge's verse in a companion piece, 'The Snake in the Oak'. Only a poet with access to an acute intellectual imagination could have composed prose works of that deep-searching order, and they came at a price.

Later, as illness took possession of his body, Ted would come to attribute the serious attrition of his immune system to this prolonged exile away from poetry in the less salutary climate of prose. By the time my letter arrived on his desk he was in his sixty-fourth year and 'jealous of every fading minute'. In these circumstances, my request that he come to speak to us at Dartington was doomed to disappointment.

But I was not. In finally writing a letter I'd first conceived many years before, I felt I'd accomplished something personally important. It made a long overdue return on years of outstanding debt – a debt of which the creditor might have been unaware but which still needed to be paid. So even a brief polite note regretfully declining my invitation would have been a more than acceptable reply: it would have become a valued possession.

A week or so after I'd posted the letter, an unexpected parcel turned up at my door. It contained a pre-publication copy of a handsomely produced book titled *Winter Pollen: Occasional Prose.* Folded inside was a single sheet of duplicating paper, both sides of which were densely covered in a spidery, cursive hand. The first line read, 'Well, you will understand well enough what a lift your package gave me.'

By then, having received thoughtful letters from previously unknown readers of my own books, I did indeed know how much it can matter to authors who spend too much time shut inside the silence of the study to hear such responses from the world into which their work has been posted. Yet none of such letters as came my way mattered to me as much as this one did. That first line instantly overwhelmed me; so too the generosity of his response to the gift of my novel. But I was still more touched by the note of personal honesty – of modesty and vulnerability even – in the subsequent paragraphs.

The letter gives an account of how the image of a gigantic woman rising from a swamp in a children's story he was writing had unexpectedly released the energy needed to accomplish his Shakespeare study. It goes on to relate how, 'as a kind of afterbirth', he later found himself 'babbling out a whole essay on Coleridge's visionary poems'. Referring to that essay, he wrote, 'I'm sending you this (it's the last piece in the enclosed book) just to show you how weirdly my interests and notions have been shadowing yours. Must be the life-in-death-hand of the Calder Valley!'

Of course there can be no doubt about which of us had been shadowing the other – I had been stalking Ted like a rare wild animal for more than half my life; and it's a measure of the man's dignity and largesse of heart that he could write so openly to this supplicating stranger about his own immense achievements without a hint of grandiosity or condescension.

Others may have less enthusiastic views of Ted's character, life and work. For me, the most apt description of my relationship to the man I never met can be found in a kind of postscript to the letter. Both sides of the sheet on which it was written were so crammed with his script there was no space left to sign it. Instead, he opened the fly-leaf of *Winter Pollen* and, beneath a generous dedicatory superscription, his signature, and the date, he wrote,

Scabby donkeys smell each other over nine hills

# Seven Haiku for a Poet

In the silent room
he sleeps: a fox is printing
blood across the page.

He calls to the sky:
through rainy light a hawk
swoops to his bare wrist.

House, hill, moorland, crag,
all blown about. He is caught
in the teeth of the wind,

Maddened by despair,
a crow caws its black grief at
the porch of his ear.

Dehorned in the crush.
Might peace be found on a farm
with a farmer's wife?

Under cold torrents
salmon of wisdom take
live bait from each line.

Though crowned with laurel
and dead as a doornail now,
he crackles with life.

# How to Refuse a
# Heavenly Mansion

This review of *The Chameleon Poet: A Life of George Barker* by
Robert Fraser (Jonathan Cape 2001) was first published in
the *London Magazine* (April/May 2002) when Barker's eldest
son, the poet Sebastian Barker, was its editor.

Towards the end of this engagingly written biography Robert Fraser
offers a sketch of his subject at home to friends and visitors in the
drinking room at Bintry House on Norfolk Saturday nights in the
1980s:

> Newcomers made their way to the hearth, where Barker held
> court, resting his left elbow on the mantelpiece, scowling at
> the company, or appraising them with an indulgent, mocking,
> come-and-get-me smirk. One by one he locked kindred spirits
> in a fervent *sumo* clasp and subjected them to eye-ball-to-
> eyeball scrutiny. They emerged from this encounter convinced
> that Barker valued them uniquely.

I recognise the moment, and the feeling, well. The picture is accurately drawn. It's George as I knew him, mellowing into his seven-
ties, liberal with his kisses, and quite capable, only minutes later, of
combusting into pyroclastic flows of rage. I'd been fascinated by his
work since I first found it in a PEN anthology and John Lehmann's
*London Magazine* of the middle 1950s, but I'd also heard stories about
the bacchanals at Bintry, so for a long time I steered clear. Yet, when
George and I met towards the end of his life, I was quickly seduced

by the aerobatic skills of his imagination, by his outrageous charm, and above all by the generosity of his heart. As a writer I remain hugely in his debt. I miss him deeply still, and for that reason it was with almost proprietorial vigilance that I began to read Robert Fraser's attempt to tell the story of his life.

Slippery as ever, George himself had declared the task impossible (while at the same time stashing away in plastic bags the evidence without which his prophecy would almost certainly have been fulfilled). It wasn't just that the trickster-poet had spent so many years blowing smoke across the past and garlanding the myths that grew around him. For, even if the facts could be established, what delicacy of tact and judgement would it take to get close to – yet keep a sober distance on – a heart known to its wearer as both 'a heavenly menagerie' and 'a butcher's cave'? How to do justice to the passionate loyalties of that heart while also chronicling its betrayals? How to honour both the deep, sacramental seriousness of the man along with his wicked gift for fun, while at the same time fathoming his reach in grief and guilt? On top of that, how to keep pace with that flashing intellect *and* the scrupulous care for language of a poet who was the master elegist of his age? And to pull this off with the fierce love of George's wife and family looking on? Small wonder that Fraser underwent 'moods of anguish, elation and despair' while trying to outflank his prey's prediction that 'it simply can't be done.'

As Barker's friend and editor, he was well aware of the difficulties, but the solution proposed in his Preface – that 'once the myths had been stripped away, I had simply to put down what had happened' – amounts to rather less than his actual achievement. In so far as those events could be put down, Fraser has done it well – though I imagine those who were there might quarrel with some of his depictions. But because he has also performed a larger service I strongly recommend this book to two classes of reader: those who seriously care about the art of poetry; and everybody else. For what Fraser unfolds is a moving, entertaining, and enlarging study of what it means to live out a life's vocation to the full, without compromise or safety nets, and with a readiness to pay the price exacted by such proud commitment.

And what a life it was! 'The poet's only hope', wrote Ted Hughes in answer to a *London Magazine* questionnaire on the state of poetry in the early 1960s, is to be infinitely sensitive to what his gift is … According to this sensitivity, and to his faith in it, he will go on developing as a poet, as Yeats did, pursuing those adventures, mental, spiritual and physical, whatever they may be, that his gift wants, or he will lose its guidance, lose the feel of its touch in the workings of his mind.'

George Barker knew very well where his only hope lay. He never lost that sensitivity, and the strict terms set by Yeats's poem 'The Choice' must have been seared on his memory. For, given his absolute loyalty to poetry, there would be no 'heavenly mansion' for him, much 'raging in the dark', and – with an increasing number of mouths to feed – a life always dogged by 'that old perplexity an empty purse'.

'I trust', he said to me once, 'you are a man of sufficient intellectual dignity whereby you would not write verses unless absolutely compelled to do so.' That he himself was so compelled was never in doubt. Fraser shows how the fate that went with such compulsion was conditioned from the start by the tension between the rebel-Irish ancestry of his hugely affectionate Roman Catholic mother and the stiff, soldierly Englishness of his Nonconformist dad. The mix was further complicated when young George began to study under the intellectually conservative Father Dale-Evans at the Brompton Oratory. It was there that this 'boy of good make and mind' encountered Newman's metaphorical description of such a boy in his account of 'the terrible, aboriginal calamity' that afflicts humankind. Ever afterwards, 'sin' – both original and otherwise – was for him a word that carried its full theological force.

Towards the end of his life, Barker confessed to having broken every commandment except the one forbidding murder. A Catholic who 'found it impossible to retain an absolutely total love of the Church', he saw himself as a renegade. Yet among his noblest achievements are a lengthy *True Confession*, an elegiac meditation *At Thurgarton Church*, and the extended prayer of *Anno Domini*. For poetry, as Fraser says, became 'a means by which he could express both his sense of religious awe and the urgency of his revolt'. Barker's heterodox vision of life as a passion play charged with immense spiritual consequence may account for the neglect of his work by a culture chary of ranging outside its own narrow scepticism. It is also the measure of his continuing importance.

Yeats must have sensed it in him, along with what he called 'a lovely subtle mind and a rhythmic invention comparable to Gerard Hopkins'. Why else would a man as spiritually serious as T.S. Eliot have taken such care over this 'very peculiar fellow' in whose genius he believed? Yet Barker won't be nailed down as a religious poet. A voice very different from his, that of Harold Pinter, hails him as 'a love poet of the highest order', and perhaps the hardest part of Fraser's task was tracking Barker through the passionate, guilt-racked love affairs behind the verse. Always magnetically attractive, George was lucky enough to win (and, for all his faults and duplicities, to keep) the love of several magnificent women. As one of the mythic love stories of the last century, his life with Elizabeth Smart was already well documented, but the course of his love for his first wife Jessica and the later attachments to Betty Cass and Dede Farrelly are less well known. So too is the story of the last great love of George's life. For almost thirty years Elspeth Barker blessed him with a loving home, anchoring his spirit there, enduring his rants and rages with indomitable devotion – 'I had never met anyone of his age who was so consistently rude and outrageous' – and clarifying and deepening the reach of his poetic vision. Fraser guides us through the turbulent passages of Barker's erotic life without flinching from his lies, yet also leaves us with a lively sense of a man 'who prized emotional honesty above everything'.

If it's madness, as the Celts used to say, to love a poet, to mock a poet, to be a poet, then Barker was quintessentially a poet in that fierce Celtic mode. So completely so that it seems impossible to speak of him except in contradictory terms. Like Blake's, his imagination was possessed by contraries, not least the paradoxical conviction that 'even love is evil, even life is good'. As much salamander as chameleon, and as gentle as he could be devastating, this impossibly endearing man was never quite one thing or the other. Always both this *and* that, betwixt and beyond, elusive, oxymoronic, polymorphously perverse, the paradisal light of his vision was invariably countered by a brimstone darkness.

Such a shape-shifting figure resists definition, yet Fraser has done a remarkable job of catching him in flight. Barker emerges as an apostate believer – a kind of unruly Franciscan in thrall to Aphrodite. We watch him resisting political affiliation and then occasioning parliamentary debate (how many poets have managed *that?*), while later pitting the prodigious charity of his imagination against Thatcher's money-grubbing corrosion of the English soul. Always his own man, we see him trading jokes and insults with artists, rogues, and writers in the Soho pubs, yet writing his finest verse out of an attentive love for the rural landscapes where he lived and worked. However disorderly his public behaviour, we also glimpse him at his desk, a diligent, solitary craftsman caring as deeply for the metrical tradition of English verse as he did for the need to make it new.

And so the arc of Fraser's story brings us movingly to the place where a life that might so often have gone down in flames ends in almost shadowless contentment. Happily married, his confession made, the ballads still tripping out after the *Collected Works* was done, the Commonwealth Prize won, and keeping company with rascals still, George even saw his long-lost first child return to join the rest of the large family he fathered.

As Fraser says, the tone of his last poems is of 'a man who has looked into the seething heart of things and rejoiced'. If the ardent adventure of George's life was not without its casualties, he paid the price in anguish for the damage that he did. It's hard to believe that he finally went unforgiven.

'You couldn't help but love him,' said Clive Sinclair; 'he made you feel more alive.' The judgement feels as true of the work as of the man, and in giving us this perceptive biography, with its careful readings of the major poems, Robert Fraser has shown us the man in all his antinomian complexity. It may be too much to hope that his book will wake up any critics still too entranced by their own aridity to recognise the range and stature of this visionary poet, but you never know. Not that George would give a damn. 'I've been to the top of Parnassus,' he used to growl with a scapegrace gleam in his eye, 'and – wha'd'ya know? – it's *flat!*'

# Sacred Monster

If anyone ever merited that oxymoronic title it's surely George Barker. In evidence, consider two statements he made about his life-long avocation. In the first he declared that 'to preserve and to enlarge the rejoicing categories of created things is the duty of the poet', which sounds agreeable enough. The second, given at the 1967 World Gathering of Poets in Montreal, may be less so. It affirms this personal credo: 'I believe the nature of the poet to be at heart anarchic, so that in the inconceivable eventuality of an Ideal Society, a society, that is, possessing no faults to which we could rationally object, it would still be the job of the poet to object.'

At the heart of such a declaration lies a resolute, creative perversity, the nature of which can be fully understood only when held in tension with the fact that, to the end of his days, this particular poet remained an ardent, if serially delinquent, believer in the Roman Catholic faith. In a sense, therefore, the uncompromising course of his dissolute life was a gamble with damnation. So, in many ways a monster, yes – but a *sacred* monster.

Much of his behaviour was certainly monstrous, and sometimes – especially when supercharged by too much booze – abominably so. Legends of his dissipations abounded around Soho, Fitzrovia, and Norfolk, where he passed his final years, while the rumours of his escapades across North America, a continent that he crossed like a priapic Johnny Appleseed, are more numerous than the children who would later claim him to be their father.

Raffish and good-looking, Gorgeous George (as he was known) radiated a louche glamour that could be as ominous as it was appealing. By the same token, the words issuing fluently from his mouth could move the heart with tender urgency, reduce you to helpless laughter, or strike with the venom of a Gila monster's bite. On more

61

than one occasion he remarked how, were he not to write poetry, he would eventually do what that mythically anus-less reptile was reputed to do – explode under the pressure of its own accumulated shit.

So not at all what you'd call a *nice* man; one – you may be thinking – probably best avoided. There was a time when I certainly thought so, even though the poet's name had haunted me for years since I first came across it in a PEN anthology that a girlfriend gave me as a birthday present in the mid 1950s. My adolescent mind swayed to the lilting cadences of his poem 'A Song of the Sea', with its bitter litany of questions to a faithless lover and to himself. Then I came across his 'Summer Song', which rued the self-inflicted pain of

> The stupid heart that will not learn
> The everywhere of grief.

Discovering that he was a friend and rival to Dylan Thomas, whose verse was already important to me, I looked for more of his work, only to find much of its declamatory syntax and apocalyptic imagery barely penetrable. Yet some time later, when I came across a paperback edition of his novella, *The Dead Seagull*, his name once again summoned me with a strangely familiar resonance.

Though I didn't then know that the story was a counterpoint to Elizabeth Smart's classic account of passion and abandonment in *By Grand Central Station I Sat Down and Wept*, I became mesmerised by the distinctive tenor of a narrative voice that enunciated an erotic drama of love and lust, guilt, contrition and rage, through prose rhythms that contrived to be both ornate and precise, aphoristic and overblown. And somehow all that must be squared with the self-mockery of a brief prefatory note that stated, 'I could have wished to have made a lot of excisions in this little book, but then, if I had done, it would be so little as to be not a book but a rather impractical joke.'

So what was it about the impassioned rhetoric of these poems and this poetic prose that stirred me so? Who was he, this disquieting figure of whom the *New Statesman* reviewer had said, 'My mother warned me about George Barker when I was a boy … my mother was, up to a point, right'? And what, above all, did he have to do with me?

I was to find that out years later in 1972 when I moved to a market town in north Norfolk and learned that the locally scandalous poet was living in a village just a few miles up the road. Despite the troubling stories I heard, some daimonic compulsion, one that I did not entirely trust, pushed me into risking a request that he give a reading to the recently arrived group of young Americans whose studies I was supervising. The fee I could offer was embarrassingly small, but together with the promise of free booze it was enough to bring him along one evening, accompanied by Elspeth, his strong, long-suffering wife.

The powerful hour-long reading, delivered in his precisely enunciated, magisterial voice, astounded the whole group to rapt attention. The poems he read, mostly from the volume *In Memory of David Archer*, the socialist bookseller who spent his inheritance supporting some of the finest poets of his generation, were by turns moving, provocative, and very funny. Included was this one, which is simply titled with the Roman numeral V to mark its fifth place in a sequence of fifty-six poems:

> I think that like many susceptible men
> I have collected several monsters that might
> – had I not fed them flesh again and again –
> very much better have been buried when
>     they first came to light.


> Six doves and a small bunch of early spring
> crocuses, a primrose and a rare
> Siberian primula I received this morning
> Persuade me that the little pretty thing
>     Calls for no less care.

But the reading was well lubricated with wine, so it wasn't long before the monsters elbowed the doves out of the room. As the students began to ply him with naïve, occasionally crass questions and comments, his eyes narrowed and his tongue began to flash with a scurrilous eloquence that had little truck with patience or mercy.

Then the brilliance of his wit darkened until there was no visible sign that here was a man who was also capable of displaying that rarer quality he once described as 'the extraordinary gentleness that prevails in the presence of men who are truly poets'.

I was wondering how best to halt the evening's tilt towards disaster when my six-year-old daughter, Maddy, who had listened in attentive silence throughout, took advantage of a moment in which George poured himself yet more wine to say with a bemused note of concerned accusation, 'You're an alco-frolic.'

Her malapropism was innocent, but so providentially apposite that everyone immediately laughed with relief. Everyone, that is, except George. Stopped in his tracks, he put down the bottle, studied the child for a moment or two in suddenly shamed wonder, then whispered gently, 'You're absolutely right, my dear,' before turning to his wife and saying, 'Elspeth, take me home.'

My own earlier exchanges with him had been friendly enough, if wary; but, as someone who had once aspired to write poetry, I now felt a shock of alarm at finding myself in the presence of a man so utterly possessed by its exacting spirit. I was uncomfortably aware that, in sharp contrast to his flamboyant poetic intelligence, my left-brain, lit-crit, university education had largely flattened my imagination into an intellectual construct. Instinctively I sensed that a serious encounter with George's penetrating gaze might bring down that flimsy edifice in flames. Having more or less closed off access to a comparable poetry of the soul, what would I put in its place? So, when, over the next few years, invitations were offered by Elspeth to join the notorious Saturday night revels at their Itteringham home, they were politely declined.

By 1980 my life had undergone further change. I had given up formal teaching, and with my new wife, who was a fine ceramic artist, I was managing a small craft gallery while trying to knock a first novel into publishable shape. Around that time I was contacted by Elspeth, who had heard that I was offering tuition to pupils who were experiencing difficulty with school. Her daughter Raffaella had walked out of high school in the middle of her A-Level course. Would I consider giving her some help to prepare for the forthcoming exams?

As the Barkers were famous for their perennial indigence, I was well aware that such service would go unpaid, but again the daimon pushed. I agreed to try a session or two, and Raffaella (who would, like her mother, become a successful novelist, journalist, and teacher of creative writing) proved to be a responsive student of the Metaphysical poets.

After a couple of weeks, Elspeth was on the phone again. She and George were so grateful for the work I was doing with Raffaella – wouldn't I join the two of them for a little drink at a local pub?

By that time, to demur would have been more than rude, so I braced myself for the meeting. Yet, soon after joining them in a cloud of smoke by the bar of the Black Boys Inn, I sensed that George too had gone through significant changes in the intervening years. Rather than the fire-breathing hippogryph who had first enchanted and then half-terrorised my students, I was greeted by the welcoming, even gracious, smile of an elderly gent who was happy to thank me for teaching his daughter – as he put it – what I loved.

It felt sincere. I began to relax. Drinking, we talked amicably of other things. Then George took two sheets of paper from a pocket. 'I gather you're rather good at literary criticism, dear boy,' he smiled. 'Tell me what you think of this.'

I looked down at a poem titled 'Ben Bulben Revisited'. Typewritten in four long stanzas, it was an elegy addressed to the memory of W.B. Yeats. I knew already that Yeats had selected one of George's early poems as the final entry in his 1936 edition of *The Oxford Book of English Verse*. Both men were distinguished Anglo-Irish members of the pantheon of poets. They had known each other before I was born, and they had kissed one another as a further link in what was (George claimed) a golden chain of kisses stretching back to Chaucer and Gower. Now the younger poet had written a memorial poem in homage to his dead master, and I was being asked to pass judgement on it.

Hesitantly, I muttered something about how he must be among the few people alive who had the authority to write such a poem – a response that George dismissed with a wave of the hand: yes, of course; but what did I *think* of the bloody poem?

After a tense moment I answered that I thought it was a bloody good poem ... for the most part. To which he growled, 'Whaddya mean – *for the most part?*'

What had bothered me was a line that described the rough beast slouching from Nazareth 'with death under its oxter'. Aware of the challenge in his gaze, I decided to say so. When he asked what I thought wrong with it, I said that Basil Bunting had got away with using that archaic word for 'armpit' in *Briggflatts* because it felt consistent with the poem's use of Northumbrian dialect words; but I couldn't see what business an oxter had drawing attention to itself here.

George drew his breath into a long sniff before slowly nodding his head; then he snatched back the pages, and I watched, aghast, as he crumpled them in his hands and threw that tight ball away across the bar-room floor.

'Are we ready for another drink?' he asked.

After a moment's horror I realised that he must, of course, have many other drafts of the poem. When it eventually appeared in his last collection, *Street Ballads*, I took some satisfaction in seeing that death had been shifted from beneath the beast's oxter to be firmly gripped under its elbow. That was some years later and by then George and I had long been friends. Perhaps I was fortunate to catch up with him at a time when his volatile temperament had mellowed and his good-natured, if still wickedly limber, wit was more in evidence than the detonations of rage when he was affronted by falsity or a lack of true seriousness over matters about which he deeply cared. The insults he gave, which were frequent and picturesque, were also wryly affectionate, and there were times – particularly if news came of the death of old friends – when the depth and gentleness of his feelings ran clear.

Listening to poetry recited well – usually in Elspeth's voice – ranked high among his pleasures, and he too was an impressive reader, and not only in perfect command of his own verse. On one visit to our house I heard him ride the demanding pitch and falls of Gerard Manley Hopkins's sonnets of spiritual desolation with such perfect attention to the rhythmic stress of each line, and such presence inside their meaning, that his reading felt definitive.

Without the gift of George's friendship, I could never have

conceived of the old poet Edward Nesbit in *The Chymical Wedding*. Even then I had to cross the country from Norfolk to live in Somerset, denying myself the complex pleasure of his company for over four years, until the novel was written and published. Had I not done so, either his presence would have overshadowed the character completely or I would have abandoned that feature of the book out of a sense of failure to catch in my fiction anything that could remotely keep pace with the actual sacred monster who had, unknowingly, modelled for the part.

I saw him again on a number of occasions before his death. At the launch of Elspeth's moving and hilarious novel *O Caledonia*, he proudly wore a plastic badge labelled with the name of the ambiguously sexed pop-star Boy George. (Could anyone else match George Barker's claim to have been to bed with both Anaïs Nin and Alan Ginsberg?) I saw him give a strong London reading from the substantial volume of his *Collected Poems* at an evening introduced by his good friend Harold Pinter. On a later visit to Bintry I found him weakened by illness and sharing a downstairs room with the television set, on which, he ruefully told me, he was forced to watch the Australian soap opera *Neighbours* twice a day because some of his kids could watch it only in the morning and the others only in the evening. That ordeal might, he opined, be accepted for time-off in Purgatory.

As I had known he would, he also smiled at the gift I gave him – a colourful first edition of the novel *Beltane the Smith*, which I had brought because on an earlier visit, after a exchange of admissions, he'd remarked, 'We must be the only writers with a modestly serious claim to literary reputation who would publicly admit to a weakness for the dubious works of Geoffrey Farnol.'

Soon afterwards, on the Feast of All Souls, I saw his coffin carried into Itteringham church by four of his sons, his son-in-law, and a bank-robber friend.

George was a veteran seeker after truth, and he knew what it means to get lost. 'In an act of exploration,' he wrote, 'the navigator does not decline to put in at the wrong islands – he merely calls them by the wrong names. Thus the poet, in the pursuit of a moral paradise, may sometimes come upon such places as the Bay of Noble

Conception or the Archipelago of Partial Sanctity. But he does not often discover the Indias of Absolute Revelation he is after.'

Who can know whether any such revelation greeted George on arrival in the next world, or what, if any, form of penitential judgement awaited him? What seems clear from some of his last words uttered to his friend and fellow Catholic, Oliver Bernard, is that his religious faith remained with him to the end. 'I am entering the kingdom,' he declared, and it's my guess that his passport for that last journey, like the grave in which he lies, was blazoned with these two resolutely defiant assertions, *Resurgam* and *No Compromise*.

# Remembering George

*1913–1991*

Passion and gesture: one arm outstretched
and fingers splayed as though a captive bird
had just been freed and flung into the sky.

    It is the words, the self-astonished words, that fly.

Or like a figure walking at you from the sun,
the whole form thrown in shadow but the hair,
which is a white-hot, flashing crown of flame.

    It is the words, the self-consuming words, that burn.

# Beyond the Literary

## Some Thoughts on John Cowper Powys and His *Porius* as a Romance of the Prophetic Imagination

A version of this essay was published in the *Powys Journal*, Vol. 27, 2017, pp. 26–43.

Thirty years after he had listened enthralled to a lecture given by John Cowper Powys (JCP) in New York, Henry Miller wrote to tell the novelist of his lifelong debt to him and suggest that the preface that JCP had written for his collection of essays, *Visions and Revisions*, should be published as a pamphlet and sent to all editors and critics the world over. As that letter was written in 1950, the preface to which it referred could not have been that of the 1955 edition, but must have been that of the New York edition published in 1915, which is more startling and combative in its assertion that 'Most books of critical essays take upon themselves, in unpardonable effrontery, to weigh and judge, from their own petty suburban pedestal, the great Shadows they review. It is an insolence!' JCP exclaims, for 'How should Professor This, or Doctor That, whose furthest experiences of "dangerous living" have been squalid philanderings with their neighbours' wives, bring an Ethical Synthesis to bear that shall put Shakespeare and Hardy, Milton and Rabelais, into appropriate niches?'

That caustic note is absent from the later version of the preface, but it seems clear from JCP's *Autobiography* that a mutual antipathy seems to have existed between him and an academic world that, with the honourable exception of a few open-minded spirits, has tended to undervalue and even ignore the scale of his achievements. This neglect might be explained in part by critical distaste for the sometimes hectoring, often unfashionably dithyrambic manner of his prose; but prophets are seldom admired in their own country, and a less comfortable reason for the neglect may lie in what, as time passes, has turned out to have been significantly prophetic in the work of John Cowper Powys.

In a time dominated by intellectual scepticism it may sound portentous to describe JCP's work as 'prophetic', so I should explain that I use the word as I believe Blake understood it, and as R.G. Collingwood defined it in his important book *The Principles of Art*: 'The artist must prophesy not in the sense that he foretells things to come, but in the sense that he tells his audience, at risk of their displeasure, the secrets of their own hearts.'

Regarded in this way, it is the business of the artist to speak out, to make a clean breast, not just of his or her own secrets but of *ours* – those things that we already deeply know, but choose to ignore or repress because of the challenge that their truth presents to the way we live our lives. It's my suspicion that JCP's work has suffered neglect because it performs, with unremitting courage and resolve, that vital duty of enlarging our consciousness in a way that presents a major challenge to conventional perspectives and values.

Even a favourable review of JCP's achievement, published anonymously in the *Times Literary Supplement* of 8 February 1974, reveals characteristic uneasiness in this respect. The criticisms it raises are principally on such literary grounds as lax, self-indulgent writing, poorly controlled narrative form, and clumsy authorial interventions; but surely JCP was sufficiently master of his craft to have put such matters right had he considered them to be important. If he chose not to do so, wasn't it because his deepest concerns lay *beyond* the literary? By his own admission, JCP's intent as a writer was propagandist, and his most passionate commitment was not to literature but to life – to 'an ecstasy of life-worship', life in all its generously varied, prolific, and polymorphous aspects, both creative and destructive. More specifically, his avowed purpose was to celebrate and promote what he called 'the magical view of life'; and if that was to be accomplished it could be done only by articulating elemental dimensions of human experience which had never previously been explored with the psychic-sensuous intensity that was his particular gift.

Such explorations required him to map great tracts of liminal terrain that conventional opinion would consider not so much debatable as uninhabitable. Even the sympathetic author of that generally positive *Times Literary Supplement* review of his work refers uncomfortably to JCP's invocation of the First Cause, Ceridwen, and the Earth-Mother – each an integral feature of his mythological vision – as 'excuses for, or maybe compulsions towards, various highly discardable views of the universe (or multiverse)'.

Note the implicit scepticism of that appended parenthesis; but times have moved on, cultural perspectives have been enlarged, and what may have seemed discardable views to the critical intellect in 1974 may, as I hope to show, seem less so today – although prevailing literary standards may still find themselves in difficulties with them.

I have chosen to concentrate on *Porius* in considering these issues, not only because I believe them to be raised most powerfully in that 'buggerly great book', but also because it demonstrates clearly how it wasn't only the themes that JCP felt compelled to explore that put him at odds with conventional literary expectations; it was also the very form – that of the romance – through which he chose to explore them.

In his *Autobiography* JCP confesses that he was always 'an indurated romanticist … first and last'. His youthful imagination was enchanted by the historical romances of Walter Scott, which he calls 'the most powerful literary influence of my life'. When he goes on to declare that 'what I wanted was that kind of romantic struggle with things and people … a struggle which takes place in an ideal region, hewn out of reality and constantly touching but never quite identified with reality, such as might be most conveniently described by the expression, *a Quest*', we are already deep into that liminal terrain which is the visionary landscape of the romance.

Remaining faithful to that youthful vision in his later years, JCP's ambition in writing his masterwork *Porius* was to give to the world 'the greatest ROMANCE of modern times'. In a century when literary scholarship would produce such celebrated critical studies as Erich Auerbach's *Mimesis*, Frank Kermode's *The Sense of an Ending*, and Ian Watts's *The Rise of the Novel*, this was far from a fashionable ambition. Each of those books sternly asserted that in the evolutionary course of Western cultural history the mythological imagination characteristic of the romance had been rendered obsolete by a more mature, accurately observant instrument of psychological and social consciousness – the novel. And if the novel had dismissed the romance form from serious current attention, it was because (to quote Kermode) the novel was more 'capable of coping with present reality', which, in a century darkened by some truly atrocious passages of history, he equated with 'the barbarous, brute, meaningless reality of things'.

Given that severe critical context, it's perhaps not surprising that a later novelist, John Fowles, should have rejected the thesis proposed by Simon Loveday in a study of his work, that his books are best understood less as conventional novels than as modern romances. The very term 'romance' has long been associated with cheap and sentimental fiction, and so strongly do reservations about the genre persist that, even though JCP, was happy to title one of his masterpieces *A Glastonbury Romance* and, from the first, conceived of *Porius* as a romance, the cover of the Overlook Duckworth edition insists on defining it as a novel.

One might question whether there is anything seriously at stake here in what could be dismissed as a merely academic matter of genre classification. A sceptical mind might also ask whether to write an Arthurian romance of the Dark Ages in a decade traumatised by the Holocaust and nuclear warfare was not a more regressive than prophetic enterprise. Yet in her lively study, *The Romance*, Gillian Beer points out how the genre has always flourished in periods of rapid change – times when, as Rilke says in the 7th Duino Elegy, 'each brute inversion of the world knows the disinherited, those to whom the past no longer belongs, and not yet the future'. The years during and after the Second World War were surely such a time. Moreover, an insightful study of the romance by Margaret Anne Doody, *The True Story of the Novel*, published much later, convincingly demonstrates that all the major narrative tropes that have been claimed as the significant achievement of the novel can be traced back to the sophisticated mode of storytelling already evident in the prose romances of the ancient world. Doody also shows how those same tropes were employed by the writers of the medieval romances that held a particular fascination for both JCP and Fowles. Arguments about the formal difference between the novel and the romance might be seen as little more than the parish-pump gossip of those who like to claim the novel as a triumph of the enlightened imagination. However, although Doody argues that what is now generally known as 'the novel' has a continuous history of about two thousand years, she also makes clear that there is a difference of metaphysical perspective between these two narrative modes. In contradistinction to the essentially secular perspective considered to be characteristic of the novel of more recent centuries, this form's roots in the ancient romances lie deep in a religious and sacred vision of life.

Drawing upon the work of the classical scholars Karl Kerenyi and Reinhold Merkelbach, who theorised that stories such as the *Metamorphoses* of Apuleius and *Ethiopika* of Heliodorus were designed to offer fictional enactments of otherwise esoteric mystery rites (originally those of the goddess Isis), Doody claims that, for their first readers, the reading of those narratives was 'in the nature of a religious experience'. If she is right, then those early romances did indeed take their readers far beyond the literary, for to engage imaginatively with the stories they told was to undergo an initiation that allowed the reader to follow and identify with the progress of a soul in the service of a god or goddess.

In this light, it becomes possible to read much of JCP's work as modern examples of the prose romance, reaching back to deep roots in the ancient initiatory tradition where the history of the novel began, yet handled in such a way as to deal with serious contemporary issues while also, in key respects, pointing prophetically towards the future.

Wolf Solent is surely undergoing such an initiatory ordeal when he makes a journey of the soul which begins with the sight of the 'inert despair' in the face of the man on the Waterloo Steps, progresses by rail through a wasteland vision of the whole round earth 'bleeding and victimized like a vivisected frog', and on into his encounters with the enigmatic figures who inhabit the Dorset otherworld where his personal mythology is tested to destruction before the final realisation that 'a change had taken place within him, a readjustment of his ultimate vision, from which he could never again altogether recede'.

That JCP's great book of Glastonbury is unashamedly a romance is avowed by its title, though some readers may be troubled by a disjunction in its pages between the quasi-naturalistic depiction of contemporary characters and the archetypal material constellated by their interactions with each other and the mythological landscape they inhabit. By the time he came to write *Porius*, however, JCP was freed to create his most powerful achievement precisely because its quasi-mythological Dark Age setting released his imagination from the constraints of the conventional social and psychological 'realism' that was, in his day, associated with the serious novel – as with most other things. That freedom allowed him to create a kind of fictional alembic in which readers can observe the timeless inward matter of the human soul and its relations with the natural world, both earthbound and cosmic, as it undergoes its processes of transformation.

Writing amid the menacing devastations of the Second World War, JCP knew that *Porius* was addressing, with full imaginative power, an earlier convulsive moment in the history of Britain – a time when the settled civilisation of the Pax Romana had been obliterated by civil strife and foreign incursions, and the people faced the challenge of forging a new destiny under the impact of alien invasion. Yet his deeper concerns were less historical than mythological, for he was attempting to dramatise in that unsettled context those elusive, polymorphous forms of evolving consciousness that resonate through the ages in ways that – even as they reveal the creative and destructive forces at work in the events of a particular period – are both timeless and contemporary.

Inexorably, the demands of that enterprise would lead his imagination still deeper into ranges of experience which, however finely articulated, would command little attention from an age largely in thrall to a hard-nosed positivist philosophy and to the technological achievements of a scientific method that reduced the natural world to a soulless state of exploitable objective existence.

As the eponymous hero of *Porius* struggles to free his beleaguered spirit from his own inhibiting constraints, among the various mysteries dramatised in the book are the release of the masculine figure

– at once animalic, human, and divine – of Myrddin Wyllt from confinement beneath the stone; the redemption of Blodeuwedd from her enchantment as an owl; and the fiercely climactic copulation of Porius and the giantess Creiddylad in whom is incarnate both the awesome power of the earth and the contrasexual aspect of the protagonist's own soul. Together these transformations prefigure the possibility of what JCP envisioned as a renewed Saturnian age of gold.

To summarise them in such a prosaic manner renders them absurd to the sceptical modern mind. Yet to translate them into the psychological language with which some of us are now more familiar would be to reduce the scale of JCP's achievement. They were, in fact, accomplishable only through the compelling, transrational power of fiction as acts of the poetic imagination. Which is to say *magical* acts – for, as JCP well understood, words *are* magical and are able to bring about such transformations as defy the laws of causality. A scientific – some would say *scientistic* – age gives little credence to magic. So an author who knew his achievements to be on a scale comparable to those of Dostoevsky, and who had once secretly hoped that his work might win what he called 'the Noble Prize', would remain a voice in the wilderness.

Yet, as the best medieval romances wisely advise us, in a world grown jaded by its own power and excesses, renewal can come out of the wilderness. It may often do so in what seems an unacceptable form, and prophets of all ages have met with resistance when, in times characterised by some turbulent crisis of consciousness in the world, they are summoned out of the wilderness.

There can be little question that ours is such a time, and that the crisis is already on a planetary scale. It's my purpose here to indicate ways in which JCP made powerful use of the romance to perform, in imaginative rather than merely conceptual terms, a transformative effort of consciousness which prefigures the work of a number of radical thinkers who, in more recent times, have sought to address an ever-deepening sense of psychological, sociopolitical, and spiritual crisis.

A few paragraphs ago, I enclosed the word 'realism' in inverted commas to query the assumptions about the demonstrable nature of objective reality on which that perspective often relies. In his provocative study, *The Philosopher's Secret Fire: A History of the Imagination*, Patrick Harpur has shown how that perspective is peculiar because it insists 'that it is not a perspective at all, but a true vision of the actual world'. Viewed from the outside, such a literalising mode of consciousness emerges rather as a *loss* of perspective, because perspective means 'seeing through' and such 'realism' fails to see through itself into its own inescapably *mythological* character. Yet confidence in its unquestioned assumptions largely abides, and in any case the meaning of the word 'myth' has long been relegated by those who regard themselves as realists to denote merely that which is false, wrong-headed, and misleading.

JCP's contemporary, Thomas Mann, valued that word more highly. In a speech given on Freud's eightieth birthday, he said, 'Myth is the foundation of life; it is the timeless schema ... into which life flows when it reproduces its traits out of the unconscious' and 'when a writer has acquired the habit of regarding life as mythical ... there comes a curious heightening of his artistic temper, a new refreshment to his perceiving and shaping powers'.

For me, one of the supreme strengths of JCP's work lies in the capacity of his multi-perspectival vision to perceive and dramatise the mythological character of the way *all of us*, not just the artists, apprehend and seek to make sense of the world through the stories to which we give credence. In so doing, he foreshadows significant aspects of post-Jungian archetypal psychology, and I want to focus for a moment on his understanding of the way we shape our cultural and our personal experience through myth, since it provides an overarching context in which to consider other prophetic aspects of his work.

Consider this statement from JCP's description of Porius reflecting on the liberating insight, which he had gained from the heretical theologian Pelagius, 'that each solitary individual man had the power, from the very start of his conscious life, not so much by his will, for *that* was coerced by other wills, but by his free imagination, *by the stories he told himself*, to create his future' (original emphasis). Then place beside it this from James Hillman's study of Freud, Jung, and Adler in *Healing Fiction*: 'The way we imagine our lives is the way we are going to go on living our lives. For the manner in which we tell ourselves about what is going on is the genre through which events become experiences.' Consider too how Hillman affirms the role of myth in our lives when he says,

> Case histories are fundamental to depth psychology. They are soul stories ... They give us a narrative, a literary fiction that deliteralizes our life from its projective obsession with outwardness by putting it into a story ... They present us with the chance to recognize ourselves in the mess of the world as having been engaged and always being engaged in soul-making ... This is the gift of case history, the gift of finding oneself in myth. In myths gods and humans meet.

Where the ancient romances tended to foreground a single god or goddess, the characters of JCP's prodigious book serve many different gods, who preside over different modes of consciousness. These range from Brochvael's loyalty to Hadrian, 'believing in nothing, yet believing in everything', which includes the classical gods and the charitable Christ of Brother John, to the priest Minnawc Gorsant's despotic deity; from Rhun's embracing of the rites of Mithras, to Woden and the Valkyrie of the Saxons; and present everywhere is the Earth Goddess revered by the Modrybedd and the reclusive Forest People.

Like Blake, JCP recognised that, wherever else they may live, the gods 'reside in the human breast' and are immortal because they remain active in every generation, presiding over those impersonal forces that James Joyce regarded as the 'grave and constant' themes of human life. What I find impressive about JCP's vision of the gods in *Porius* is the degree to which it invokes the nature of each of them as they shape the destinies of those who serve them, and are evaluated in the protagonist's questioning consciousness. By accomplishing this, JCP anticipates in imaginative terms the conceptual insights that James Hillman later brought to what he called 'polytheistic psychology' – a psychology that, in contrast to the emphasis placed by monotheistic psychology on the virtues of balance, integration, and wholeness, demands what Thomas Moore (in *The Essential James Hillman*) calls 'a stretching of the heart and imagination' towards a patient and flexible tolerance of the complicated and ambiguous and is 'the theatre where many stories are enacted, many dreams mirrored'.

One might almost think that in making his case for the polytheistic psyche Hillman had eavesdropped on what Porius says to Medraut on page 733:

> Isn't it safer and more sensible, as well as kinder to ourselves and others, to take things as we feel them and see them? Isn't it better to take for granted that there's a host of worlds and a host of gods and a host of consciousnesses and more universes than we can imagine; and get rid, once and for all, of the unnatural and confining notion, however logical and rational it may be, that there's only one God and only one opposite of God?

This passage indicates the degree to which all the gods and characters in the story can be read as members of Porius's own complex, evolving nature, as well as illuminating the generously humane reach of JCP's prolific imagination. By extension it iterates his vision of the cosmos as a *multiverse*, a concept that may have been influenced by the pluralistic thinking of William James, but which the *Times Literary Supplement* review of 1974 enclosed in sceptical brackets because it seemed absurd to the consensual view of reality as a single unfolding history. Today, however, it seems to prefigure the multiversal perspective of what theoretical physicists have called 'the many worlds theory'. Yet JCP's vision differs from that of those quantum scientists who posit that wave functions never collapse but split apart to creative alternative actualities, thus construing reality as a series of forking paths, such that, at every moment of decision (for example, the one you don't remember in which you decided not to read this paper) it splits into mutually inaccessible universes each doing their own thing. The myth of reality produced as a logical consequence of such mathematical theorising feels, to my small understanding, futile and devoid of meaning. By contrast, JCP's generous vision of the multiverse opens the imagination to the astounding variety of life with all its plural forms of consciousness and manifold dimensions of meaning, and does so through imagery that contends in scale with the vast perspectives on time and the cosmos offered by the age-old myths of the Hindu religion, while also addressing Western culture on its own historical and mythological terms.

In recent times the nature of consciousness has become a matter of focused study. It is a peculiar strength of serious fiction that it can investigate and attempt to dramatise the workings of consciousness as it manifests in our experience of the world. An essay on *Consciousness and the Novel* by the academic and novelist David Lodge traces the various devices by which novelists have attempted to convey the mental states and inward feelings of the characters they create before it goes on to consider how the very idea of the person has recently been called into question by both science and the humanities. Lodge notes 'a certain affinity between the poststructuralist literary theory that maintains that the human subject is entirely constructed by the discourses in which it is situated, and the cognitive science view that regards human self-consciousness as an epiphenomenon of brain activity'.

One can almost hear JCP snort as he shrugs off such a diminished picture of consciousness. Through the energetic psychosensuousness of his own rich imagination he was able to dramatise many varied inflections of consciousness in diverse individuals, each of whom is thoroughly realised in unique personal terms. In the masculine world these range from Medraut's world-despairing love of death to Taliesin's bardic vision of himself as a being set apart from others 'to reveal to the world what only the *mystery* poetry could reveal'; but even more impressively JCP enters the minds, feelings, and souls of female characters as strong and diverse as Morfydd and Euronwy, Sibylla and Nineue, and the three Aunties who worship the omnipresent Earth Mother.

After centuries in which it was ignored or demeaned, the feminine principle as manifested archetypally in the figure of the Goddess has seen a resurgence in our time. But it was already active in the pages of *Porius*. By dramatising the conflict between the patriarchal tradition of the line of Cunedda and the matriarchal authority of the Modrybedd, with the consciousness of Porius at stake between them, JCP confronted the timeless questions that came sharply into focus around gender issues in the decades after his novel appeared.

The public attention those issues have demanded in recent years are not only a matter of feminist politics and the gender debate, important though they are. In *The True Story of the Novel*, published in 1998, Doody felt free to describe the wide, generous embrace of the novel form in a detailed ekphrastic portrait of the Goddess of the Novel, standing with her head rayed like the moon in a field at the edge of a skyscrapered city, with Eros playfully wrecking a garden behind her, and a half-eaten cheese sandwich at her side as she holds what may be a mirror or possibly a computer screen.

By that time the Goddess was already becoming a familiar figure. Seven years earlier, in 1991, Richard Tarnas had published *The Passion of the Western Mind*, a book that examines the entire, predominantly masculine tradition of Western philosophical thought, from the mythic vision of the Homeric era to the many perspectives of the postmodern age, and concludes that the true passion of the Western mind is 'to recover its connection with the whole, to come to terms with the great feminine principle of life: to differentiate itself from, but then rediscover and reunite with the feminine'.

In the same year, Anne Baring and Jules Cashford wrote in their lucid and comprehensive study *The Myth of the Goddess* that 'it seems clear that a new *poetic* language has to evolve to allow back into consciousness a sensibility that is holistic, animistic and lunar in origin, one that explores flux, continuity and phases of alternation, offering an image not of exclusive realities, nor of final beginnings and endings, but of infinite cycles of transformation. In other words,' they insist, 'it is only through Imagination that the reunion of the goddess myth with the god myth can take place'. This seems an apt description of the act of imagination which JCP had performed fifty years earlier.

Yet his explorations into consciousness were not confined to human relations. Perhaps his most significant authorial achievement was the astonishing reach of his empathic sensitivity in presenting the natural world – animal, vegetable, mineral, climatic, and cosmic – as a sentient concourse of living intelligence with which human life is always, whether consciously or unconsciously, vitally interactive, and on which our sanity and survival depend.

As he stands over Brother John's grave, staring at a patch of greenish-white moss, Porius seems to look through into

> the secret roots of life ... for in this glimpse of reality seen through this white moss he saw ... all creatures as composed of a natural human clay and of a natural human spirit activating that clay ... with desires, purposes, instincts, impulses that were on the whole not only natural but absolutely necessary if the individuals composing the human race were to enjoy as well as endure their short and troubled lives.

Such a comprehensive degree of consciousness, both receptive and creative, is made incarnate in what is probably JCP's most extraordinary creation – the figure of Myrrdin Wyllt, who is so closely in touch with the animal world that he is almost subhuman and yet so far-reaching in his prophetic vision that he is superhuman too. By the end he is acknowledged as divine by Porius, who comes to share something of the magician's power of penetrating the animate nature of all existence. In the closing pages of the book, Porius stands beside

> this titanic creature of whose essential being he knew so little, and fancied he could catch moving up to that mountaintop a vast, multitudinous murmur, groping up, fumbling up, like a mist among mists, from all the forests and valleys of Ynys Prydein, the response of innumerable weak and terrified and unbeautiful and unconsidered and unprotected creatures, for whom this ancient accomplice of Time was still plotting a second Age of Gold.

What Myrddin and Porius are hearing here is 'the voice of the earth' – a phrase that Theodore Roszak chose as the title of the book in which he stated the principles of a challenging new school of psychology which has emerged as a response to our accelerating desecration of the planet (see pages 232–4).

Ecopsychology posits a layer in the human psyche deeper than the personal and the collective unconscious, where its substance is coextensive with the material form of the natural world of which it is inseparably a part, and can both respond to it and communicate with it. Viewed this way, human consciousness is no solitary epiphenomenon but a filament of the planetary intelligence that generates and sustains all life.

Both the wisdom of the traditional peoples of the earth and the Romantic poets who were attuned to the poetic basis of mind had long been alert and responsive to this reciprocal bond between the human soul and the soul of the earth. In our time, the development of James Lovelock's Gaia hypothesis has pointed to a renewal of such understanding, while the work of such ecological visionaries as Roszak, Thomas Berry, and Aldo Leopold has explored its implications for a deeper understanding of the human psyche. But it took a crisis of planetary proportions to waken the industrialised world to what JCP had long since urged us to recognise: that through the unchecked activity of the analytic mind the crime of vivisection, about which he expressed such passionate outrage, has been committed on the living body of the earth.

Back in 1938 JCP declared in *The Pleasures of Literature* that 'Nature in a manner totally beyond our comprehension, possesses a consciousness of her own, a consciousness not less but more than human.' Just a few years later he completed *Porius*, a major novel in which passage after passage makes clear that the landscape of North Wales is not just a vividly depicted backdrop to various human conflicts: it is a sentient presence interacting with, and subtly modifying, the consciousness of its human inhabitants. So vividly is this awareness quickened in the sensory imagination of the reader that one may doubt that the consciousness of nature is quite so utterly beyond human comprehension after all.

A sceptical mind may reasonably ask how JCP can know the things that he claims to know. A more sympathetic mind might ask: how can he have known them so far in advance of recent cultural developments in thought? The answer is that there is more than one way of knowing, and most of them thrive beyond the self-imposed limitations of detached scientific objectivity. The kind of knowledge to which JCP had access was provided by his highly developed gift of empathic psychic-sensuous imagination and by his willingness to do as the giants in his story advised and 'tread amorously on the earth'. It's the kind of knowledge that reveals itself to an imagination that is firing on all four cylinders – thought, feeling, intuition, and sensation – and refuses to jam out of consideration those freely available sources of life-intelligence which reach deep into the psyche from what is experienced by us self-conscious human beings as the outside world.

Ted Hughes, who was, like JCP, a shamanic figure, puts this well in his essay on 'Myth and Education' when he says of the works of great artists 'that in them the full presence of the inner world combines with and is reconciled to the full presence of the outer world. And in them we see that the laws of these two worlds are not contradictory at all; they are one all-inclusive system ... They are the laws, simply, of human nature.'

Richard Tarnas amplifies this insight, arguing that it's 'only when the human mind actively brings forth from within itself the full powers of a disciplined imagination and saturates its empirical observation with archetypal insight that the deeper reality of the world emerges. From within its own depths,' he says, 'the imagination directly contacts the creative process within nature, realizes that process within itself, and brings nature's reality to conscious expression.'

JCP spent an entire lifetime tempering his sensibility to become a finely tuned instrument for that evolutionary creative process, and in his doing so his imagination became prophetic. So, as Jeremy Hooker suggests in *Imagining Wales*, there are good reasons why 'we may cautiously apply to Powys the definition of the story-teller (*cyngarwydd*)' given by Alwyn and Brinley Rees in *Celtic Heritage* as 'originally a seer and a teacher who guided his hearers through the world of "mystery"'. Being of a less scholarly, and therefore less cautious, disposition, I'm inclined to apply it unreservedly. Though *Porius* may be a formidably long and demanding read, I believe that the effort is deeply rewarding and that open-minded readers will find themselves imaginatively engaged by a complex initiatory drama in which are unfolded the emergent – indeed the increasingly urgent – issues of our time.

In JCP's time such issues had for too long been almost unthinkable and were still largely unsayable. By resolutely speaking up, with a writer's consummate skill, on vital matters dismissed by the intellectual mainstream both of his day and our own – the mythological nature of our perception of the world, the multiversal dimensions of its reality, the polytheistic aspects of the imagination, the elemental power of the feminine principle, and beyond all this the animate participatory consciousness of the planetary environment – JCP told us profoundly important yet disastrously repressed secrets of our hearts. In doing so he performed a challenging act of consciousness on behalf of us all. Much will depend on how seriously we respond to it.

# Wise Old Codgers

This review of *Proteus and the Magician: The Letters of Henry Miller and John Cowper Powys*, edited by Jacqueline Peltier (Powys Society, 2014), was originally commissioned by and published in *Resurgence & Ecologist* and later adapted for publication in the *Powys Journal*.

At first glance, members of the Powys Society might be surprised to encounter a book that brings the visionary author of *A Glastonbury Romance* into close association with a writer principally notorious for the explicit sexual ebullience of *Tropic of Cancer*. In some ways the preoccupations of these two novelists may seem as far apart as the landscapes depicted on the book's cover – the Welsh hill country above Corwen and that of Henry Miller's home on the Californian coast of Big Sur. Yet in a time when so much fiction is written in a lean, almost anorexic prose, it's salutary to recall how once, and not so long ago, there were novelists who appealed to their readers' senses as well as to the intellect by regaling them with a feast of language. Prominent among them were these two writers, of different generations but kindred temperament, whose imaginations travelled far beyond the current vogue for ironical scepticism in their need to articulate a vision of cosmic range.

Henry Miller has so long been renowned for the unabashed gusto with which his books demolished sexual taboos that it's hard to imagine him as the shy, would-be novelist, uncertain of his gifts, who attended the public lectures on the inseparable themes of life and literature which Powys delivered with astonishing eloquence to American audiences in the 1920s. Miller never forgot how Powys's passionate hwyl had made his own imagination combust with visionary delight. In later life, with his own (then scandalous) literary

85

credentials established, he wrote to the almost eighty-year-old Powys expressing his grateful admiration. The next twelve years saw a mutually affirming, life-enhancing exchange of letters between two men who rejoiced in the shared conviction that, as Powys once wrote, 'it is wisdom in us terrestrial mortals to make what imaginative use we can of *every phase* of our earthly condition', and also that 'everything in life is sacred and everything is a huge jest'.

The Powys Society has performed a valuable service by making their correspondence fully available in English for the first time, and Jacqueline Peltier has done an exemplary job of editing the letters. Her insightful introduction places the friendship in the context of both lives, while her textual notes clarify possibly obscure points and references. Facsimiles of some letters are also provided along with three appendices and bibliographies of the major works of both authors.

Correspondence between friends is not intended for publication, but these two daimon-driven writers are far too genial to leave the reader with any sense of intrusion, even when Miller asks his friend not to share with others the pained feelings he confesses over the breakdown of his marriage. Powys's missives are like mighty rambles, gathering thought as they go, taking in reflections on the giants of world literature and philosophy, his peculiar sexual proclivities, his devotion to ritual, his *pro*-Semitism, his love for the landscape around Corwen, and much else. A virile honesty is the mark of both men (even though Powys describes himself as 'old-maidish'), along with a huge openness to a world that took scant note of their prolific existence.

Both writers lived their lives as matters of serious spiritual consequence, Miller drawing inspiration from Zen Buddhism, while Powys felt more kinship with the Taoist tradition, though in many ways his vision was closer to his intuitive apprehension of Druidic wisdom. Yet both are larger, more elusive figures than such generalised labelling suggests. They have their differences of perspective too. Powys challenges Miller's advocacy of 'love' – a word he considered hopelessly debased – and by countering Miller's unitary view of things with his vision of a pluralistic 'multiverse', he anticipates the later insights of archetypal psychology into that imaginal polytheism which illuminates consciousness as the poetic basis of mind.

What emerges throughout, however, is the warm affection with which each of these wise old codgers recognises in the other a fellow pioneer into the vast terrain that, after the great achievements of the nineteenth century, remained to be explored through fiction. Above all, the book is a timely reminder of how many of our finest writers drew their creative energy from a profound and exalted sense of the sacred and from the lived experience of the human imagination as a vital participant in larger orders of being.

# An Allegiance to the Wild

## Some Thoughts on the Work of John Fowles

This is an extended version of a review of *Wormholes: Essays and Occasional, Writings* by John Fowles, edited by Jan Relf (Jonathan Cape, 1998), that was published in *Resurgence*.

In his introduction to the revised version of *The Magus*, John Fowles writes of his admiration of Alain-Fournier's novel *Le Grand Meaulnes* and its capacity to provide what he calls 'an experience beyond the literary'. Surprisingly, having confessed his desire to imbue his own story with that elusive quality, Fowles goes on to dismiss that desire both as 'a characteristic longing of adolescence' and as what he considers to be an irremediable mark of 'failure' in his own enigmatic book. Yet it seems significant that it was precisely that characteristic of Fowles' work which most excited his readership, and perhaps it did so because in novel after novel his efforts to go beyond the literary opened up startling perspectives on initiatory aspects of our experience as individuals and on the dislocating cultural relativities that shimmered across the second half of the twentieth century.

Certainly, it was because I was stirred by that quality in Fowles's work that his novels exercised a pronounced influence on my own development as a storyteller. Contrary to his own dismissal of the longing for that quality as merely adolescent, I took it as a sure sign that he was preoccupied with serious adult issues – ethical, psychological, social, political, existential, erotic, and, above all, imaginal. If I tried to learn something from a respectful study of his work, it was because I believe (as D.H. Lawrence also did) that it's the willingness to advance beyond merely literary concerns that makes the novel more than a complicated means of entertainment, though of course it must be that too. Such willingness can turn the telling of a story into an athletic adventure of the imagination, one that can transform it into an experience akin to a rite of passage – a voluntary, dream-like ordeal through which the reader enters a realm governed by ambiguous tutelary figures, and from which one may emerge with a sense of life deepened and enlarged.

Novelists who perform that service for us have always been rare, and perhaps never more so than in recent years. At a time when few serious English writers have been willing to risk more than a coldly dissociated complicity with the general pessimism of the age – enlivened perhaps by a pyrotechnical brilliance with words – Fowles took larger, braver gambles. His care for the beauty of the language and his willingness to experiment with narrative form were always put in service to more important and consequential values. His was an interrogative imagination, sceptically alert, often tangential and ambiguous, sharpened by a lively sense of irony, and rarely to be found wearing its heart on its sleeve; yet it was always reaching after a fuller, more exacting sense of humanity. To read one of his novels is to be confronted with pressing aspects of our predicament and to be made uncomfortably aware of our vanities and fallibility while being denied the consolation of easy solutions – even as one's faith in the transforming power of the imagination is strengthened and exhilarated. The stories that Fowles tells care, and care deeply, about questions of moral and erotic justice in human affairs, about the future of the species, and about the fate of the natural world which he loved and celebrated with a sensitive eye for detail.

This is not to say that I don't also have reservations about his work. For all its imaginative vigour and compelling writing, many readers have found the both the structure and the conclusion of *The Magus* unsatisfactory, and some critics were exasperated by the presentation of alternative endings to *The French Lieutenant's Woman*. Both issues seem to me to indicate what may have been an unresolved conflict in the author's mind. In both those books, as in *The Aristos* and later in *Daniel Martin*, Fowles firmly took his stand in that secular tradition of humanist thought which is rooted in the combined energy of the will and the power of compassion as fundamental values, neither alone being sufficient to answer the complex demands of the human condition. Taken on their own terms, such values seem unexceptionable. The question is whether those terms reach deeply enough into the impersonal unconscious processes that flow like hot magma beneath the surface of our experience; and that question is of pressing importance in novels concerned, as those of Fowles are, with dramatising the ordeals of personal transformation.

My suspicion is that, as was characteristic of the intelligentsia of his generation (and remains so in today's intellectual mainstream), Fowles's imagination was arrested by an ingrained wariness that, unless one kept one's intellectual defences in good order, a boundary might be crossed beyond the secular realm into territory more closely related to the spiritual. In consequence, the possibilities for deeply transformative renewal – possibilities that seem implicit in the unfolding stages of the stories he tells – are aborted by conclusions in which this reader at least is left more with a frustrating sense of coitus interruptus than with a narrative consummation devoutly to be wished.

Perhaps related to that issue is a second concern aroused by the peculiar erotic presentation of women in Fowles's books. I'm particularly struck by the way that the central male characters of the novels are sexually excited by the presence of female twins (in *The Magus*) or of sexually available sisters (in *Daniel Martin*) or of close female friends (in *The Ebony Tower*). Rather in the way that poorly focused eyesight creates a fuzzy doubling of images, this sexual fascination with the twinning of women in the novels suggests that Fowles himself may have had imaginative difficulty in bringing the female into focus. Again, the consequence is that the narratives tend to remain arrested within a literalised, somewhat voyeuristic and self-regarding sexuality rather than moving through into a deeper relatedness.

In that respect, the central male characters in Fowles' novels exemplify a more general cultural problem: the difficulty experienced by men in relating to women as human beings rather than as objects of sexual desire. Behind that difficulty lies the deeper issue of the failure to honour the elemental power and dignity of the female principle in the lives of both men and women. The consequences of that failure reach into many areas of life, not just those of sexual interaction, and should surely rank among the most urgent concerns of a serious novel in our time. Consciousness of this has evolved somewhat in the half-century since Fowles's work appeared, and it should be said that, whatever reservations one may have about the limitations of his approach, there is never any doubt that his novels (unlike many published in his time) are firmly on the side of life as an imaginatively creative, evolutionary process intimately grounded in the natural order.

A number of engaging non-fiction works by him reveal his life-long love of nature. A particular favourite of mine is the little volume titled *The Tree*, which includes among its many wide-ranging reflections a wondrous description of Wistman's Wood on Dartmoor. Towards the end of his life, with the help of his editor and friend Jan Relf, Fowles collected under the title *Wormholes* various occasional pieces written between 1964 and 1996. This book offers, in Relf's words, 'a chronicle of the various matters that have plagued, preoccupied, or delighted Fowles throughout his life'.

A novelist's collection of essays will largely revolve around literary themes, and Fowles never fails to intrigue when considering the condition of the writer and his own creative process. Admirers of his novels will enjoy 'Notes on an Unfinished Novel', which follows the evolution of *The French Lieutenant's Woman*, and 'Behind *The Magus*', which includes an early passage written on Spetsai which was to prove to be 'the sperm and egg, the very genesis, of the as-yet unwritten – indeed unconceived – book'. A brief autobiographical squib called 'The J.R. Fowles Club' tells amusingly of his birthright membership of a querulous order that he never asked to join and often wished he hadn't. But Fowles also writes with committed, unacademic verve about other writers who matter to him. He is especially eloquent about Marie de France, about his great spiritual forebear and neighbour Thomas Hardy, and about his friend and exemplar William Golding.

I was particularly grateful for the loyalty of heart with which, in his commentary on that late, brief masterpiece *The Man Who Died*, he insists on a respectful valuation of the often infuriating, but always enlarging, visionary courage of D.H. Lawrence. 'The human side of the world, *our* world, is very sick, and has become several times worse since Lawrence himself died;' he wrote, 'and I believe we need, desperately, whatever our own religious beliefs, to listen to his message. He isn't trying to shock us; but trying passionately, like all good preachers, to save us.'

As was evident from his challenging statement of personal philosophy in an early work of non-fiction, *The Aristos*, Fowles shared that sense of moral and spiritual urgency. A passionate naturalist and a man who sometimes seemed at his happiest when working alone in the large garden that owned him, he was resolutely alive to green issues. *Wormholes* offers a number of essays that will engage the ethical and philosophical intelligence of the least literary of environmental activists.

Fowles saw each of these occasional pieces as a 'little square of mosaic in my general portrait'. Brought together by a challenging and sympathetic editor, they reveal him as a complex, exactingly truthful man, aware of his strengths and his failings, and conscious that in various ways he is in 'exile from normality'. I closed this book wishing that there were more among us with his power to convert serious moral purpose into provocative and imaginatively enchanting stories; and many more too who identified with these words from his essay 'The Nature of Nature': 'I truly venerate, behind my inadequacies, the wild; and pity the ignorance of all those who deem themselves so superbly evolved that they judge they can do without it.'

Such a statement reaches far beyond the literary; it is on the strength of such committed allegiance to the irreplaceable value of what is untameably wild in the natural order that our own sane survival as a species will finally depend.

# A Stone from Heaven

## Wolfram's *Parzival* – a Myth for Our Time

This is a revised version of the afterword that I wrote for
*Parzival and the Stone from Heaven*, originally published by
HarperCollins in 2001 and republished by the Godstow Press
in 2011.

At some point towards the end of the twelfth century, Chrétien de
Troyes, a northern French poet writing under the patronage of the
Count of Flanders, began to put into rhyming verse a mysterious
story that he considered to be the best of tales that were told in royal
courts. Frustratingly, we know almost nothing about either the oral
or written sources on which he was drawing, and – even more tanta-
lising this – the story was left unfinished at his death, Its title was
*Perceval*, yet Chrétien also referred to his romance as *Li Contes del
Graal*, and through a fusion of ancient Celtic lore with the newly
evolving courtly ideals of the amorous Latin temperament he created
an appetite for a chivalric myth – the story of the grail – which magnetised the imagination of medieval Europe and has never since
quite lost its fascination.

It seems characteristic of the elusive nature of the grail motif that
almost everyone has heard of it and no one has ever come up with a
definitive idea of what it is. Some of the confusion arises from the
fact that so many other imaginations have improvised round Chrétien's themes that a complete account of the influence of the myth
on European culture is probably now impossible. Any attempt
would certainly have to take into account the work of such diverse
figures as Robert de Boron, whose *Joseph d'Arimathie* solemnly Chris-
tianised the once pagan vessel by associating it with the chalice used
at the Last Supper and the vessel in which Christ's blood was carried

from the cross; the Nazi war criminal Heinrich Himmler, who instituted his obscene SS as an order of 'grail knights' with its own lugubrious ritual centre at Wewelsburg Castle; and the Monty Python team, unforgettably urging on their invisible horses in quest of the further reaches of human absurdity.

When a symbol becomes so diverse in its application that it can be variously interpreted as a relic of an ancient pagan fertility cult, a coded reference to the bloodline of Christ, and an emblem of psychological integration, while journalists have come to rely on it as a useful cliché – 'the holy grail of sustained growth and low inflation' – then one may reasonably ask whether there can be any virtue left in it at all. Yet were there none, how else to explain its continuing grip on the human imagination?

Of all the authors who have seized on the themes first assembled in written form by Chrétien and put them to their own purposes, there is one – Wolfram von Eschenbach – who has long exercised a particular enchantment over my own imagination. It was his version that I chose to dramatise when I was licensed to write a two-part, three-hour version of the grail story for broadcast by BBC Radio 4 on Easter Saturday in 1995.

Wolfram flourished in the brilliant first half of the Hohenstaufen period of medieval German culture around the turn of the thirteenth century. He was a knight ministerialis, bound in service to a feudal lord, whose family hailed from Eschenbach in Franconia but who considered himself a Bavarian. Writing under the patronage of the Landgrave Hermann of Thuringia, he was a highly accomplished poet who declared himself to be illiterate. This may have been no more than a joke directed against the pretensions of his more learned rivals; the many qualities of his writing reveal a man with broad cultural horizons, and one whose feeling for the integrity of the individual conscience was always enlivened by a humorous vision of life which was widely tolerant in its sympathies.

Writing at a significant moment in the evolution of Western consciousness, Wolfram demonstrated a subtle awareness of the links between the erotic and the spiritual dimensions of experience. At a time when the Holy Roman Emperor was resisting the claims of a corrupt papacy to political supremacy over Christendom, it's significant that the orthodox institutions of the church have almost no part to play in a story that sets out to dramatise a knight's solitary quest for redemptive meaning in a wasteland world.

Like all great art, Wolfram's *Parzival* transcends the age in which it was written. It's not surprising, therefore, that it has exercised a particular fascination for writers, artists, and thinkers across the centuries and has furnished the narrative underpinning of works as diverse as Wagner's opera *Parsifal*, Thomas Mann's novel *The Magic Mountain*, and George Lucas's film *Star Wars*. I was first drawn to it when, as an undergraduate, I chose to study the period from 1066 to 1385 and became an amateur medievalist. I already knew and loved the poetry of Chaucer and the Gawain Poet and was acquainted with Langland's *Piers Plowman* and many of the lyrics and ballads, but even so my reasons for setting out on this year-long pilgrimage through the literature of the Middle Ages were far from clear to me. I just knew I had to go.

During the course of that year I read many other medieval romances, from the exquisite lays of Marie de France, through Chrétien de Troyes' witty and insightful adventures of the heart, and on to the virile, turbulent prose of Malory's *Morte d'Arthur*. It was through those enchanted stories that I started to gain a larger perspective on the kind of interior landscape that had first been opened up to me many years earlier by my entranced reading of *Grimms' Fairy Tales*. As a student newly awoken to the problematic life of the mind, I began to glimpse in its contours something that had largely been banished from serious consideration by the post-Holocaust world, for reading those old stories felt like studying a map of the soul.

No doubt there was an element of escapism in my appetite for them, but I can't believe I'm alone in thinking that the attempt to escape from what William Blake called 'mind-forged manacles' is a fairly sane response. And – intuitively at least – my imagination was beginning to understand how the themes explored by the medieval romances might have a direct bearing on some urgent, unsolved problems of my own troubled times. I think that was why I cared about them. I *know* that was why, much later, they would encourage me to shape similar stories of my own.

Nowadays I would go so far as to suggest that the romance writers of the twelfth century were laying down an agenda for the development of Western consciousness which was as crucial for the welfare of its heart as that of the ancient Greeks had been for the sharpening of its intellect. It's an agenda with which we're still struggling today, and on which – if the dismal state of mutual misprision between the sexes, the degraded condition of the planet, and our ignorance of the unconscious forces that propel us towards calamity are anything to go by – we have made far too little progress.

The themes of that agenda can be briefly resumed under four related headings:

- the need to renegotiate the balance of power between the masculine and feminine principles (not only in outward relations between the sexes, but inwardly, as aspects of our individual being, whatever our biological gender);
- the need to renegotiate the relationship between civilisation and the natural order (in particular the need to recognise that renewal often comes out of the wilderness, and sometimes in ways we don't recognise or consciously desire);
- the need to renegotiate the balance between the ambitious claims of the ego and the larger, more exacting claims of the soul;
- the need to renegotiate relations between conscious awareness and the neglected resources buried in the dream world of the unconscious mind.

In a sense, the last heading subsumes all the others, and perhaps for that very reason many of the romances were overtly cast in the form of dream books. Even the ones not presented in that way tended to take the form of dreamlike journeys between the everyday world of social reality and a mistily ambiguous otherworld where the big transformations happen. These days we have to remind ourselves that, for the courtly medieval audience, knights and castles and tournaments were the stuff of social realism. The otherworld was something else, and it's possible to regard accounts of strange adventures there as merely a more or less sophisticated form of courtly entertainment. They certainly were that, of course, and all the more enjoyable because of it, but I prefer to take a larger view, one that takes them seriously within that visionary tradition of Western writing which has always valued the wisdom of dreams and which insists on the primacy of the imagination in the shaping of our world.

Generally speaking, that tradition has been more openly championed by poets than by prose writers, particularly in recent times. But, as Margaret Anne Doody shows in *The True Story of the Novel*, the narrative tropes of the medieval romance have much in common with those of the modern novel as well as such ancient prose fictions as the *Metamorphoses* of Apuleius. So much is this the case, she argues, that the distinction between romance and novel is far less severe than has been suggested by those critics who regard the social and psychological 'realism' of the novel as a more mature mode of storytelling than the romance with its unabashed taste for initiatory marvels.

In any case, when I set out to be a novelist, I knew where the springs of my own imagination lay. Two of my novels were conceived as contemporary variations on ancient Gawain stories, and during the course of writing my radio play, *A Stone from Heaven*, as a free adaptation of *Parzival*, I was possessed by the curious sensation of having embarked on a heavily fictionalised form of autobiography. The more I progressed with it, the more strongly I began to feel that Wolfram wasn't just telling my own story but also that of many of my contemporaries.

Like Parzival, many of us who were born around 1939 were separated from our fathers by war and left in the anxious company of mothers frightened by the violence of the times. Much the same thing had happened to our own parents twenty-five years earlier at the start of the First World War. It was as though we had inherited their affliction, and there has never been a day's peace across the planet since 1939. In fact, our view of life has been so largely shaped – it would be more accurate to say *distorted* – by the atrocious history of the twentieth century that there is a sense in which, to a more or less terrible degree, we are all casualties of war.

My generation grew up in an increasingly materialistic society where the standards of masculinity were set by an aggressive patriarchy organised into companies that carried on their trade with martial zeal. (Consider how many knights are now champions of business!) Almost nothing in our education was designed to give us an understanding of the feminine perspectives that might be available to men, still less of the activity of a masculine spirit within women. We knew almost nothing, that is, of the role of the unconscious in shaping our experience. Nor, for many of us, was there any vital sense of a spiritual dimension to life. The history of industrialised slaughter in both World Wars, together with the ever imminent possibility of total destruction through thermonuclear conflict, left most of us convinced that the existence of a benevolent God was beyond belief. The scientific worldview seemed to make a nonsense of many religious claims, and, apart from its use to describe a stirring form of music, the word 'soul' had no apparent referent. If there was any meaning to life – and that itself was an open question – then it was entirely self-created by the power of human reason.

So we set out on our journeys into adulthood armed with a bright weaponry of rational logic, defended by our scepticism, and possessed of large ambitions – for love, for success, for wealth, happiness, and perhaps even fame – yet largely ignorant of our own nature and utterly estranged from any vital sense of the sacred. Whether we were 'idealists' trying to change the world or 'realists' accepting and working with its injustices, we were each questing for a viable sense of personal meaning in what a selective reading of T.S. Eliot had long since persuaded us was a Waste Land time.

We were also on a collision course with those refractory, undomesticated aspects of life that flourished outside our tightly managed scheme of things. Such anyway was the case with me, and it was only through the changes brought about by such collisions that my perspectives began to widen. Emerging from them in a renewed effort of self-recognition, I saw that the insights of *Parzival* might offer a relevant myth for people in such an errant condition.

Of course others had seen it so before me. In his *Memories, Dreams and Reflections*, C.G. Jung spoke of the importance of the story in his own life, recording how his memory of his father was 'of a sufferer stricken with an Amfortas wound' that would not heal. Likening his boyhood self to a 'dumb' Parsifal witnessing this suffering, he admits that, 'like Parsifal, speech failed me'. Laurens Van Der Post has suggested that the story of the grail quest anticipates in dramatic form Jung's theories of the lifelong quest for individuated consciousness, though it was Jung's wife Emma who made a detailed psychological study of the tale in collaboration with Marie Louise von Franz. Approaching it from a different angle, the great mythographer Joseph Campbell saw in *Parzival* 'the earliest definition of the secular mythology that is today the guiding spiritual force of the European west'.

My own sense of the continuing power of this story has been reinforced by the time I've spent using its themes as a stimulus for writing workshops at Dartington and elsewhere. Participants in those events were asked to monitor memories from their own lives which were aroused by listening to the incidents of the story, to explore them in conversation, and then to write out of an imaginative fusion of their own experience with motifs borrowed from the tale. It's a technique called 'midrash writing' after a rabbinical method of exploring untold parts of scriptural stories through imaginative improvisation, and it can produce startling results.

One man came to the workshop because a dream had told him to think about 'wolfram'. As an engineer, his only association had been with 'wolfram' as another name for the metal 'tungsten' (which means 'heavy stone' in Swedish). It was only when he'd chanced upon a translation of *Parzival* that the wider implications of the dream came clear to him. Having done no imaginative writing since his schooldays, he was far from relaxed about trying again now. But I have an unforgettable image of him reading aloud a moving piece, written from the point of view of Parzival's horse, in which he reflected on his own failures of trust and his often injurious reliance on the will. Another man found himself writing out of the still livid wounds of a twenty-year marriage to what he called 'a man-hating woman'. After several intense hours of imaginative work with words, relating Gawain's story to his own, he came to the realisation that, whatever else their conflicts might have meant for her, his exwife had been desperately mirroring the rage and fury of his own long-neglected soul.

The women who attended those workshops also found in the

images of the story new ways of examining the ambitions and confusions of their own questing spirits, while at the same time confronting the pain inflicted on them by the illusions and insensitivities of men. Indeed, much of the value of the work came from dialogues between men and women across the gender divide as they reacted, positively or otherwise, to the archetypal figures of the story and strove to find their way towards a more empathic attention to each other's experience.

Any good story can be made to work this way but, for some of us at least, the very form of the Parzival story seems to offer a metaphor for life as a mythic journey into meaning through the liberating spaces of the imagination. There are particular qualities to its themes and motifs which encourage us to approach that journey in an adventurous spirit of self-renewal.

A good place to start is with the acceptance that the people in this story are not presented as the kind of fully rounded characters we expect to find in a novel. They are less individuals than archetypes, each representing in dramatic form some important element in the structure of the human psyche. Interplay between them offers a working model of the human soul, revealing contrary aspects of its nature and its often painful struggle to reconcile them.

Once this is recognised, the Parzival story can be read in the way that certain schools of dream analysis suggest we should try to read our dreams. Using this method, we identify not solely with the figure who seems to represent us in the dream, but with all the other figures who appear there too. The assumption is that each of them, along with all the impersonal motifs and situations of the dream, illustrates some not yet conscious aspect of our nature with which our dreaming mind wants us to become better acquainted. Thus, when we dream about our fathers and mothers, our spouses, lovers, friends, and enemies, it's not those actual figures, living or dead, who have chosen to spend part of the night with us, but symbolic representations of them that have a vital part to play in the unfolding drama of our interior life.

Having grown up in an age that tends to think literally, we are poorly educated in this kind of thinking. 'If dreams mean anything why can't they just say what they mean?' is typically the positivist's response – a response that fails to realise that dreams do exactly that, though the language they speak is that of the imagination. Its syntax is subtler and more flexible than that of rational logic, and its vocables are drawn from the timeless store of symbols. It is, in fact, our native language, though our schooling has largely estranged us from it. But, as with all languages, one grows fluent by practice, and once we make the effort to see through literal appearances in this way we maximise our imaginative use of the resources that the unconscious spontaneously offers. At the same time – and this goes to the heart of the matter – we are reminded that our personal lives are continuous with the life of everything around us, that the presence of everything else is the condition of our own existence, and that for all our experience of ourselves as separate and isolated individuals we are also members of one another.

In modern times, Lawrence Durrell attempted a mode of story-telling which encompasses this kind of insight. The various characters of his *Alexandria Quartet* and *Avignon Quincunx* seem to meld and flow into one another as the novelist calls the existence of the discrete ego into question in order to explore the poetics of the soul. But a more direct parallel to the emblemology of the Parzival story may be found in the Major Arcana of the tarot deck. Each of the symbols depicted in that vivid procession illustrates an elemental aspect of human experience. The order of their sequence dramatises the gradual education of the soul, from the condition of untutored Fool, through an initiatory cycle of changes, to the integrated wisdom of the wiser Fool.

Parzival's history clearly follows that trajectory. He begins as the uneducated green man, more or less a wilderness creature, perfect in his simplicity and, as far as the world is concerned, a hopeless fool. The obedient innocence of his youth cannot cope with the ambiguous impact of experience. He is gradually matured by the ordeals he undergoes until he achieves a compassionate wisdom won from knowledge, grief, and silence. But an important part of that journey is delegated to his soul-brother Gawain, whose erotic adventures act out those aspects of life which Parzival has left unlived.

Rather than puzzling over a discontinuity here, it makes larger sense to think of these two figures as twin aspects of a single soul –

aspects that are in conflict with one another, yet both of which are necessary to the soul's wholeness. Without access to Parzival's loyalty of heart, Gawain is a mere libertine; without Gawain's amorous encounters, Parzival remains a solemn prig. But the two natures can be reconciled only through a crisis of consciousness which the story presents as armed combat.

In much the same way, Parzival only attains the grail when, after a life-and-death struggle that extinguishes his hitherto triumphant ego, he is united with his dark brother, Feirefiz. That is to say, he approaches the state of wholeness only when, through hard-won self-recognition, he assimilates the values associated with his previously unconscious shadow side.

Just as the male figures of the story are confined within the variously inflected archetype of knighthood, so the female characters are barely differentiated as individuals. In ways that must seem quite dismal to the evolved feminist thinking of our time, they remain maidens in need of rescue, for example, or prophetic hags. It's more profitable to read them not as portraits of women but as elemental constituents of the human psyche – the beleaguered values of the soul and the power of intuition among them – and to consider how those various aspects of the soul complement one another.

The demure figure of Condwiramurs, for instance, remains only partially realised at the time of her marriage to Parzival. Her own otherwise unexpressed life – her rage at being abandoned by her husband, her fury at his bone-headed commitment abroad to what (were he less driven by his will) might have been found with her at home, and her own ambiguous, sometimes promiscuous feelings about men in general – all these bitter passions are acted out on her behalf by Gawain's beautiful tormentor, the Lady Orguleuse. Yet that proud Duchess will find no peace until her own injured heart dares open itself to the risk of love again.

The word 'behalf' gives the clue. Without each other's energy to complement their own weaknesses and strengths, Parzival and Gawain are, at best, only half themselves, and much the same is true of Condwiramurs and Orguleuse. The structure of the story seems to suggest that to approach wholeness as a person, whether male or female, one is required to assimilate all of these different aspects into a conscious unity that leaves nothing out of count, however stressful the contradictions. That this is a process fraught with difficulties is clear from the general context of strife, loss, and injury – particularly sexual injury – in which the principal characters of the story pursue their destinies. That context is both generational and cosmic in its reach, for as the story unfolds we discover that conflict on earth mirrors the conflict in heaven, and that the wounds of this conflict will be passed on from one generation to the next until an evolutionary act of consciousness opens up a genuine possibility of renewal.

For this reason, Wolfram's story, unlike Chrétien's, begins not with Parzival but with his father, Gahmuret. Long before Parzival is born, Gahmuret loses his own father to the violence of the times yet he is driven by a restless ambition to emulate his father's martial accomplishments. He shows only a casual concern for the feelings of his distraught mother and finds it impossible to sustain a mature relationship with either of his two wives. Having lived his father's life, Gahmuret dies his father's death, passing on to his sons responsibility for all that has been neglected by the narrow preoccupations of his self-glorifying career.

For a time it seems as if the cycle must repeat itself. Despite all his mother's neurotic efforts to protect him, and perhaps because of them, Parzival sets out into the world in much the same cavalier way. His crass encounter with the Lady Jeschute amusingly caricatures his father's callous way with women. Signune's inability to let go of her lover's rotting body mirrors the manner in which Parzival's own neglected soul metaphorically carries his father's corpse about with him – a dreadful emblem of that masculine vitality which has fallen into decay and must somehow be revivified. He has to find ways of coping with the mockery and authority of the world, yet his efforts to emulate the one-sided achievements of his absent father bring the youth into collision with the capacity for loving feeling which he has inherited through his mother. His ignorance of the values associated with his feminine side is vast. He doesn't know that his self-absorbed departure has left his mother dead behind him. In his eagerness to prove himself a knight he doesn't know that his first act has been to kill a kinsman. Nor is he aware that he has a larger destiny than that of a crack jouster, for not only must he redeem both his own and his father's failures of the heart, he will have to find a way of healing the sexual wound that blights the family of the Grail – a family of which he does not yet know himself to be the spiritual heir. Meanwhile the dumb obedience with which he conforms to the expectations of those around him only brings Parzival into increasing conflict with the claims of his own essential nature.

As the story unfolds, he will be made aware of the extent to which he is the prisoner of his own ignorance, yet the access of that knowledge brings with it such pain and derangement that it seems as if the sudden light of consciousness itself comes as a kind of wound. If so, it is a wound for which the only cure is greater consciousness. In his quest for that, Parzival will encounter forces far more impersonal than those embodied by his relatives and friends.

Because almost everything in our education conspires to identify the separate ego as the centre of consciousness (with reason as its trusty sword for keeping anarchy at bay), we tend not to believe in such impersonal powers these days. Wizards and witches, monsters, ogres, angels, once relegated to the nursery, now populate fantasy novels and films, but even there they are entertained only as 'figments of the imagination'. So imperious is the fallacy of literalism, we forget that it is by means of such unsettling figures that the imagination mirrors hidden aspects of ourselves – aspects that will break out, resentfully, angrily, violently, if they are ignored. Stories like *Parzival* wisely bring them back into play, reminding us that what matters is that we recognise their archetypal power and find ways to integrate them.

The further Parzival and Gawain venture beyond the known world, the more urgently do they encounter the problem of harnessing the raw, amoral energy of such figures in service of higher values. But the jaded civilisation of Arthur's court has already lost its sense of purpose and direction. Its formidable defences are porous to the haunted wilderness of the otherworld. And it's from there that both the challenge and the possibility of renewal come.

To begin with, it comes in the form of Parzival himself, the roughly clad green man, barbarously armed. But he covers his wildness with the Red Knight's armour, tears himself free of his roots, and, taking Gurnemanz for his mentor, becomes a conventional knight. Living as his father lived, forsaking his wife for adventure, he is on a collision course with larger, more impersonal forces.

Anfortas, the Rich Fisherman, lies in wait for him. The Grail Castle looms on its savage crag. Divested of his armour and dressed as a woman, Parzival the wanderer is admitted to a dreamlike ritual of wonders. He is given a sword – bright symbol of the penetrating intellect – that will break when he most needs it. He is shown the bleeding lance and the table of the grail. He sees Anfortas unable to stand or sit or lie because of the grievous wound in his groin. Everything seems charged with an energy that is both sacred and sexual, yet that energy is arrested, impotent, unfruitful. Later we will learn how Anfortas was given that wound, and about Gramoflanz who gave it to him – the usurping King of the Wood who has, through violence, seized control of what belongs by right to the feminine principle. We will learn about the shadowy castrate Klingsor, whose malevolent enchantment holds the women of the kingdom in thrall at the Castle of the Marvels and has cast this blight across the lands of the grail. Like Parzival we dimly discern a mysterious pattern of relationship between a sexual wound, a lance that bleeds, and a cup of generation. But like Parzival we find it hard to bring them through into consciousness, to speak about them. And so silence prevails, the dark powers win again, the possibility for renewal fails. But nothing is quite as it was before. Sigune may still grieve over her decaying lover, but the unconscious has sprung open like a wound. Soon blood is everywhere.

Later we may come to ponder the connection between a tender, three-night-long initiation into married sexuality, a pattern of blood on snow, the inability to take advantage of a ferryman's willing daughter, and a magic bed where raw animal energy has to be overcome and transformed if a spell is to be lifted. Our guide in these matters of the heart will be the hideous sorceress Cundrie, the boar-tusked guardian of hag wisdom, who has burst into the arrested castle of the mind with threats and challenges and scornful demands that we wake up from our immature dreams of conquest, that we try to become fully human.

Here in the dark feminine, rendered angry and monstrous by

neglect, is the transforming power source of the story. Yet Cundrie will be assisted in her endeavours by a quietly reflective male figure, one who has turned his back on the life of action and delivered himself over to solitary contemplation. He too is a wilderness creature, living away from the violence and temptations of the world, striving to make his soul. The hermit Trevrizent may not himself be the spiritual prince who will bring renewal to the blighted land, but without access to his hard-earned wisdom that prince will never find his way back to the Castle of the Grail.

So here we come to it at last – the question of the grail. What is it, and what are we to make of its arcane mysteries in sceptical times such as these? To approach an answer, let me take, in the time-honoured tradition of knights errant everywhere, a somewhat roundabout route.

Perhaps the most extraordinary achievement of Wolfram's poem is the powerful act of the imagination by which it enfolds the story of the evolution of an individual human soul within a larger, cosmic myth that offers metaphorical insights into the evolution of consciousness. *Parzival* is a story about renewal, the kind of renewal that comes when, and only when, apparently irreconcilable powers are in fact reconciled – when contradictions have received their complete expression, fought each other to a standstill, then re-perceived one another, no longer as hostile opposites but as polar complements.

Through such a process of reconciliation something new can get made for life. We take for granted the fact that it happens biologically when the often conflicting powers of male and female come together and a child is born. We find it harder to conceive how, by a parallel inward process, an individual soul might renew its vitality through the difficult reconciliation of its contrary elements. As the epidemic violence of history daily reminds us, we find it harder still to imagine how a similar process might hold true for the social, political, and spiritual conflicts of the age – though the problems there are vertiginous in scale. Yet it is to all these possibilities that Wolfram's story speaks, and it speaks to them through the creative power of the imagination.

Central to the unfolding narrative of *Parzival* is its firm grasp on two different aspects of the imagination: the inventive aspect by which some new vision is conceived for life, and the ethical aspect that enables us to empathise with others and thus ground our understandings in compassion. In Wolfram's story the invisible champions of the imagination are the neutral angels – those who refused to join the war in heaven which had threatened to tear the universe apart. Whatever sources he was drawing on – and there are elements that relate it to pagan, Christian, Cabbalistic, and Islamic traditions – Wolfram's gnostic myth of the grail as a sacred stone from heaven is staggering in the reach of its vision. For a universe where one is forced to take sides, where one spiritual power can triumph only at the expense of another, is unacceptable to an imagination large enough to understand that truth is found only where contradictions meet.

This, in Wolfram's vision, is the place of the grail. This is the virtue of the stone. Everything in his story heartens us to live with the tension of such ambiguity. Thus the powers of both light and darkness are built into the fabric of the stone. Both a black queen and a white queen are needful to produce a true champion of the grail. Both black chess pieces and white are used as weapons for Gawain's otherwise disarmed defence in the fight at the Castle of Ascalun. Parzival (whose very name is a play on words meaning 'pierce through the middle') follows his inner light until it leads him into utter darkness; only then does he begin to find his way back to the Castle of the Grail. Before that journey can be completed, Parzival, the champion of light, must yield to his Moorish half-brother Feirefiz, whose skin is dappled like a magpie, being both black and white.

It seems that only when that which has split apart is brought back together, and everything has been afforded its rightful place in the scheme of things, only then can the wound in consciousness start to be healed – that is, be made whole again. This is not a problem capable of a solely intellectual solution. Though the healing presence of the grail can be evoked only by the asking of a question, it is a question that is prompted by a compassionate motion of the heart.

Earlier I suggested that Wolfram's story offers a map to the landscape of the human soul, but there is something in its emblemology of opposites which seems to correspond to the very fabric of our bodies too. We are twofold creatures: our brains, torso, limbs, and organs are delicately stitched into a sturdy and fragile unity from almost symmetrical halves. Even the heart is made up of left- and right-hand chambers like that vessel called a 'pelican' in which the alchemists strove to solve the problem of the opposites and thereby attain the Philosopher's Stone, the elixir of life itself.

Foremost among the apparent contraries that the alchemical process sought to reconcile was that of matter and spirit, body and soul, and there are many alchemical references in Wolfram's text. He certainly had a poet's understanding of the hermetic connection between the vessel and the stone, on the one hand, and the human heart and soul, on the other. He may have had an initiate's understanding too.

In *The Myth of the Goddess*, Anne Baring and Jules Cashford luminously relate the emblem of the grail to Gnostic and Cabbalistic alchemy and to the processes of renewal and rebirth which were celebrated in the ancient mystery rites of the Goddess. 'What is the Grail then,' they ask, 'but the inexhaustible vessel, the source of life continuously coming into being, energy pouring into creation, energy as creation, the unquenchable fountain of eternal being?' In affirming the power of Wolfram's vision of the grail, they add, 'There had been other images of the source of creation, but no myth before this had linked that image to the spontaneous outpouring of an individual heart.' Here we approach both the heart of Wofram's particular genius and its resonance for our time.

The wound that must be healed in the grail story is a bodily wound, a sexual wound, but it mirrors that dualistic splitting of the mind which is the price we have to pay for our consciousness of ourselves as separate beings. Our analytical powers increased enormously with the evolution of such consciousness, but it also estranged us from the wisdom of the heart and the lived experience of that sense of unity with the world around us which is the deep ground of our being. Like Parzival, we cut ourselves off from the primal union with the mother and set out on our quest into life armed with the sword of the divisive intellect only to find that 'things fall apart, the centre cannot hold', and with the world thus turned centrifugal on us we are uncertain how to find our way back home.

Writing in a time when the power of the church and a hierarchical system of government claimed to offer a coherent picture of the universe, Wolfram confronted a predicament common to many of us today: the anxious awareness that the way to authentic being cannot lie in obedience to external authority, but has to be found through each individual's loyalty to the often contradictory truth of personal experience.

It may not always be a reliable guide but, for many of us, it's all we have. Often enough it leads us into dissidence from the powers that be. Whether coded or not, Wolfram's account of the sources of his story (he claims to have got it from the astrologer 'Flegetanis' in Muslim Spain through the Provencal and therefore possibly Catharist poet 'Kyot') places his imagination in heretical terrain. The prelates of the Christian church have no place in his story, and the power of his vision brought him to an almost Taoist understanding that all the fury and mire of human complexity must dissolve into a receptive emptiness of heart before renewal can take place.

Such a vision makes each life an individual project of the imagination – a gnostic process of self-discovery and self-transcendence, which is deeply grounded in the compassionate awareness that we live in the plural, that we are answerable for one another.

So when Parzival asks what ails his uncle he is also implicitly asking, 'What's wrong with us? Why can't we hold it together? Why do we cause such injury in the world?' And because his attention is focused not on his own plight but on another's, he is immediately admitted to the presence of the grail. Which is to say that the renewing energy of life itself comes to meet him in joyful response.

But all the ancient mysteries have been profaned these days. We no longer have such accessible rites of passage and or any universally accepted myths. It's a time for openness, for sceptical questioning, a time when nothing can be taken on trust. In such a time the activity of the analytic intellect has put enormous powers at our disposal, yet most of us feel paradoxically impotent within a scarily fissive world. Our technological skills present us with choices for which we are ill-prepared, and ingenious things get done in the name of scientific enquiry that leave us ill at ease. We find it hard to trust in the virtue of our politicians, our judges, our religious leaders, our scientists, our artists, our intimate relationships, the food we eat, the water we drink, sometimes even the air we breathe.

Some of us recoil from the uncertainty and bewildering moral relativities of this situation into the consoling absolutes of one or other form of fundamentalism – each of which tends to be violently opposed to another. Meanwhile much of the population of the earth is eroding the natural environment in a struggle for profit or subsistence, and in the prosperous North-West, like a deep bass note trembling under everything, there is a sense of impending disaster. We know we've got things wrong. We don't know what to do about it. And so, apart from occasional upsurges of charitable outrage, we shut our eyes against the suffering and aridities of a wasteland time, and hope for the best.

Yet this is not the whole picture, for we also live in a time when two hopeful and apparently contrary motions of the human spirit are seeking to converge.

The first of these is the widespread need for the discovery and assertion of personal identity which has emerged in recent years. For all the vanities and delusions that may attend the many various regimens of self-development, there has never been a time when so many individuals have made such a vigorous commitment to the difficult process of self-transformation. Each of them is a knight errant seeking their own path through the dark wood, and in the process they are discovering imaginative new ways to come together.

At the same time, as the fine flower of our sense of environmental crisis, we are witnessing an unprecedented increase in ecological understanding. With it has come an ever-increasing awareness that we are all in this together and that our decent survival as a species depends on the welfare of the entire planetary community.

Furthermore, the kind of thinking required and encouraged by these perspectives is of a subtler order than the old 'objective' positivism. Subject and object, self and other, inside and outside, can now be perceived as parts of an inclusive field. Like it or not, we have seen that what we do to the other we do also to ourselves, and the accompanying evolutionary shift in consciousness seems to be from ego-centrism to eco-centrism, from the divisive perspective of the separate ego to the confluent perspectives of the soul.

Like all transitional times, ours is an age fraught with perils and possibilities, but so high are the stakes these days that the outcome is full of doubt. Perhaps what is needed in such a time is a vital response from the imagination. Don't we need to keep the intelligence that reaches us from the outside in living relation with the insights arising from within? Don't we need to temper our talent for invention with a compassionate awareness of how things stand with others than ourselves? Don't we need to remember that the imagination is a faculty that seeks to hold contraries together in creative tension instead of letting them split off into destructive conflict, and is therefore a resource sorely needed by many warring couples, divided families, and embattled communities? Fortunately, like the ability to dream, it is also a faculty to which we all have birthright access, though it will prosper only to the degree that we take pains to keep it exercised. As I indicated in 'Imagining Otherwise' (see pages 10–29), much will depend on the kind of stories we choose to tell each other.

Eight hundred years ago Wolfram von Eschenbach composed a narrative poem that examples us all in imaginative endeavour. The magical stone for which its hero seeks is an emblem of the transforming power of the imagination. For, properly understood, magic *is* the activity of the imagination – that power which conjures doves out of darkness, redeems the tormented soul from its cabinet of knives, and brings about change in ways that seem to defy the rational mind.

Like all true myths, Wolfram's *Parzival* is a lively oracle of change. The presiding spirit of its vision – startling in its invention, wryly humorous in tone, anti-fundamentalist in its metaphysic, and tolerant in its embrace – demonstrates the gains that can be made for life when an individual sets out in quest for an authentic sense of being. Following his heroes through the landscape of the soul, the poet bravely explores the range of his creative power in ways that are enriched by a hard-won, deep-searching knowledge of the self and by compassion for others. The question this fable poses to the imagination is not, 'What is the meaning of life?' Rather it asks, 'How can we best live our lives so that they feel rich in meaning?' In this, as in so many other respects, *Parzival* remains a contemporary story and a salutary myth for our own troubled and exhilarating times.

# Parzival at Dartington

Birdsong, stirrings, incidents
of air attend the loaded heart
this February day of crocuses
and soft uncertain Spring.

I bring about my person images
I know I'll find: the coupled swans
entwined above the tiltyard stair,
the matron stone, and Flora garlanded.
Green emblems of the heart, they beckon
inwards where an unexpected sparrowhawk
alights and perches on a sprung-braced stick
to preen and squint in wind. She mews;
the broken jesses ring and stop my breath,
for what is on her huntress mind is death.

And then (as once in dream I sensed
my father's corpse drag lax and heavy
at my side) I meet a grieving woman
with a dead man in her arms, whom once
she loved and lost before the world
could make things new in them.
She charges me with bitter fault –
a faithless mind; a tongue that utters
nothing when a feeling word might quicken
the arrested air; a heart withheld.

*O father, time has long since found*
*a stop in you; and you and I are almost*
*almost of an age these days. I rage*
*across the generations of this hurt to see*
*how long it takes your open wound to heal in me.*

# In Praise of Dreams

This is a revised version of a review of *Private Myths: Dreams and Dreaming* by Anthony Stevens (Hamish Hamilton, 1995), which originally appeared in *Resurgence* under the title 'Rituals of the Night'.

Traditionally, the Senoi people of Malaya have attached such importance to the role of dreaming in the human story that each of their mornings begins with a kind of breakfast clinic in which the elder males listen to their children's accounts of their dreams and then interpret them as an essential feature of their education. By contrast, here in the North-West, for all that psychoanalysis has taught us about the unconscious mind, we still tend to identify ourselves almost entirely with the activities of waking consciousness, tending to regard our dreams as sometimes engaging, more frequently discomfiting, aberrations of the night. But isn't it the case that we human beings are, so to speak, amphibious creatures, adapted to two different and complementary modes of being, and that each time we enter sleep we forgo conscious control of our identities to become for a time whatever it is that our dreams need us to be? On occasion it can even feel as if we lie at the mercy of these involuntary rituals, exposed in the wildest glades of our being, beyond the reach of everything except the daimonic imagery of the soul. So, do these nocturnal rites mean well by us or not? Do they mean anything at all?

We know that by wiring us up to electronic circuitry and patiently watching us snooze in dream laboratories the scientists have confirmed to their own satisfaction what India long ago intuited from experience: that there are three distinguishable states of mind: wakefulness (vaiswanara), dreamless sleep (prajna), and dreaming sleep (taijasa), in which state we spend about a quarter of each night's slumber, on and off. Thus around six years of an averagely long life will be passed in the enigmatic otherworld of dream. By any standards this is a major investment of time. We are relatively helpless throughout it, outwardly unproductive, and may feel we have more pressing things we might prefer to do with such a substantial portion of our lives.

Yet nature insists that we sleep and, while we are sleeping, that we also dream. It's not surprising therefore that the dream scientists have finally proved what the romantics among us always knew – that dreaming is as needful to our lives as eating. But the essential mysteries surrounding dreams remain. Where do they come from? What are they for? How best to interpret their often ambiguous imagery?

Let no one be in doubt that these questions matter. To agree with the seventeenth-century doctor, Sir Thomas Browne, that 'We are somewhat more than ourselves in sleep and the slumber of the body seems to be but the waking of the soul' is to live in a very different universe than do those who share the nineteenth-century view expressed, according to Freud, by W. Robert that a dream is no more than 'a somatic process of excretion of which we become aware in our mental reaction to it'. It's hard to imagine Browne and Robert are speaking of the same phenomenon even; but dreams are paradoxical, and perhaps, having got the sorts of dreams they deserve, dream theorists proceed to base their judgments on them!

In our own time, when James Hillman assures us that their 'unending, embracing depth is one way that dreams show their love', while at our other shoulder Francis Crick sceptically insists they are merely a way of getting rid of superfluous information – that 'we dream in order to forget' – what are we to make of this perplexing, enlarging, least public, most intimate and occult of our activities?

Anyone who has read my novels will know where I stand on the matter. I'm convinced that a life, as much as a story, can turn on an important dream. It was a dream that ushered me out of a relatively safe teaching job into the challenges and generative anxieties of the writing life, and since then dreams have often come to my aid when I get lost inside the stories I try to tell. So I'm inclined to agree with Edward Nesbit's perhaps extravagant declaration in *The Chymical*

*Wedding* that 'dreams have a knack of undermining the ego's self-esteem. They offer nightly demonstrations of what malleable stuff reality is made. Their invention is endless, insatiable, because they insist on the truth.'

With greater confidence I would back Yeats's resonating utterance that 'in dreams begins responsibility'; but then poets have always been champions of dreams and have often been patronised as 'dreamers' for their pains. These days it seems that a different sort of authority is required to affirm the dignity of dreams – one able to approach their elusive world in the questioning spirit of scientific rigour, yet tactfully too, and shrewdly, with something of their own multivalent nature. Ideally such an approach would call on the combined resources of scientist, healer, psychotherapist, medium, and poet. It would refine a scientific training in biology and psychology with an educated love of the arts and a familiarity with evidence from many cultures and traditions, while enlivening such scholarship with the kind of insights only imagination brings. It would, moreover, combine open and honest self-scrutiny with a compassionate attention to the testimony of others and be concerned to do justice to all aspects of the issues involved while also bringing to their consideration an informed intelligence that is eloquent, witty, and wise.

A tall order, yes, but in the author of this wonderful book we are fortunate to meet a master dreamworker uniquely qualified for this delicate task. *Private Myths: Dreams and Dreaming* draws impressively on all these qualities and resources. Its comprehensive and accessible account of dreams in our life also meets one of the urgent needs of the time.

Anthony Stevens is an evolutionary psychiatrist and a distinguished Jungian analyst. His sensitivity to the mythic, symbolic, and sacred aspects of human experience is anchored throughout to both a precise biological sense of our material existence and a sophisticated understanding of the role of natural selection in the formation of our complex brains. While acknowledging the foundational role in dream theory of Freud's magnum opus *The Interpretation of Dreams*, he goes on to trace fascinating links between Jung's theory of the archetypal structure of the psyche and the evolutionary adaptations the species must have undergone to ensure its own survival. In so doing, he makes a convincing case for the symbolic images of dream as the only language in which the old, dumb, instinctual brain can speak its word, thus keeping open 'the lines of communication between the neocortex and the limbic system, enabling the dialogue between conscious and unconscious functions to occur'.

Yet there is nothing reductive about this book, and among its many engaging qualities is the degree to which its writing has been shaped by the dream process itself. When he began work on his book Stevens dreamed of a 'poetry machine' which counselled him to keep his dominant bent as a scientist attuned to the essentially poetic nature of work with dream. As he approached the end of his task, sleep took him on a stupendous 'shamanbird's' flight over his beloved Devon coast in a lucid vision that corrected a left-brain tendency towards over-intellectuality and recalled, to both mind and heart, the sacred ground from which dreams, consciousness, and the need for meaning rise. Without pretension the reader is thus left assured both of the personal honesty of the book and that it is all the richer for the impersonal wisdom of those dreams. That wisdom is, moreover, delightfully balanced by the author's willingness – as in his hilarious account of an oneiric encounter with Asklepios – to show himself ticked off by a dream for a less exemplary moment of personal weakness.

Through such judicious self-disclosure he brings us into living touch with the dream world and enlivens what might, in less confident hands, have been a less animated survey of the history, theory, and practice of dreamwork from the time of Gilgamesh up to the present day. Among its other virtues the book is an excellent introduction to the development of dream science and gives a thorough grounding in psychoanalytic theory which acknowledges both Freud's pioneering endeavours and Jung's wide-ranging explorations in this field.

Dr Stevens' chapter on 'The Dream Work' is perhaps the liveliest corrective to what he recognises as Freud's 'pessimistic and reductive cast of mind'. It gives a brilliant account of oneiropoesis – the way dreams invent themselves with the fluent, improvisational, syncopated play of a two-million-year old imagination that is infinitely resourceful in its capacity to relate the exigencies of our individual lives to the organic needs of the species. More diligent than a tedious nightshift filing clerk, and far subtler than the most sophisticated computer, this version of the dreaming mind places the activity of poet and myth-maker at the integrating centre of all our lives. It makes us all authors of our own deep story and thereby lends wider dimensions of meaning to Shelley's claim that the poet is 'the unacknowledged legislator of the world'.

Throughout the book Stevens insists that interpretative work with dreams is not a science but an art. His chapters on 'Dreams in Therapy' and 'Practical Dreamwork' demonstrate the range of his artistry, care, and skill in ways that will be of invaluable service to practising therapists, to those in therapy, and to those who simply find their waking lives deepened by the private effort to learn the idiom of dreams. He calls on the wide resources of his culture and critical intelligence, along with a passionate emphasis on wholeheartedness, to give luminous readings of some of the big dreams that have shaped the career of human creativity, the inflections of our evolving sensibility, and even the course of history. In a time that has become critically aware of the limitations of Cartesian thought, readers may be particularly struck by the interpretation of an important dream recorded by René Descartes which reveals the schizoid disposition of a mind that was a major influence in establishing scepticism as the principal virtue of the scientific method.

There are other, more urgent reasons why this book matters. 'To work on dreams', Stevens declares, 'is not a petty form of indulgence, but a spiritual ritual of cultural and ecological significance.' He is aware that many of the personal dreams with which we are individually preoccupied might strike the dreamworkers of traditional societies as trivial in comparison with the big dreams that once magnetised their world. But in the heroic pursuit of consciousness we have stepped outside the sacred ground of myth and dream and 'the only myths left to us are the personal myths we create in sleep; the only ritual left to us is the intimate ritual of analysis'. Even in these depleted circumstances, by its insistence on linking our psychic life back to its roots in nature, this remarkable book opens us again to the knowledge that we are the instruments of nature's quest for self-awareness and that the voice of nature speaks to our personal, and sometimes our collective, situation most clearly through our dreams.

Out of his desire to acknowledge and celebrate the mysteries of existence, Stevens not only urges us to listen to that voice; he shows us how to do so more feelingly and leaves us more finely tuned to its subtle frequencies. Whether we listen or not is up to us, but, like all true rites, our dreaming rituals of the night seek to reunite us with the procreative ground from which they spring, and on which our own free-ranging lives finally depend. Like the great public myths whose narratives dramatise the passions of the soul, they are oracles of change. Keyed to the needs of each individual in the privacy of sleep, their images return us to that ancestral place where existence becomes numinous with a sense of commonality. And so they can lift us, if we are prepared to go, beyond our narrower ambitions out towards the larger need of our species to be at one with this most beautiful and mysterious of worlds.

Many centuries ago, in his *Oneirokritika*, Artemidorus of Ephesus instructed the ancient world in the importance of its dreams. In an age dominated by the sceptical intellect, books that quicken the heart with serious reminders of that are indispensable. Among them, Stevens's *Private Myths* is a lucid, careful work in which scholarship and wisdom meet, a feeling intelligence speaks its word as a healing force, and art and science – far too long estranged – come home once more to dream creatively together.

# In Dreams

*for Dr Anthony Stevens*

Artemidorus, I recall how once
you almost wept when speaking of
the animals and ancestors that nightly
gather in the darkness of our sleep
to mourn for us and for the ruin
we are making of their home.

And then in laughter aimed against
yourself you told how once in Greece
you boasted that Asklepios would come
to you in dream. He did, and shot you wide
awake in shame at his rebuke for using
him to prove your ego's point.

For nothing speaks more truly than a dream,
and where else, in the spin and jangle
of a time so fast to change that even
wisdom seems redundant, shall we keep
those secrets that the soul discloses
for our welfare while we sleep?

# Blake

## A Man without a Mask

This is a slightly edited version of a review of *Blake* by Peter Ackroyd (Sinclair-Stevenson, 1995), originally published in *Resurgence*.

If prophets are rarely honoured in their own land or time, it may be because there is something essentially seditious in the nature of their task. Properly performed, it has less to do with foretelling the future than with speaking out those secrets of the heart that few wish to hear. Not surprisingly, therefore, the handful of artists who accept this dangerous responsibility meet with little acclaim in their life-times, though if their work is done well they may eventually come to be valued as agents of eternity rather than simply as products of time.

Inexhaustibly provocative and inspiring, and in many ways still as much an enigma to conventional thought now as he was in the first quarter of the nineteenth century, William Blake stands large among such vital spirits. 'There is no doubt this poor man was mad,' Wordsworth opined after perusing *The Songs of Innocence and Experience*, 'but there is something in the madness of this man which interests me more than the sanity of Lord Byron and Walter Scott.' Blake's close friend and colleague, John Flaxman, saw no reason to doubt Blake's sanity, though he was often bewildered by him and must have foreseen how his long years of devoted, uncompromising labour would bring little but hardship, neglect, and incomprehension such as might have left a less resolute spirit rankling with bitterness. Yet, recording the old visionary's late reflections on the manner in which he had pursued his solitary course through the darkness, Crabb Robinson heard him declare, 'I should be sorry if I had any earthly fame, for whatever natural glory a man has is so much detracted from his spiritual glory. I wish to do nothing for profit. I wish to live for art. I want nothing whatever. I am quite happy.'

That calm, philosophical self-judgment meets with the assent of Samuel Palmer, the most gifted of 'The Ancients', the loyal band of young painters whose devoted enthusiasm came as a vital confirmation to the aged Blake. 'He was a man without a mask,' wrote Palmer, 'his aim single, his path straightforward, and his wants few; so he was free, noble and happy.' For the Ancients this extraordinary old man was not the 'Poor Blake' pitied by so many of his baffled acquaintances, but 'Michael Angelo Blake'; and the two rooms in Fountain Court where he passed the last years of his life were known to them as 'The House of the Interpreter'.

One hopes that in the eager, reverent attention of those poetic young spirits, Blake found – if any were needed – sound intimations of the enduring value of his work for future generations. For, with an astonishing vigour quite distinct in its transforming power from that of almost any other poet or painter one can think of, William Blake lives on. The words of his great hymn, 'Jerusalem', stir the souls of schoolchildren, environmentalists, socialists, and members of the Women's Institute alike; and the publication of Peter Ackroyd's biography was accompanied – I imagine he would have hated this – by a television programme.

Blake's own vision was, of course, of quite another order. It insisted on the primacy of the imaginal realm and reached so deeply through into that realm that, more than two centuries after he came into the world, it may well be that his true contemporaries are yet to be born. In the meantime it seems that those seriously engaged with the dilemmas of evolving consciousness sooner or later find themselves as deeply in conversation with Blake as he himself was with the Old Testament prophets Isaiah and Ezekiel.

The spread of his influence has been wide and deep. In his own efforts to further what he called 'the revolt of the soul against the intellect', W.B. Yeats discovered that Blake had already tried to forge a mythology adequate to the ordeals of that mighty struggle. The Four Zoas dramatised in Blake's Prophetic Books can be interpreted as significant precursors of Jung's attempt to discriminate the contrary and complementary functions of the human psyche; and, though Blake was no egalitarian, champions of the political left such as E.P. Thompson have drawn stimulus and inspiration from his vision. Meanwhile explorers of Druidism, syncretist mythology, and the hermetic tradition find that many of the themes and images that excite them today already figured large among Blake's preoccupations. One glance into the rigorous glitter of his gaze, however, reminds us that he would have had as little patience with the flakier speculations of the New Age and its Spectre as he would have done with the way in which his works have become grist to the academic mills.

It is a measure of Blake's enduring importance that, for all his obstinately guarded singularity (indeed as a living celebration of it), he is also a vital link in the Golden Chain by which Wisdom survives the efforts of successive generations to erode its demand that life be experienced as an evolutionary drama of immense spiritual consequence.

'The Ages are All Equal,' he insisted. 'But Genius is Always Above the Age.' In this comprehensively researched, finely written study, Peter Ackroyd acknowledges the timeless dimension of the man's achievement, but as a biographer his emphasis tends to fall elsewhere. 'Blake was the poet of eternity,' he says, 'but he was also the poet of late eighteenth century London.' In that apparently self-evident assertion lies the main difficulty facing this (and perhaps any other) attempt to do justice to Blake by chronicling his personal history.

Apart from the conflict with John Scofield which brought him briefly and scarily up against the power of the state, his life itself was relatively uneventful. In the faithful company of his extraordinary Kate, the outward span of his experience was that of the solitary engraver, imaginatively detached from a world that often filled him with 'nervous fear'. Though he was far from indifferent to the social and political issues of the time – and his prophetic vision was profoundly revolutionary in its assertions – his distrust of rationalism, and his vigorous championing of individuality and diversity, kept him at a significant cultural distance from the mainstream of contemporary radical thought. For this reason, although Ackroyd's effort to characterise him as a 'Cockney visionary' in an established tradition of urban dissent may serve as a useful corrective to a woolly view of

Blake as an eccentric mystic, it also has a vaguely reductive air.

Ackroyd is conscious that Blake would have been resistant to such a localized and circumstantial approach to his life. Writing of the moral character of the metropolitan culture of the time, he admits that 'Blake himself rarely alludes to such things, and so the biographer must mention them for him – even if, in the process, he becomes one of those whom Blake denounces for their blindness to the true and spiritual state of the world.' One is left wondering what sort of marginal comment such sleight of mind might have elicited from its subject had Ackroyd's book been more generously graced with margins than it is. (Perhaps: 'A Very Clever Sentence,' as Blake scribbled once in his copy of Joshua Reynolds's *Discourses*, 'who wrote it, God knows').

Nevertheless, one of Ackroyd's strengths in this book (as in his novels) is its well-documented, atmospherically charged feel for the period. He does a fine job in evoking the streets and fields of eighteenth-century London as they must have struck the rapt gaze and vivid imagination of the boy growing up in the parish of St James. Ackroyd's diligent research has also turned up details that throw fresh light on specific images in Blake's work. In the bloody-armed women plying the butcher's trade in Carnaby Market, for example, he has found the possible 'lost originals' of those seen disembowelling a fallen man in a plate in *Jerusalem*; and he contemplates the burnt-out ruin of Albion Mill in Blackfriars Road as a looming prototype of the 'dark satanic mills' that Blake so powerfully condemned in his visionary hymn.

Ackroyd is equally good on the character and feel of an engraver's workshop, with its smell of nut oil, varnish, and lampblack, its pots and pans, tallow candles, racks of needles and gravers, rags, pumice stones, the square wooden press itself, the stacks of fine paper and the plates 'which were the thickness of a half-crown'. Good too on Blake's method of engraving and the part it played in his imaginal process. He describes how 'Many of the *Songs of Experience* are etched upon the other side of the copper plates for *Innocence*,' and points out that in this way the 'two contrary states could be held, as an object in the hand'.

These and many other insights are intriguing, yet one is left with the uneasy feeling that, in trying put Blake the man into perspective, Ackroyd is stronger at seeing the sun as 'a round disk of fire somewhat like a guinea', so to speak, than he is at bearing witness to the heavenly host chanting their hosannas. In both his fictional version of Oscar Wilde and his biographical study of Charles Dickens, Ackroyd has demonstrated his skill at portraying imaginative men of this world, but the figure of Blake presents a more formidable problem. Doubts that this biographer's visionary range is adequate to his subject begin to grow on hearing a beautiful and difficult sentence from the Platonist philosopher Thomas Taylor casually dismissed as 'standard alchemical doctrine'. They are confirmed when one watches him back quickly away from the truly radical implications of Blake's insistence to the Revd John Trusler that 'To Me This World is all One continued Vision of Fancy or Imagination'.

As our own generation gradually wakens from Newton's sleep, and counts the terrible cost of those errors of perception which Blake long ago recognised and opposed with all the visionary power at his command, surely it is here, in his insistence on the imaginal dimension of the world and the responsibilities that arise from that recognition, that his voice is most urgently alive for us? For a deeper understanding of what that difficult, enlarging vision might mean in these transitional times, one must turn not to this – the best biography of Blake presently available – but to the fierce light still burning from the hot forge of the poet's own imagination. It is there, in verses and plates celebrating the holiness of all life, that we will find the energetic, contrary states of his soul most vigorously portrayed – along with the uncovered secrets of our own bewildered hearts.

# The Alchemy
# of Imagination

This is an edited version of a lecture given at the Adam Mickiewicz University in Poznan, Poland. It was later published
in *Polish Studies in English Language and Literature* and then in
*Medievalisms: The Poetics of Literary Re-reading edited by Liliana Si-
korska (Peter Lang, 2008).*

Generally speaking, we English are a sceptical lot, particularly the
intellectuals among us, so the words 'alchemy' and 'alchemical' are
rarely used in serious discourse these days except with metaphorical
force. This isn't greatly surprising, for even in the work of Isaac
Newton and Robert Boyle, two of alchemy's most celebrated inves-
tigators, we can already see the tide of energy shifting away from the
study of matter in the sacred tradition of the medieval worldview
towards the new 'sceptical chemistry' and the development of the
scientific method of replicable experiment. The evolution of Enlightenment thinking was entirely opposed in spirit to the hermetic
nature of alchemical assumptions, vocabulary, and imagery, and if
this tradition still holds sway in academic circles, it's not only among
the strict minds of the scientific community.

Scholars of English literature, for instance, are comfortable
enough with the satirical view of alchemy evinced in Chaucer's
'Canon's Yeoman's Tale' – which may have furnished us with our
derogatory term 'crackpot' – as they are also with the corrupt version of the alchemical art humorously portrayed in Ben Jonson's
play *The Alchemist.* Many of them also delight in the use of alchemical
imagery as the stuff of poetic conceits in the verse of the Metaphysical poets. But they tend to be less happy with the awkward fact that

the interest shown in alchemical modes of thought by such great twentieth-century poets as W.B. Yeats and Ted Hughes was, for them (as for earlier poets such as Donne and Vaughan), a matter of more than just literary importance. Indeed it seems to have been integral to their way of seeing, feeling, interpreting, and recreating their vision of how things are.

Now it's possible to dismiss such apparent regression into a medieval way of thinking as a quaint eccentricity, a quirk of their creative imaginations – odd, yes, but forgivable as a perhaps necessary stratagem for the generation of new poetic energy. But I doubt that either Yeats or Hughes would have been content with such a reductive view of what was a dynamic aspect of their personal experience and the very ground of the worldview out of which they wrote.

Nor is it just our poets who present such a problem. Novelists such as James Joyce, Malcolm Lowry, John Cowper Powys, Patrick White, and Doris Lessing have all drawn deeply on hermetic modes of thought in order to articulate in fiction their experience of the world. In this respect they lie closer to the European tradition of hermetic writing achieved by such major figures as Wolfram von Eschenbach, Novalis, Goethe, Baudelaire, Rimbaud, Thomas Mann, and Hermann Hesse than to the drier vision of sceptical academics. Not that we should glibly dismiss such scepticism, for even C.G. Jung, who did more than anyone to restore the dignity of alchemical enquiry, came away from his first encounter with the weird cavalcade of green lions, hermaphrodites, and self-consuming serpents depicted in alchemical texts with the opinion that they were 'something off the beaten track and rather silly'. Only later, motivated by a powerful dream, did he return to them in a more committed spirit and begin to realise that the serious alchemists were not only his precursors in the evolution of psychology as a science of the soul but were also engaged in an imaginative enterprise towards the resacralisation of what orthodox theology regarded as the fallen state of the material world redeemable only through the suffering of Christ.

It's part of Jung's heritage that the culture of the late twentieth century saw a revival of interest in the art of alchemy, and if, as I believe, such a development represents more than a recoil into quasi-medieval credulity, it seems that only a confluence of a slowly turning tide of cultural transition with the urgent demands of personal experience might lie behind it. Such was true of the growth of my own interest in alchemy, so I hope you will come to understand my reasons if I speak to my theme in personal terms before attempting a more generalised consideration of what its implications may be for a wider evolution of consciousness in our time.

Back in 1987 my first novel was accepted for publication. Telling the story of a white man's ordeal of initiation through an encounter with a witch in West Africa, it had originally been a dense text more than five hundred pages long entitled *Nigredo* after that arduous transitional phase of the alchemical opus in which darkness prevails and everything threatens to go wrong. But earlier disappointing responses from publishers had persuaded me to strip the novel down to half its length and change the title to *Sunday Whiteman*. In that form it proved acceptable to the editors at Jonathan Cape; but the book still had the look about it of being the only egg this chicken might lay, so before the contract was signed I was asked whether I had anything else in progress. As it happened, I did have drafts of a couple of stories that had both got stuck at an early stage. Conceived under the heavy influence of John Fowles's powerful novel *The Magus*, one of them told of an initiatory encounter between a young poet and an old poet and was a loose reworking of the medieval story of Sir Gawain and the Green Knight. The other idea I had begun to sketch out in the form of a novella based on the true story of the nineteenth-century alchemist Thomas South, who insisted that his daughter Mary Anne burn all the copies of her own remarkable book, *A Suggestive Enquiry into the Hermetic Mystery*, because he felt that her text revealed too much of the alchemical secret.

I was puzzling over which of these two still undeveloped ideas to submit when it occurred to me that the film of Fowles's *The French Lieutenant's Woman* had done an interesting job of combining one story set in the nineteenth century with another set in the twentieth. Could I do something similar? So I rewrote the openings slightly, sandwiched the start of the nineteenth-century tale between the opening two chapters of the twentieth-century one, made up a list of chapter headings to give the impression that I knew exactly where this interwoven narrative device was taking me, and submitted the job to Cape. The result excited them more than the first novel had done and I was committed to spending the next three years inside a bewildering hermetic labyrinth, trying to find the way out. The book eventually became *The Chymical Wedding*, which is the reason I was invited here today.

I have three reasons for sharing this somewhat disgraceful confession with you. Firstly – and I shall have more to say about this later – because the initially arbitrary conjunction of two apparently unrelated stories illustrates a principal theme of this talk – that something new can get made for life through the difficult process of the mysterium coniunctionis – the reconciliation of opposing forces. Secondly, because it gives a hint that one cannot begin to write imaginatively *about* alchemy without the writing itself becoming a work *of* alchemy. Even though I'm a novelist not a practising alchemist, the alchemical theme on which I had chosen to write put me through a sometimes gruelling process of personal transformation before the work itself could be accomplished. The end result may not have been pure gold but the struggle did give me some experience of what I'm trying to talk about. (I should perhaps add as a footnote – and a caveat – that a talk about alchemy, if it is to be true to its theme, may also have something of the character of an alchemical treatise, proceeding not by the usual means of conceptual logic but through a sequence of images designed to elicit responses at levels deeper than that of the managerial intellect.) Lastly, I share the anecdote with you because it may give you an indication of the degree to which alchemy had begun to play an active part in the evolution of my personal consciousness long before I came to write the novel. But to say more about that I will have to speak more personally still.

Almost half a century ago I entered King's College, Cambridge as a woolly-minded, working-class nature mystic yearning to be a writer. I came away both with the conviction that there was not much hope of that, and with an alternative commitment to the tradition of sceptical humanist thought, which took me as a teacher to newly independent Ghana, then on, out of a conviction of the urgent need for social change, into work in further education with students on release from industry and commerce. Employing the heavily rational system of values I had acquired at Cambridge, I became a member of that gallant band of liberal-minded intellectuals – a sort of unofficial lay clerisy – who believed they were transforming society by spreading the word of reason across the land.

At that time, I became the kind of young liberal-minded intellectual who believed that the world would be much improved if only it paid careful attention to his rational solutions for its problems. But my naïve belief in the power of reason was on a collision course with the refractory pressures of married life and the working world. By the age of thirty those pressures had pushed me into an increasingly withdrawn, more or less schizoid state of false consciousness which exploded into sudden breakdown with the failure of my marriage.

Because I had been so unconscious of what was happening to me and around me, the collapse of my masculine ego was as unexpected as it was dramatic, Over the course of two days and three nights, I felt myself impelled on an arduous inner journey of transformation. The bewildering reality of such an experience is largely unpublishable, though there are passages in my novels where I've tried to offer fictional versions of what it felt like to undergo that ordeal of change. It embarrasses me to employ such terms as 'ego-death' and 'rebirth', and yet that experience redirected the whole course of my life in radical and lasting ways. From my previous tightly managed, self-protective mode of living, I emerged into an almost virginal, deeply receptive sense of the flow of life, a flow of which my own being was seamlessly a part, and which felt richer in meaning and affirmative value than anything I had experienced since childhood. Even as my collapsed ego began to build back again, I knew that the rest of my life would be conditioned by loyalty to that experience, and it was necessary therefore to try to gain a fuller understanding of what had happened to me.

The search for that understanding eventually led me to Jung's writings on individuation, and through them I found my way into the rich store of emblems by which alchemy speaks of transformation. Like all who try to approach that elusive and enigmatic material through the analytic intellect, I quickly found myself confused by the twists and turns of its tutelary deity, that slippery fellow Mercurius

Duplex, who dissolves into thin air just when you think you are about to pin him down. But what gradually emerged into focus was an enlarging sense of the beauty and subtlety of the alchemical vision and the degree to which it offered a vocabulary of images which resonated with, and confirmed the value of, my own recent experience and enabled me to relate to it in fuller recognition and with greater imaginative energy.

Much later I tried to convey something of the urgent excitement of that discovery in a longish speech I gave to the old poet Edward Nesbit in *The Chymical Wedding*. Trying to persuade his sceptical young friend Alex Darken of the contemporary relevance of alchemy, Edward says,

> Materialism leaves us trapped in a world that won't hold together. It's centrifugal. It splits at every turn into the Ten Thousand Things each neatly labelled with a PhD thesis. In the meantime we become more and more obsessed with what we mistake for our real needs, hopes, fears, and more and more estranged from our birthright membership of a coherent universe … We can't live that way – not for much longer … We have to find a vision that will help us to change … One that reconciles matter with spirit, heart with mind, the female in us and the male, the darkness and the light. That was the problem which engaged the spiritual intellect of the true alchemist. That was the Elixir, the Stone, the Gold. They are all symbols for what cannot be said – only experienced.

And he ends with the declaration that 'the Hermetic tradition has always offered a vision whereby men and women might recover their experience in its wholeness. It offers a technique for achieving that vision – and we need to know how to know it now, for that is how things deeply are, and not only human life depends on it.'

Now the language in which the old poet expresses himself may be a touch hectoring and over-dramatic but I believe that his heart is in the right place and there's a good deal of truth in what he has to say. So, what were the main themes that emerged from my own investigations into alchemy at that time?

Firstly, I drew from them a vigorous confirmation of the visionary insight that had been borne in upon me immediately after my breakdown when I walked out into the quiet water meadows of a sunlit morning to be met by a profound sense of the unitary nature of all being. The world felt one, singular and whole, and I was no longer apart *from* it but a part *of* it, my own soul resonating, as it had not done since I was a child, in answer to the living soul of the world around me. Everything else would follow from that experience. In my attempts to assimilate it, I later discovered that nowhere outside the lines of the most sublime poetry was that vivid sense of unitary nature expressed more clearly than in the magisterial declarations of that seminal alchemical text, the *Emerald Tablet* of Hermes Trismegistus: 'What is below is like what is above, and what is above is like what is below, for the performing of the marvels of the one thing.'

As I have already mentioned, Mercurius Duplex is the presiding spirit of the alchemical vision – an elusive figure embodying a complex of opposites, forever unchanging yet never quite the same, as unstable as quicksilver and impossible to pin down. So there could be nothing fixed and permanent about that insight into the unitary nature of being except the degree to which it had altered my way of perceiving things. Otherwise it kept, and still keeps, slipping back and forth across the boundary between the conscious and unconscious mind. With this came the understanding that, though all things are interrelated through the great chain of being – the delicate web that supports our life – the various phenomena of the world around us are in quite different states of evolution towards consciousness.

Furthermore, the insights of the alchemists suggested that all things are an interfusion of matter and spirit, each seeking to realise and celebrate its part in the union with the whole. Because we too are an integral part of that seamless process, we do to ourselves what we do to the world that appears to be outside us, and what we do to the world we also do to ourselves. Our inward condition inescapably projects itself in and upon the world, and if there's an unholy mess out there, then it mirrors the state of confusion inside us.

The aspirations of the alchemists also seemed to demonstrate that by a proper use of the creative imagination we can raise the value of both inward and outward experience through a disciplined process of necessary change. But such work could only be done successfully, they insisted, by entering into right relations with the right material at the right time.

The various alchemical texts all agree that the one thing required to begin the work is the prima materia; they are, however, confusingly diverse in their assertions about just what that mysterious first matter is. Some of them, like the *Gloria Mundi* of 1526, confidently assert that it is to be found everywhere and is therefore despised by all, though next to the human soul it is the most precious thing on earth. The material was given so many disparate names – mercury, sulphur, salt, lead, earth, water, fire, dew, virgin, dragon – that the alchemists were clearly speaking in symbolic terms rather than of some literal substance.

By the same token, the secret 'fire' that is needed to perform the alchemical processes – 'a fire that does not burn' and that has to be extracted from the first matter and yet is also, at the same time, the means of its extraction – is clearly not what we usually understand by the term.

I confess to having found the enigmatic nature of the alchemical texts as perplexing as the next person; and yet their language and emblems worked, and still work, a curiously exciting enchantment over my imagination, as though, like the elusive images of dreams, they speak to something inside me deeper than the reach of the analytic intellect. If their language is paradoxical it's because it strives to hold together apparently contrary forces. That creative tension, it seems to me, goes to the very heart of the alchemical enterprise.

In describing the method of alchemical procedure, one formula tends to recur throughout the texts: 'Solve et Coagula', which in synoptic form instructs the would-be adept that the prima materia must first be dissolved into its constituent elements before it can be unified again. Another version of this formula tells the alchemist 'to make the fixed volatile and the volatile fixed.' In chemical terms, this apparently refers to the process of reflux distillation by which liquid is heated until it evaporates into a gas, which rises, cools, and condenses into a liquid, which is then fed back through the retort into the original liquid with transforming effect. If we translate this into psychological terms, it refers to the process by which consciousness arises out of the darkness of the unconscious, illuminating the conscious ego with insights that then allow a more complete discrimination of unconscious contents into still larger consciousness. For the alchemists the two processes – one external and material, the other internal and spiritual – were identical; the outer transformation could not happen without the same process working inwardly, thus affirming the essential unity of matter and spirit.

As anyone who has seriously engaged with these processes will confirm, the effort required is long, arduous, and at times extremely painful; for when one begins to dissolve a complex situation into its constituent parts by bringing them into the light of consciousness, one soon discovers that some of those elements are in a state of profound contradictory tension with one another, to such a volatile degree that they continuously threaten to tear apart – or, in alchemical terms, to burst the crucible in which those tensions are held together.

A simple analogy may make the process clearer. A man and woman fall hopelessly in love in what they take for a blissful state of union which leads them into marriage. After a time uncomfortable aspects of their relationship of which they had been unaware begin to oppress them. Conflicts emerge and develop. When efforts to resolve those conflicts prove ever more difficult, the situation deteriorates until divorce begins to seem a desirable option. Only if a massive effort of honest self-disclosure along with mutual recognition and acceptance is undertaken and sustained can true reconciliation and a new, more conscious union be achieved. It also requires a withdrawal of projections and a measure of self-sacrifice amounting at times to a kind of ego-death on both sides. The difficulty of that process is evidenced by the divorce statistics of a world that remains largely uneducated in such transformational dynamics.

When the alchemists sought to speak of such matters as they saw them at work both in their alembics and in their own souls, they did so in archetypal terms, illustrating their procedures through the changing nature of the relationship between a King and Queen, for example, or of Sol and Luna, Sun and Moon, which represent the often combative relationship between the masculine and feminine principles, both inwardly and outwardly. Thus a marvellous illustration to the sixteenth-century text *Aurora Consurgens* depicts figures of the Sun and Moon jousting with one another, he armoured and riding a lion, she naked on a gryphon's back. Each seeks to unseat the other with a lance, yet both are protected by shields. The subtlety of the illustration consists of the fact that the Sun carries the emblem of the Moon on his shield, while the Moon is protected by the emblem of the Sun on hers.

The picture illustrates the first stage of the alchemical work in which the King and Queen, Sol and Luna, are in a volatile state of opposition with one another, a conflict that leads through the course of many distillatory circulations to a state of death and putrefaction – 'a black blacker than black' known as the Nigredo – in which the opposed forces are dissolved so that each loses their separate identity. Out of that blackness a scintilla of white light eventually appears, heralding the cleansing stage known as the Albedo, through which, if the tension of contrary forces has been properly sustained, is eventually achieved the Royal Marriage of the Rubedo – the mysterium coniunctionis, in which all the contraries are reconciled and an enlarged sense of life, a newly unified state of consciousness – the Gold, the Elixir, the Philosopher's Stone – mysteriously arises.

These were the themes and processes I tried to explore in *The Chymical Wedding*, which is, I suppose, a kind of alchemical text for our time presented as fiction. Its title, borrowed from a celebrated seventeenth-century text, is another emblem for the reconciliation of the opposites. By structuring the book around two initially disparate stories set in different time frames but on a collision course, I sought to dramatise the process within the dual form of the narrative. The plain fact that I was largely unconscious of this aim when I first conceived the idea of the novel is an indication of the degree to which the three years of often bewildering work on the project mirrored my own struggle through into a larger degree of consciousness.

Now it's all very well for me to speak of the self-imposed tribulations of a novelist in this regard, but I'm sure that many of you will already be questioning whether the true alchemists were speaking in symbolic terms of mystical techniques for the raising of consciousness when they wrote of these things, or whether they were in fact offering a coded account of procedures by which base metal could indeed be transmuted into gold. An intriguing account by the physician and alchemist Helvetius, reputedly endorsed by Spinoza, insists that he both witnessed and later replicated such an operation; but, as I've said, I'm not a practising alchemist, so am not qualified to answer the question with any authority. I would suggest, however, that the divisive either/or terms in which it is posed may be missing the point, for it's possible they were doing both.

As a pioneer of depth psychology, Jung tended to view the hermetic texts in psychological terms, interpreting the events that the alchemists observed in their alembics as projections of the unconscious contents of their minds. But in paragraph 394 of his great work *Psychology and Alchemy* he records how Martin Ruland's 'astounding definition' of the imagination as 'the star in man, the celestial or supercelestial body' suggested other possibilities. Imagination, Jung declared, 'is perhaps the most important key to the understanding of the Opus', for it is 'a physical activity that can be fitted into the cycle of material changes that brought these about and is brought about by them in its turn. In this way the alchemist related himself not only to the unconscious but directly to the very substance which he hoped to transform through the power of imagination'.

Thus the alchemist operates simultaneously in the psychic and the physical realms and changes are being brought about in both – an interaction of the observer and the observed which seems to prefigure the discovery of quantum physics that the behaviour of matter at molecular levels is conditioned by the approach of the scientist observing it.

What Jung was attempting to articulate here may not be easy to grasp, but it lies, I would suggest, at the heart not just of alchemy but of all genuinely creative imaginative activity. Part of the difficulty we have in grasping it arises from the fact that our culture tends to reinforce only a limited understanding of the nature of the imagination.

Those of you who have heard me speak before will know that I champion an older, larger view of the imagination, one that was articulated by Romantic poets such as Coleridge and Blake, and by the alchemists and philosophers of the hermetic tradition before them. In that view, what we take for reality is not something fixed and

impermeable, simply there, but a product of our vision, and is therefore porous to the transforming power of the imagination. Thus,
when Ruland the Lexicographer of alchemy defined imagination as
the 'star in man' he was affirming a creative link between human
nature and the nature of the cosmos that goes back through the medieval worldview, to the Gnostics, to the mythopoetic imagination
of the ancient world, and perhaps even further to the primordial
animistic vision of our inalienable involvement in the living intelligence of the universe.

My view of the imagination is allied to this ancient tradition. I regard it as the means by which, with more or less psychic energy, we
conduct a process of negotiation between our inner world and the
intelligence reaching us through the senses from the outside, and
thus shape our vision of the world and our place within it. What
matters is the degree to which we are conscious of what we are doing. The real problem, as Ted Hughes says in his essay on 'Myth and
Education',

> comes from the fact that outer world and inner world are in-
> terdependent at every moment. We are simply the locus of
> their collision … and whether we like it or not our life is what
> we are able to make of that collision and struggle. So what we
> need, evidently, is a faculty that embraces both worlds simul-
> taneously. A large, flexible grasp, an inner vision which holds
> wide open, like a great theatre, the arena of contention, and
> which pays equal respect to both sides. This really is imagina-
> tion. This is the faculty we mean when we talk about the im-
> agination of great artists. The character of great works is ex-
> actly this – that in them the full presence of the inner world
> combines with and is reconciled to the full presence of the
> outer world. And in them we see that the laws of these two
> worlds are not contradictory at all: they are all one inclusive
> system.

So, the proper exercise of the imagination is an energetic process
of negotiation between the outer world and the inner world through
which we strive to hold together their often contradictory pulls. By

engaging in that process we begin to work extraordinary changes, for it is through the meeting and reconciliation of opposites – the process the alchemists described as the Coniunctio – that something new can get made for life.

In that respect the alchemical process can be understood, in its most sophisticated form, as *both* an attempt to transmute base metal into gold *and* a highly concentrated spiritual discipline through which the alchemist sought to raise his own consciousness towards a visionary experience of the unity of being. In accounts the alchemists gave of their work Jung found a precursor of his own understanding of individuation – a process through which 'every living thing becomes what it was destined to become from the beginning'. This process of self-actualisation involves the often painful, and always difficult, recognition and integration of hitherto unconscious elements of our being as part of the lifelong effort to become more fully human.

In Jung's account of the individuation process, what he called the Self (with a capital 'S') is both the origin and the goal of ego-consciousness, just as, for the alchemists, Mercurius, the presiding deity of their art, was both the beginning and the end of the great work. In an age attuned to the logic of philosophical positivism, such tail-swallowing paradoxes can seem little more than a complex of contradictions, encouraging sceptics to dismiss the claims of the alchemical imagination as obscurantist nonsense. Our secularised, democratic age, with its Freedom of Information Acts and appetite for exposure, is also suspicious of a tradition that insists that the secret of the alchemical operation can only be passed on from one adept to the next in a golden chain of shared experience. There is an amusing story of one alchemist, Thomas Charnock, who was initiated into the secret by an adept and then subsequently *forgot* it – though that doesn't greatly surprise me when I recall how often I myself forget, or seem to lose living contact with, insights that once felt securely understood. (Hermann Hesse's fine novella *The Journey to the East* dramatises the way this can happen, so tenuous is our grasp on things that most deeply matter to us.) And the language of alchemy is very elusive indeed because it speaks not in concepts but in symbols, and a symbol is, as Jung says, 'neither abstract nor concrete, neither rational nor irrational, neither real nor unreal. It is always both.'

Notice how Jung turns a series of apparent negatives – 'neither this nor that' – into the implied positive 'both this and that'. The novelist Thomas Mann described sentences constructed this way as 'lunar syntax', an alchemical metaphor by which he emphasised their effort to bring things together in relationship rather than discriminating them by their differences in the analytic or 'solar' mode of thinking with which the European intellectual tradition tends to be more comfortable. That capacity to hold apparently contradictory elements together in creative tension is at the heart of the alchemical enterprise, and as Jung says right at the start of his final master work, *Mysterium Coniunctionis*, 'the factors which come together in the *coniunctio* are conceived as opposites, either confronting one another in enmity or attracting one another in love'.

It's in this way, as a continuous attempt to reconcile the contrary elements of our lives – inner and outer, spirit and matter, ego and soul, the masculine principle and the feminine, the conscious and unconscious regions of our being – that the alchemists understood the imagination as the truly creative principle of our lives – the secret fire that lay behind all their work. I believe they still have a great deal to teach us – not least in the example that their frequent failures give us of just how difficult the processes of transformation can prove to be.

When the alchemists sought to speak of such matters, as they saw them at work both in their alembics and in their own souls, they did so in archetypal terms, illustrating their procedures through the changing nature of the relationship between a King and Queen, or of Sol and Luna, Sun and Moon. Descriptions of the alchemical opus record those changes in metaphorical terms as a series of distillatory circulations through which, if the tension of opposing forces has been properly sustained, is eventually achieved the mysterious reconciliation of the opposites as a newly unified state of consciousness. I say 'mysterious' because that is the nature of the process, but we should also remember that, although we all think we know what it means to be conscious, the nature of consciousness itself remains deeply mysterious.

As the sixteenth-century text of the *Rosarium Philosophorum* (which Jung used as a guide to understanding the psychological process of the transference) puts it: 'In hora coniunctionis maxima apparent miracula' – 'in the hour of conjunction the greatest marvels appear' – a declaration that reminds us how closely it is related to the symbolic act of the hierosgamos, the sacred marriage celebrated at the climax of the ancient mystery rites – rites that held a transformative power recognised by some of the greatest minds of antiquity.

As an elemental archetype built into the structure of the psyche, the mythic image of the sacred marriage lives in and arises from the timeless world of the unconscious. For this reason the woodcuts illustrating the Coniunctio in the *Rosarium Philosophorum* show the alchemical King and Queen copulating underwater in the presence of submerged images of the sun and moon, a symbolism that affirms that their coition is happening in the deeps of the unconscious as a psychic event – the merging together of the masculine and feminine principles, of solar and lunar energy – rather than as a physical sex act between a man and woman. The image does draw its power from the highly charged nature of human sexuality, but it does so in a manner quite different in character from the plethora of pornographic images that crowd our world today. Those images offer only a degraded simulacrum of the mystery, one that retains the capacity to seize the imagination but merely arrests it in a wistful, addictive trance devoid of any transforming significance. Yet, through such graphic pictures in films, magazines, newspapers, and advertisements, this elemental archetype insists on reminding us of its power and presence even as such desacralised erotic imagery *literalises* our perception of sexuality and thus deprives it of deeper and richer levels of meaning.

As I have indicated, the language of alchemy is not literal but symbolic. Like the way our dreams are the symbolic language of the soul and do not come complete with neat explanations like the motto in a cracker-barrel (see pages 113–18), it offers irreducible images upon which we have to exercise our imagination if they are to reveal their significance. The problem is that by and large we are not well educated in thinking symbolically these days, and there is a reason for that.

One of the supreme achievements of human consciousness has been the development of the method of rational enquiry by which we analyse the material phenomena of the world, measuring and classifying them, making significant discriminations between them and coming ever closer to an accurate definition of their components. So successful has this process been, and so great the power that its effect on technological progress has put at our disposal, that it tends to be valued above all other means of relating to the world. The consequence has been a relative devaluation of the imaginative faculty, which the rational intellect tends to confuse with fantasy or ingenuity. But if it is the imagination that responds to symbols, and if symbols are the native language of the soul, then a depreciation of the imagination may lead to an erosion of the soul.

As I understand it, the truly creative state is one in which all four Jungian functions – thought, feeling, intuition, and sensation – are working together in a complementary, sometimes mutually corrective partnership that stops thinking getting lost in the head, feeling drowning in sentimentality, intuition indulging in fantasy, and the senses saying, 'To hell with it all, let's get drunk, stoned or screwed.' Instead, the creative imagination is firing simultaneously on all four cylinders, harnessing the four functions together in readiness to concentrate and direct our faculties towards a particular goal.

My novels are preoccupied with the difficult problem of reconciling contradictory aspects of our experience as a way of allowing something new to enter life. Just as a child is born from the coupling of an intimately reconciled man and woman, so a fuller sense of individual being can emerge from the balancing of masculine and feminine principles inside each of us. The ending of apartheid in South Africa and the peace agreement in Northern Ireland have shown how extraordinary things can happen in the political realm once space is opened for the process of reconciliation to begin. In each of these contexts a deeper process of reconciliation between the conscious and unconscious minds is at work; that process is accelerated once we understand how our lives are founded on archetypal forces that can overwhelm us with their impersonal power if we fail to admit them into consciousness.

My novels have sought to dramatize ways in which such issues play themselves out within and between individual lives, but as I wrote those stories I became keenly aware of the important part played in the drama by the landscapes in which they were set. This awareness was intensified by my discovery of the psychological implications of deep ecology. The pioneering work of writers such as Theodore Roszak has revealed a view of the unconscious mind which reaches deeper than the realm of Jung's collective unconscious, into our rootedness in the material order of the natural world. Ecopsychology has alerted us to something that our ancestors intuitively understood and we now urgently need to remember: that there is a continuous process of participatory communication between the human mind and the animate intelligence of the planetary environment to which we inextricably belong. In my view, the hotline of that communication is the Imagination, and if that is the case, then to enter the creative state will pose some powerful questions that will require courageous answers. Am I alert to frequencies of intelligence other than those of my own conscious intellectual preoccupations? If I'm not, how true am I being to my own essential nature and direction in this life? And above all, in engaging with the Imagination, am I making the effort to see life whole in its manifest contradictions, and how seriously am I trying try to hold those contradictions in creative tension?

The Imagination speaks to us, and through us, not in intellectual concepts but in images and symbols. The word 'symbol' derives from the Greek 'syn ballein' – meaning 'to throw together'. Thus it carries the sense of unification, of relating things in an intimate and meaningful connection and holding them together, as opposed to its etymological opposite 'diabolic', which means to pull them apart. Similarly, the word 'religion' with its roots in the Latin 'religare' – 'to bind back' – also has the overlying sense of reunification or reunion. Each of these words seem to speak of the recovery of a lost sense of wholeness. To me, they suggest that the state of inspiration is one in which the artist briefly abdicates the divisive sovereignty of the ego and enters the service of a larger consciousness of which personal consciousness becomes a living filament.

For much of our busy, ambitious lives we remain unconscious of that universal source. Perhaps the unconscious may be more wisely understood not simply as the repository of repressed experience but as the almost, but not entirely, forgotten presence of a universal, even divine, intelligence within the deepest quick of our life: that which relates us inseparably to everything else as the true ground of our being; that which abides when the hopes and fears, the ambitions and delusions of the solitary ego have evaporated, and which is most alive in those rare moments of self-forgetfulness when we are delivered over to wonder and to awe.

Isn't this why we revere our saints and poets, for it is through them that such awareness is most manifest? Is it possible that the state of full imaginative creativity is one in which, by a transfiguring paradox, the usual polarities are reversed, so that, for however brief and precious a moment, one is unconscious of what one has long mistaken for oneself, the ego recedes, and in the space it has evacuated one is, consciously, an active participant in that wholeness which is the deep, all-embracing ground of our being?

Jung may have been speaking of such an experience in his account in *Memories, Dreams and Reflections* of the moment when he was gazing at gigantic herds of animals, silently grazing on the Athi Plains in East Africa as they had done for countless millennia, and felt himself identified with 'the first human being to recognize that this was the world, but who did not know that in this moment he had first really created it'. That moment led to his realisation that human consciousness is 'indispensable for the completion of creativity', that we ourselves are the second creators of the world because it is through us that the world comes to consciousness of its own existence. In his *Answer to Job*, Jung dares to takes this insight even further by suggesting that God too needs human beings because it is through the effort of our struggle into consciousness that God becomes conscious of himself and his creation.

Such a coherent vision of the unity of being – of what the alchemist Gerard Dorn called the 'unus mundus' – is perhaps the greatest achievement of human consciousness. It can be won only by confronting the opposites creatively and then making the effort to reconcile their apparent contradictions in the wholeness of the Self. This is the mysterium coniunctionis – the mystery of the conjunction at the climax of the alchemical opus – but it is also the personal goal of the individuation process in every consciously lived human life. It is also, I believe, an increasingly urgent demand of the times in which we live.

We only have to listen to the news to be reminded how the peaceful life of the planet is continuously violated by the failure to hold contrary forces in creative tension, allowing them instead to split off into destructive conflicts that can only sow the seeds of further conflict. The fissive power of nuclear weaponry, the shadow of which still hangs over all our lives, is the terrible emblem, menace, and potential consequence of such failure. Seen in this context, far from being merely philosophical issues over which we might dispute to our hearts' content, these are matters on which all our lives may depend.

The Nobel Prize winning physicist Wolfgang Pauli, whose dream-life furnished much of the material for Jung's *Psychology and Alchemy*, declared that he considered 'the ambition of overcoming opposites, including a synthesis embracing both rational understanding and the mystical experience of unity, to be the mythos, spoken or unspoken, of our present day and age'. It is certainly the underlying mythos of my own creative endeavours. The eminent Jungian analyst Edward F. Edinger has this to say in his *Introduction to Jung's Mysterium Coniunctionis*: 'In antiquity, drama was part of a religious ceremony in the worship of Dionysus. When a play was bad, it was greeted with the remark, "That has nothing to do with Dionysus." My thought is that the future may generate new standards of thought and action derived from a new myth, and that those new standards will be based on the *coniunctio* as the highest good. From that standpoint,' he says, 'the profoundest criticism will be: "It has nothing to do with the *coniunctio*."'

The affairs of this world are still governed by an outworn patriarchal tradition of thought, infatuated by its own technological power and in thrall to a dim materialism on the one hand and a literal-minded fundamentalism on the other. So great is the destructive power wielded by these forces that the changes we need may seem impossible. Yet a significant evolution of consciousness does appear to be trying to happen in our time. It may often falter in its attempts to find a language adequate to the demands of its own often confusing processes, yet at its best it represents not a regression into irrationality but a movement through into transrationality – a new conjunction of solar and lunar modes of apprehending the world, one that values all the gains for consciousness that have been made by the methods of rational enquiry, yet seeks to bring them into closer, creative relation with those less quantifiable aspects of our experience that have been undervalued.

The imagination, both inventive and ethical, is the function through which we have access to these aspects of our being. Artists sensitive to their own creative process will tell you that it is through the effort to reconcile the often contrary pulls of the inner and outer worlds, and to allow something new to arise out of their conjunction, that new work gets made. In their day, the wisest alchemists were artists of that creative order, attempting to bring about a practical conjunction of scientific enquiry and imaginative poetic insight in a transforming vision of the world. I hope I have managed to share my sense of the continuing relevance and value of their work for our own transitional time.

# The Mythic Imagination

## From Ancient Troy to the Present Day

An edited version of a talk delivered in 2011 as one of the series of Chapel Lectures organised by Ebenezer Presents at Burrowbridge in Somerset.

In *The Company We Keep*, a book that reflects on the ethics of fiction, the literary scholar Wayne C. Booth quotes what Benton Lewis, an Apache Indian, had to say about the role of story in his culture: 'Stories go to work on you like arrows,' Lewis insists; 'stories make you live right; stories make you replace yourself.'

The more I think about those simple statements the more powerful they become. When you hear or read a good story, you know that something forceful has entered you. It can even be a painful experience, piercing you to the heart, making you experience what the French philosopher Gaston Bachelard called 'a homeopathy of anguish'. The second of Benton Lewis's assertions insists that a good story has ethical force. It has moral consequences for the way we behave – something that seems too often forgotten by those who purvey stories filled with violence and sensation for the entertainment of the young. Finally, and most startlingly, Benton Lewis declares that story rightly told has the power to transform us – that the person who comes out of the hearing or reading of a good story is not the same as the one who went in. The experience has replaced us.

In today's relativistic, postmodern culture, where all the grand narratives of the past are under serious question, and the frequently phantasmagorical nature of events can make fiction seem puny by comparison, few novelists would dare to make such claims for the stories they tell. Yet I wonder whether Benton Lewis's traditional wisdom doesn't have more useful things to say about the true value of myth and story to our confused and confusing times than the almost impenetrably codified language of academic literary theorists?

Myths are the stories through which a culture tries to answer the otherwise unanswerable big questions of our existence. Where do we come from? Why are we here? Why are things this way? What happens when we die? Both our sense of the reality we inhabit and our understanding of it are shaped by the myths in which we believe, and for that very reason it can be hard to recognise them as myths at all – especially in a culture so convinced that its intellectual method of objective enquiry gives it access to a true vision of the world. Other people may live inside myths, we seem to insist, but we are realists and our world is real. It's part of the burden of this lecture to suggest that myth is inescapable and that every paradigm shift that takes place in the course of cultural development is, in effect, the displacement of one myth and its replacement by another. Yet some myths seem to act on the human imagination with such enduring power that they command attention from generation to generation across the centuries and across cultures even as the world changes around them.

The complex of stories associated with the Trojan War clearly have such power. Ever since Homer sang of that war several hundred years after its probable date, great writers such as Euripides, Virgil, Chaucer, and Shakespeare have reworked its themes. As recently as 2011 Alice Oswald published a remarkable long poem titled *Memorial* which is a moving elegy for those who were killed in the fighting at Troy. The myths generated by the passionate conflicts of that war are gripping stories, of course, but how to account for their continuing ability to excite both the creative and the responsive imagination in such vivid ways?

My own belief is that certain events seem to exercise such powerful effect on the collective emotions of a culture that, as memory gets to work on them, they begin to transcend literal reality and take on a form that corresponds to archetypes built into the very structure of the human psyche – that amazing software with which we all come issued at birth. What's more, they do this so indelibly that those same archetypal responses can be activated thousands of years later within the psyche of people who live in utterly different cultures.

The story of the fall of Troy has lived on this way for three thousand years or more because it is the myth of the West's first great war. It moves the heart and the imagination still.

But did such a war – a war of which the stories have proved so enduring in their impact that it feels realer to us than many more recent conflicts – ever really take place? Did the long siege of the city ever actually happen, or were Homer, Euripides, Virgil, Chaucer, Shakespeare, and the others simply drawing on, and adding to, the prolific realm of the inventive imagination? The question has divided scholars for centuries: sceptics remain dubious that there could be any historical truth behind such heroic legends; romantics insist that the strength of oral tradition, and its abiding power to move us, must derive from the experience of actual figures whose lives were shaped by world-changing events. When the question of whether or not such a war was fought at Troy is put to the archaeologist Manfred Korfmann, who supervises the Projekt Troia dig in Turkey, he simply says, 'Why not?' And that's probably the most satisfactory answer we'll ever be able to give.

But there certainly was such a city – it's still possible to visit its ruins, to read records of archaeological research conducted there, and to see pictures of how its citadel might have once looked like based on an imaginative reconstruction of what remains. Ancient historians such as Thucydides certainly believed in the historical facticity of the Trojan War and by classical times there was a well-established tradition that Hisarlik in western Anatolia was the location of that doomed city. It was on that hill – its name means 'the place of the fort' – that Heinrich Schliemann began to dig in the 1870s. His adventurous approach to the work, though creating many problems for later archaeologists, revealed a site of enormous historical significance. Not everyone shared his confidence that he had discovered the ruins of Homer's Troy or that the jewels in which he photographed his wife had indeed once belonged to Helen; but patient, more scientific work continues there to this day, and a picture is emerging of a larger, wealthier city than Schliemann conceived – a city of around six thousand people, which commanded the trade routes to the Black Sea and would have been a very tempting prize for the aggressive warlords of Mycenae and Argos.

Part of the difficulty of establishing the historical truth of the Trojan War arises from the fact that we know so little about our principal source for the stories. It seems probable that Homer (if there ever was such a single figure) flourished in the ninth century B.C.E., which places him at least two or three hundred years later than the likeliest date of the war; so the stories were already ancient by the time he came to sing of them. But we do have other, less poetical sources of information, most significantly the extensive archive of clay tablets on which the bureaucrats of the Hittite Empire kept their records.

A number of these, dated around 1300 B.C.E., speak of the Hittites' touchy diplomatic relations with a people of a country they called 'Ahhiyawa'. This name sounds tantalisingly close to the 'Achaiwoi' (or Achaians), which was a name that Homer gave to the people who followed Agamemnon to Troy. Archaeological digs around the sites of Mycenae, Pylos, and Tiryns in Peloponnesian Greece long ago revealed a powerful warrior culture that was at its peak between 1300 and 1200 B.C.E. Around that same time the Hittites maintained a trading alliance with a prosperous city on the Hellespont which was known to them as 'Wilusa', which again echoes intriguingly the name 'Ilios' (or Ilium), the Homeric name for Troy. It seems possible then that such a city stood on a fault line between two contending imperial powers, one to the east and one to the west, and eventually fell victim to a Western invasion.

We know from Hittite records that the Emperor Hattusilis was troubled by attacks made by the Ahhiyawa on the coastline of Asia in the thirteenth century B.C.E. The site at Hisarlik revealed evidence that the citadel was conquered, plundered, and destroyed around that time. But whether the conflict that took place between the people we know as the Greeks and a city-state that we call Troy was such a war as Homer sings of – a war that began with the abduction of Helen and ended with the stratagem of the wooden horse – that's another matter.

'We *do* care about the authenticity of the tale of Troy,' Lord Byron declared. 'I venerate the grand original as *the truth of history* … and of place; otherwise it would have given me no delight.' Yet Byron might have been wiser to acknowledge that the stories of Troy transport us into that luminous and elusive region of the imagination where myth and history intersect. We know from contemporary experience that vivid tales tend to accrue around strong individuals and dramatic events, and not all of them are strictly true. Consider, for instance, the stories that have grown up around John Kennedy's assassination or the virtual immortality of Elvis Presley. Isn't 'the truth of history' itself a matter of continuing interpretation and dispute, and doesn't a strong myth carry an imaginative truth of its own? So, if the stories of the Trojan War have inspired generations of great artists since Homer sang them almost three thousand years ago, and still resonate in our own violent times, isn't that because the human truths they celebrate – their accounts of passion and ambition, courage and cruelty, aggression and destruction, triumph and defeat, loss and grief – are constant matters of the human heart?

I began to write my own retelling of the stories in *The War at Troy* just as the war in Iraq was gathering force, and that conflict gave my work a sudden contemporary relevance. I watched the televised 'shock and awe' attack on Baghdad as I was thinking about the fall of Troy and was appalled at how little we seem to have learned over the last three thousand years. The ancient stories understood well enough that war is never inevitable unless we choose to make it so, and that the stated causes of a war may not be the real reasons why it is fought. One version of Helen's story, for example, declared that she was never in Troy at all, only a phantasm of her which was so powerful in the minds of men that the Greeks believed she was there. Something of the sort was also the case, you may remember, with the much-vaunted but never discovered weapons of mass destruction in Iraq.

Those old stories of Troy also seem to understand that it is much easier to get into a war than it is to get out of it, and that, no matter how many acts of courage it may evoke, warfare eventually harms and corrupts everyone involved in it. So my novel *The War at Troy* begins with the quarrel among the goddesses over the golden apple, and the judgement of Paris on Mount Ida, but it quickly gets caught up in the hot broil of human passion as Paris betrays his friend Menelaus out of passionate love for the latter's wife Helen, and from there it descends inexorably into the hideous carnage of war.

But it also felt important to honour the Greeks' understanding that the gods have a part to play in warfare. My solution was to honour them as archetypal powers that are always present and active within us and between us, from one generation to the next.

Christianity has taught us to use the word 'God' as the subject in such sentences as 'God is Love', but the Greeks used the word 'theos' with predicative force, saying by contrast, 'Love is a god' or 'War is a god'. Such archetypal energies were invested with divine status by the Greeks because they *are* immortal. We mortals die; those impersonal powers never die. They engage each generation in those passionate conflicts that constitute what James Joyce called 'the grave and constant' matter of the human heart. Nor can we avoid them except at a cost to our own vitality; so it seems wiser to bring them into consciousness and try to relate to their power creatively rather than allowing our lives to be driven unconsciously by them without our understanding what is happening and why.

This seems to me to be the real force behind the myths of the Trojan War. Those stories don't speak about a contest between two warring factions for control of the trade routes to the Black sea. They trace the origins of the war to a quarrel among three goddesses over a golden apple and the judgement of Paris as to which was the fairest. What could such an improbable beauty competition be about and what might it have to do with us now?

Many commentators have remarked that a beauty contest between three goddesses behaving badly seems an unsatisfactory account of the cause of a war that generated some of the greatest stories of all time. If that was all that was happening, I'd be inclined to agree; but the story may be better understood if we remember that the feminine principle was dramatised in all its rich complexity by the attributes that the Greeks assigned to those deities who gave it immortal form. We should also be aware that not just three goddesses are active in the story of the judgement of Paris, but four. The three visible presences are Hera with her matronly bounty, Athena with her strength and wisdom, and Aphrodite, whose talents and qualities are of a quite another order. Each of these goddesses is powerful in her own way and each makes manifest a form of feminine power which is attractive to men. But the fourth invisible figure concealed behind them is quite different.

She is Eris, the dark figure of Strife or Discord, twin sister to Ares, god of war. It was she who began the quarrel among the goddesses because, alone among the divinities, she had not been invited to the wedding of Peleus and Thetis, the parents of Achilles. Here is the moon's dark face, bitter, angry, and excluded. This is the aspect of feminine power which we men prefer not to confront because it leaves us fearful and uneasy. Far simpler to dismiss her as a harridan and shrew. Better still to pretend that she can have no serious claim on our attention; even that she does not seriously exist. This is why Eris is rarely invited to the wedding, though she does, of course, often prominently figure in divorces. But gods who are derided and ignored don't simply go away. Spoiling for trouble, they withdraw into the shadows. And the place where the dark aspect of the goddess tends to be most severely repressed is inside men.

Once the power of the goddess is demeaned inside a man's soul she becomes visible in the resentful and embittered faces of the women around him. If she remains unattended, then her energy can turn distorted and crazy inside him, manifesting in unfeeling lust, in sexual violence – the vain attempt to seize by force what can only truly be won through mature relationship. Worse still, at the collective level, it can be seen in the malevolent effort to turn the power of myth against the people of another tribe or nation or race by withholding compassion and projecting a hostile negative shadow on to them, thereby dragging the world into war.

Yet if such realisations were brought into consciousness, and properly assimilated through mature understanding, might it be possible that the male capacity for aggression could be converted into energy available for the cultivation of the feelings; that the savage glory of the warrior might be seen for the destructive force it is; and that the darkened, life-giving power of the feminine principle might begin to shine in creative ways once more?

In *The Return from Troy*, my version of the *Odyssey*, Circe presents herself to Odysseus in many aspects – as bounteous provider, as passionate lover, and as wise healer; but the main thrust of her rites is to launch him on that arduous night-sea voyage whereby the centre of his consciousness begins to shift from the ego to the soul.

Such a shift can happen only when all his resources of pride and cunning are exhausted and he has been reduced to the condition of Nobodysseus – a man with no fixed identity, an almost vacant space in which the feminine values, both light and dark, that have long been ignored inside him can at last begin to find room to breathe and express themselves.

Because of our industrial capacity for violence on a devastating scale, these issues of evolving consciousness are more urgent than ever. Yet we live in a world run by a terminal patriarchy that stubbornly resists demands for change. The time for such a transformed, newly creative relation to the feminine principle is perilously overdue.

William Blake once wrote that it is 'the classics, the classics, that desolate Europe with wars.' He was thinking of Homer, and – though a larger, more comprehensive explanation for our violent history is clearly required – when one considers the generations of gallant young men brought up on the *Iliad* who have been inspired by the ferocious glamour of Odysseus and Achilles to seek death or glory, it's not difficult to see what Blake meant. Yet it's in the essentially metamorphic nature of myth never to take a fixed and final form, and it seems to me significant that recent reworkings of the Troy story such as John Barton's *Tantalus*, Alice Oswald's *Memorial*, and my own Troy books all find the poetry of war in its pity and suffering rather than in its futile glory. Which brings me back to the recognition that, because we always live inside myth, our sense of reality is shaped – and can be *reshaped* – by the stories to which we chose to give credence.

Once this is recognised we begin to see that, as my friend Jules Cashford puts it, 'the world is not given to us as fact but is inhabited through interpretation'; that reality is not simply out there, fixed, obdurate, and impervious – it changes according to the stories we tell about it. Which is to say that reality is always porous to the imagination.

In *Healing Fiction*, James Hillman says that 'the way we imagine our lives is the way we are going to go on living our lives', but that we don't have to carry on telling ourselves the same story about ourselves or the world around us. Once we energetically engage with both the inventive and the compassionate aspects of the imagination we can begin to work extraordinary changes in our lives. In that respect, the imagination is related to a word that comes from the same root – 'magic' – the power to conjure things into existence and to bring about changes in the world which can seem to defy the normal laws of causality.

So here is a myth about the mythic imagination itself, one that views it as a continuous attempt to reconcile the contrary elements of our lives and nature – inner and outer, the masculine principle and the feminine, spirit and matter, ego and soul, the conscious and unconscious regions of our being – in order that something new may arise from that reconciliation. It's in that spirit that I pursue my career as a novelist, and it's in that spirit too that I've been working for some years in Northern Ireland as part of an effort to encourage the telling of different, more humane stories than those which left the divided streets of that province running with blood. I believe that it's through such committed exercises of the creative imagination that arrested situations, be they personal or political, are most likely to be transformed. In looking for inspiration, encouragement, and guidance in that belief, I turn often to the world's marvellous store of mythological stories. Myth is a living force in our lives, which, however rational and sophisticated we take ourselves to be, simply won't go away. May the gods forbid that it should ever do so, because the universal tensions and possibilities of this difficult process of transformation are vividly expressed in myth's powerful stories.

Writing about myths, the Roman historian Sallust said, 'These things never happened but always are.' Some two thousand years later James Joyce wrote something similar in *Finnegan's Wake*: 'utterly impossible as are all these events, they are probably as like those which may have taken place as any others which never took person at all or are ever likely to be'. Which sounds very Irish, but is teasingly true and reminds me of what a little Irish girl once wisely said on the subject: 'Myths are stories which are not true on the outside but are true on the inside.' I can think of no better definition of what myths are and why they remain so important as an abiding source of wisdom, nourishment, and inspiration in our lives.

# The Unbearable Brightness
# of Being

This review of *Memorial* by Alice Oswald (Faber & Faber)
originally appeared in *Resurgence* in 2011.

Whether at the Menin Gate, or at the Arlington Cemetery in Wash-
ington, or in a quiet corner of some English country churchyard,
there are few more sobering experiences than to stand mindfully
before a war memorial and read the names of the dead. In those
silent accusatory lists are made manifest both the pathos and the
folly of warfare, along with its legacy of waste and grief and its persistently ignored admonitions. 'Why', they seem to ask, 'do we keep
doing this to ourselves?'

The opening pages of Alice Oswald's magnificent poem *Memorial*
consist of such a list, a stark roll-call of men who went to war at
Troy some three thousand years ago and there encountered the
death that 'was already walking to meet them'. All the names are
drawn from Homer, some of them famous still, others more obscure, but, as each stirring elegy in this poem makes plain, each of
them had some distinguishing characteristic – a gift with horses, the
way he wore his hair – and each was at one time dear to his family,
his comrades, and the community from which he came. Through a
disturbing and compassionate act of the imagination, Oswald has
exhumed them from the ashes to which their bodies were consigned,
and the living spirit of her verse has given a newly recollected lease
on life to even those of whom nothing is known but the name.

Yet there is nothing remotely sentimental here. The brutal facts
of each death are recorded unflinchingly and without indulgence, so
that you can see, for example,

the hole in the helmet, just under the ridge
where the point of the blade passed through
and stuck in his forehead
letting the darkness leak down over his eyes.

These brief, often shocking accounts are counterpointed with an antiphonal sequence of similes drawn from the natural world, which rolls through the poem like the impersonal surge of life itself.

The first of these, the movement of its verses enacting the waves of energy passing through wind, through water, and across the land, 'wishing and searching / Nothing to be found', sounds the deep bass note of the poem. And each of the subsequent images is so vivid in its impact on the senses that the immediate desire is to re-read it – a desire instantly gratified by the text's insistent repetition of lines. The effect is liturgical, refunding each brief 'flash of flesh' back into the ever-changing, always unchanging embrace of the nat-ural world. The poem ends in a dying fall of poignantly observed similes that expire in a breathless, echoing moment:

> Like when god throws a star
> And everyone looks up
> To see that whip of sparks
> And then it's gone.

Alice Oswald is a poet who is also a classics scholar, and what she has achieved here is the return to vital currency of the Greek concept (one might more truly say the *experience*) of 'enargeia'. In her brief introduction to the poem she translates this as 'bright unbeara-ble reality.' It's the word used 'when gods come to earth not in dis-guise but as themselves' – those gods who demand not belief but recognition (and, as Roberto Calasso insists, 'a life in which the gods are not invited isn't worth living'). It's a word that opens our gaze on the impersonal archetypal world that is the elemental substrate of our being. It's a word that, in its capacity to hold together both the luminosity of life and its essentially tragic nature, reveals the deep ground of all true poetry.

The verses of Homer, Shakespeare, and Blake arose out of that ground; in our own time it has been made manifest in the work of Ted Hughes; and now here again in the precision of Alice Oswald's words. Although her love for Homer's great poem is evident throughout *Memorial*, this poem is far more than what some reviewers called a 'filleting' of the *Iliad*. It exists sui generis as a powerful contribution to the enduring stock of poetry which has sounded out across three millennia from the unforgettable tragedy of Europe's first great war.

# Adventures in the Underworld

This essay originally appeared in *The Gist: A Celebration of the Imagination* (The Write Factor and Arvon, 2012).

Like that of many other novelists, my storyteller's imagination was first fired by a childhood encounter with the folktales told for centuries by the peoples of Europe. Unsigned, free from all claims of ownership, the birthright property of everyone, they have been passed on from one generation to the next until they have grown smooth as pebbles in the passing. Some of their features may even have sprung from those early ancestral moments when people first began to shape their experience of the world by telling stories. Their elemental magic can still illuminate and enchant our lives today. For that reason, the colours, feel, and smell of the copy of *Grimms' Fairy Tales* which my mother bought for me from Woolworth's remain alive to my senses nearly seventy years later.

I clearly remember the way story after story opened on a bright, heraldic realm that was far removed from the industrial landscape of northern England where I was growing up, yet evidently accessible within it. One simply opened the door of the book and passed through into a dreamlike terrain where improbable and contradictory things seemed to happen with such fluency that one happily took them for granted. It felt as though they were obeying laws of nature different from but as powerful in their way as those which prevailed in the world outside. Though fashions have changed and those old stories no longer figure in children's bedtime reading as strongly as they once did, they have survived for so many centuries precisely because they offer to each new generation life-quickening images of

157

the way those laws can work for us.

Consider, for instance, the story of 'The Three Feathers', a tale that appeals to me as a writer because a feather was for many centuries the standard writing implement. The story tells how a sick and ageing king was uncertain which of his three sons should be his heir, so he set them to compete on three separate quests, dropping feathers to see which direction each should take. On the first quest they were sent to bring home the finest carpet. The eldest son followed the feather that blew to the east, the second son chased his feather westwards, while the third and youngest son – the simpleton – watched his feather merely fall to the ground at his feet. Looking down, he saw a previously unnoticed trapdoor, opened it, lowered himself into the empty space, and climbed down a shaft deep into the earth where he came upon a wise toad that gifted him what proved to be the most splendid carpet of the three. To his brothers' disgust he emerged as the winner of the second quest too when the toad presented him with a priceless ring. The last prize to be gained was a future queen, and the simpleton rewarded the toad for all its help by choosing the creature for his bride. On their return to the surface, his loyalty of heart was rewarded in turn when he saw the toad transform into the most beautiful young woman anyone had ever seen. Needless to say, he won the kingdom as well as a good wife.

If you have been educated into the literalistic conviction that such things are impossible in a world where tadpoles may turn into toads but on no account are toads allowed to turn into princesses, then you may dismiss this tale at first glance as a childish piece of hokum. But small children don't have that problem – not, that is, until adults put it in their way. Nor do they judge such stories at first glance. They listen to them again and again, and their delight often visibly increases at each repetition. Given that stricter minds than mine have reservations about whether tales that feature princesses in distress, cruel stepmothers, feral beasts, and violent death are fit for children, why should this be?

I think it's because they intuitively understand that such stories nourish their powers of imagination just as surely as their bones are strengthened by milk. What's more, the pleasure that such stories give them may have less to do with the fascination of strangeness than with the surprise of recognition. Yes, the story I've just told is about a king and his sons, the feathers, and a talking toad; but isn't it also about our talent for bringing something new to life through the mysterious processes of self-discovery? And if so, doesn't it offer important truths about the nature and laws of the imagination? For when things seem insolubly stuck or in decay (that is, in the idiom of the story, when the king is sick), then for renewal to happen change will be required, and change is what the active power of the imagination is all about. Often enough, such change is accomplished not by casting about on the surface of things but by risking a descent into the dark places of the underworld where the seeds of new life lie. To make such a journey successfully we must rely on what is youngest inside us – our primal innocence with its willingness to be thought simple or stupid in its loyalty to unworldly values – but also on what is oldest, the wise, serpentine power of the instincts which have their origin deep in the unifying intelligence of the earth. For toads, as Shakespeare reminds us in *As You Like It*, can sometimes have precious jewels in their heads.

Such tales about transforming journeys to the underworld are found worldwide in folktales, myths, and what we have been taught to call 'high art'. A very ancient Sumerian poem tells of the descent of Inanna into an underworld where the laws are 'perfect and not to be questioned'. Book XI of Homer's *Odyssey* tells how the hero entered Hades to consult the shades of the dead. In Virgil's *Aeneid* the hero descends into Hades, where he is granted a prophetic vision of Rome's future; and in the first part of his *Divine Comedy* Dante is led by Virgil into the underworld of the *Inferno* and is there shown a Christian vision of the torments of Hell. More recent fictional accounts, though not immediately recognisable as underworld experiences, follow a similar katabatic pattern. What else are Conrad's voyage into the *Heart of Darkness*, Hermann Hesse's *Journey to the East*, Doris Lessing's *Briefing for a Descent into Hell*, and John Fowles's *The Magus* but twentieth-century forms of the Hades journey? Each of those stories is like a trapdoor through which we are invited to descend. Whatever the particular character of the events awaiting us there, we are, at the same time, drawn into deeper imaginative acquaintance with what was once called the underworld or the otherworld,

159

but which was courageously explored during the course of the twentieth century as the archetypal structure of the unconscious mind.

The prevailing spirit of our time is so identified with the actions and ambitions of the conscious ego that we tend to forget how much of the business of living is almost entirely the duty of the unconscious. The metabolic processes of the body, on which our lives depend, go about their business with scarcely a moment's conscious thought; even when we are wide awake much of the information reaching us from outside is registered in not the conscious but the unconscious mind; and for a third part of every day we give ourselves to sleep. It has been calculated that we spend six years of our life in the secluded world of dream, which is such a considerable investment of time that we might fairly regard ourselves as amphibious creatures, equally at home in both conscious and unconscious worlds, and deeply in need of both. It's possible, of course, to regard dreams as merely a form of psychic excretion, a clearing of the system ready for a new day; but both the wisdom of many cultures and the witness of a host of individuals insist there is a richer story to tell about them – that dreams too are helpful trapdoors opening on the underworld of the unconscious, which is the deep ground of the imagination.

Because they remain impenetrably private experiences, all accounts of dreams are inevitably anecdotal and may concern only the dreamer. And not all dreams, of course, are pleasant. Yet the archetypal psychologist James Hillman insists that our dreams mean well by us, and if we share that view we can begin to see them as profitable conversations held with our deepest being in an arena beyond the narrow claims and control of the conscious ego. They can also be lively oracles of change.

'In dreams,' said Yeats, 'begins responsibility,' and this has certainly been my own experience. It was a powerful and disturbing dream of Yeats which first summoned me out of the relative security of full-time teaching and demanded that I respond to the call of the writing life (see pages 249–67). Much later, one of the key formative influences on *The Chymical Wedding* was an enlarging dream that came at a time when I had failed to find a satisfactory answer to a child's demand to know what could be done about the terrifying fact that the world was imminently threatened by nuclear warfare. And I might never have come to write my later novel *The Water Theatre* at all had it not been for the impact of a dream so powerful that my imagination worked with it for many years until it became the starting point for the narrative and the matrix from which the whole novel gradually emerged.

Unsurprisingly, therefore, I believe that our adventures in the underworld of dream are not only occasions for self-examination but can also prove to be a source of inspiration. But because they cannot be publicly observed and are so fugitive in their nature they are frequently disregarded or undervalued – like some other significant dimensions of our experience to which the poet in us may have clearer access than the abstract thinker.

Jung has described the four principal functions by which we apprehend the world. Thinking certainly figures among them; but so too does feeling (by which I mean not raw emotion but the means by which we get 'the feel' of a person or event and thus evaluate our experience of them). We would be utterly lost without the faculties of our five senses to navigate our way through the world, but we also rely on intuition, however irrational it may seem, as a way of grasping the meaning in situations without prior conceptualisation. It's at those times when we fire on all four cylinders at once that we are fully alive – alive in all our senses, thinking clearly, feeling vividly, and open to other frequencies of intelligence through our intuitive power.

That fullness of being is, for me, the vital activity of the imagination by which we give shape and coherence to our world and charge our experience with meaning and value. One might also describe it, therefore, as the creative activation of the soul. I use that word 'soul', without invoking any particular religious creed, to evoke that central core of our being which opens a deeper perspective on life than the personal preoccupations of the executive ego. (To sceptical readers who question the reality of the soul on the grounds that there is no objectively demonstrable proof of its existence, let me suggest that there is no demonstrable proof of the ego's existence either, but can anyone doubt that it makes its presence felt in the world?)

The interrelated activity of soul and imagination is the kind of creative energy of which Yeats was speaking when he talked of the necessary revolt of the soul against the intellect. Creative individuals, whether artists or scientists, have always intuitively understood this power of the imagination – William Blake, for instance who declared that 'man is all Imagination'; Samuel Taylor Coleridge, who insisted that 'the imagination is the prime agent of human perception'; and Albert Einstein, who declared, 'imagination is more important than knowledge. Knowledge is limited. Imagination encircles the world.'

Imaginative activity is responsive to the frequencies of intelligence reaching us from what we experience as the outside world, but it has roots that reach deep into our unconscious life and is informed, therefore, by metabolic sources other than those which spark mere ingenuity. What this seems to intimate is a participatory relationship between the individual human soul and what Plato called the Soul of the World, the Imagination being the vital link between them. To go further, one might suggest that, in a sense inimical to the contemporary taste for novelty, the Imagination's capacity for creation is *original* in that it reaches into, and arises from, the mysterious origins of things – even the creative origins of life itself.

As part of the educational work of the cross-sectarian Pushkin Trust in Northern Ireland, I was asked to lead a workshop for teachers on the theme 'What do we mean by Creativity?' Rather than trying to pin the concept down with abstract definitions, we decided to stalk it like a natural history unit, looking for the kind of habitat in which it thrives, and spotting things likely to scare that wild creature away.

The latter were quickly identified. First, authority figures who keep it under critical scrutiny, either outwardly in our lives, or pontifical ghosts we have internalised from bad experiences in the past. Then there are oppressive expectations that can induce an inhibiting fear of failure or ridicule. And rife in the culture as a whole are certain tendencies that tend to restrict the free range of the creative imagination. Among those are demands to comply with conventional patterns of thought, such as reductionism, that overly pragmatic insistence on 'nothing-but-ness' with its consequent demeaning of the sense of wonder and mystery; literalism, which is an inability to see through the surface of things for lack of a metaphorical sense of experience; and scientism, the tendency to validate only that which can be quantified, replicated, and evidentially proved – criteria that leave little room for such important and incommensurable aspects of our lives as, for example, love. The presence of any of these factors can drive creativity back into hiding, maybe beyond recall.

But when and where do creative thoughts arrive most easily? Some answers were: in the bath, out walking, while travelling, during hypnogogic moments while falling asleep or hypnopompic moments on waking. All of these are states of reverie where new associations of thought and imagery are freed to form without censorship or obedience to conventions. They are liminal states – on the threshold, neither here nor there, betwixt and between – and many artists deliberately try to seek them out. Thus John Keats (who celebrated what he called Shakespeare's 'negative capability', his readiness to live 'in uncertainties, mysteries and doubts without any irritable reaching after fact and reason') used to try to trick himself into creative activity by dressing to go out, opening the door, then rushing back to his desk and starting to write.

Creative ideas seem to come in moments when the customary habits of thought have been disinhibited in ways that permit entry to fresh possibilities. In such conditions of diffused focus, often heightened by sensory awareness (the play of light, the warmth of bath-water), new patterns emerge out of a soft, receptive chaos in which one is tolerant of diversity and ambiguity, even of contradiction. Such a state can, of course, be a vulnerable and sometimes deranging condition, particularly when life has visited a grievous affliction on us – a defeat, an illness, a bereavement or breakdown, some forced descent into a dark underworld that throws us into a gruelling degree of confusion but may eventually, though not always, prove generative of new endeavour.

Though I spoke earlier of the active imagination in terms of experiencing 'a fullness of being', I do recall, paradoxically, that the more I reflect on such transformative, liminal experiences (and the ways in which they may relate to those precious moments at my desk when I feel more like a pipeline than an engineer), the less they seem to speak of *fullness* than of a transitory *emptiness* of being. Such, it feels to me, is the essential nature of those moments – moments scarcely of time at all – when one has become, beyond conscious volition, a vacant, receptive space, tuned into new frequencies through which something fresh and unanticipated can enter and find form. To go back to the old story with which I began, this state of imminently creative emptiness is the shaft down which the prince descends, not knowing quite what he will find. Peter Brook writes cogently about the vital importance of 'The Empty Space' (in his eponymous book) as the arena of imaginative invention and discovery in theatre; and George Barker catches the spirit of it in these lines from *Villa Stellar:*

> Not in the poet is the poem or
> even the poetry. It is hiding behind
> a broken wall or a geranium
> or walking around pretending to be blind
> seeking a home that it cannot find.
>
> Into the ego that has emptied out
> everything except its abstract being
> and left only a shell, the poem then
> moves silently, foreseeing
> its purpose is to haunt the shell like singing.

In that alert state of emptiness it is as if the illusory veil or boundary that seems to separate us from all else is momentarily suspended and there is no division between inner and outer, conscious and unconscious, perceiver and perceived, the poet and the poem. In those moments all things co-inhere and the imagination apprehends that mutuality of being so feelingly that it is not only the prime agent of perception, it is the agency of compassion too.

None of this is to imply that one can simply sit back waiting for the poem or novel to arrive. Far from it. The delicate nature of the operation that takes place beyond the usual conscious control of writers yet within the receptive gravitational field of their being is caught in the poem 'Soror Mystica' by John Moat, who understands these things well:

At the outset
It is a moment too soon
One could not say anything for certain
She has her finger to her lips
The sign of caution.

When the work is under way
One cannot risk uttering a word
The least distraction and the moment might be missed
She has her finger to her lips
The sign of concentration.

At the conclusion
It is already too late
The moment can never be repeated
She has her finger to her lips
The sign of the secret.

So writers must work, and keep on working carefully, at their craft. 'Without unceasing Practice nothing is gained,' said William Blake; 'Practice is Art.' Such work is a way of tuning oneself like an instrument on which language and the Imagination can perform what they need to say. May it be that in that way the writer escapes the ego's sovereignty and enters the service of a larger consciousness of which personal consciousness is but a filament?

'Not I but the wind that blows through me,' D.H. Lawrence declared. To the Greeks the wind was 'anemos', which also meant 'breath', and from that word the Romans derived 'animus' and 'anima', 'spirit' and 'soul'. The Latin for 'breath' is 'spiritus', and for 'breathing', 'aspiratio', to which is related 'inspiration'. To breathe in is to inspire, but the Latin word for 'inspiration' is 'afflatus', the breath or wind of the muse or a god. In the traditions of India, the word 'Atman', besides referring to 'soul', can also mean 'wind' or 'breath'. So something universal seems to be indicated here – an acknowledgment that when the imagination is fully activated and one finds oneself in the creative state of inspiration, one is drawing breath from a universal source in order to express it – to breathe it out – in personal terms.

Such matters remain an essential part of the wonder and mystery of language and the potential for imaginative activity with which each of us arrives in this world. This essay, like others in this book, speaks for, and from, a way of relating to the Imagination which may be as old as poetry itself. Its allegiance is to an ancient wisdom tradition no longer fashionable in a time when our world is dominated by the activity of the ascendant left brain, which has different priorities of its own – priorities that, as Iain McGilchrist argues in *The Master and His Emissary*, are having increasingly corrosive effects on our personal and cultural lives. It's also a time when, as Blake lamented in his own day, such wisdom is most often to be found in 'that desolate market where none come to buy'. But then the tradition of the Imagination, which is profoundly indigenous to vernacular culture as well as finding expression in the arts, is not, and has never been, a saleable commodity. Like the folktales that have preserved memories of its wisdom down the centuries, it's an inalienable part of our birthright, freely available to everyone and, for that reason among many others, valued pricelessly among those who have come to care deeply for what it has to say.

# Going the Last Inch

## Some Thoughts on Showing and Telling

This piece was first published in *The Creative Writing Coursebook* edited by Julia Bell and Paul Magrs (Macmillan, 2001).

A novel is a game for two players. The book may get written in solitude but it kicks into life only when a reader's imagination collaborates with that of the writer, so in working out how best to secure and sustain that collaboration writers might usefully recall what most engrosses them as readers. In the early drafts of a piece, you're still working out what you're trying to say to yourself, and too much mental trafficking with an audience at that stage can inhibit the flow of your imagination. But if you mean to go public, then sooner or later you have to consider the legitimate needs of your readers, and a large part of the process of revision will be about making sure that you have given *their* imagination all the room it needs to work.

In this respect, Henry James offered the novelist three key words of advice: 'Present, present, present.' His disciple, Percy Lubbock, turned the recommendation into a rule by insisting that 'the art of fiction does not begin until the novelist thinks of his story as a matter to be shown, to be so exhibited that it will tell itself', and the cry of 'Show, don't tell' still rings across writing workshops. To understand why, you need only ask which is more immediately engaging – to witness an event for yourself or to be told about it afterwards by someone else.

A brief example will *show* what the distinction between showing and telling can mean for fiction. If, in a first novel, an author had written, 'The boy broke down and began to cry so wretchedly that the other small children started howling too,' he would, rather dully, have *told* us something. When, in *The Lord of the Flies*, William Golding wrote that 'his face puckered, the tears leapt from his eyes, his mouth opened till they could see a square black hole … The crying went on, breath after breath, and seemed to sustain him upright as if he were nailed to it,' he has unforgettably *shown* us something. By which I mean that he has brought us so closely into the presence of the weeping child that we can see him and hear him and feel our own inconsolable portion in the sense of universal grief he disturbs in the other 'littluns'. Who could prefer the told version to the shown?

Yet forty years after Lubbock's book on *The Craft of Fiction*, Wayne C. Booth pointed out in *The Rhetoric of Fiction* that showing is itself only one among the diverse strategies of telling, and that direct telling can work potent magic too. Consider, for instance, the opening of Paul Auster's *Moon Palace*, with its recklessly overt résumé of the story we are about to read – all telling, every word of it, but told to magnetic effect.

What's more, if we insist on showing everything, especially things that might more effectively be told, then it won't be long before we start to bore the reader. The error shows itself in the common tendency of young writers to begin in the wrong place, so that we must watch the leading character get out of bed, stare in the mirror, eat breakfast, and so on, to the point where we begin to lose interest long before some intriguing encounter seizes our attention. In those dull circumstances, the collaboration with the reader will end before it's properly got started. So what seems to be in question is the right choice of narrative strategy *at any given moment*. Do I tell the readers this, or should I show it? Which approach will most effectively draw them into the dream of the novel and keep them there till the dream is done?

Reading and dreaming have much in common. In both we generate images out of a limited visual field. These images move and disturb us because we feel immediately involved with them, at times more intensely than with our everyday experience, yet they arrive without overt explanations and require us to work for meaning. Also, unlike those of film, the images we find in books and dreams are unique to each of us, the work of our own imagination. So my Heathcliff does not look like yours, and when either of us tries to tell someone else about a dream we've had, or a book we've read, we know just how much gets lost.

Dreams remain a great mystery, but their vocabulary of images seems to allow the oldest, preverbal parts of the brain to speak to the neocortex, thus opening a channel of communication between the conscious and unconscious minds. By flexing all the inward senses of the imagination, fiction can tap us into that hotline too. When that happens, good writing literally works like a dream. And what may most deeply excite us about it is the fact that we have been set free to dream the story for ourselves.

This freedom of the imagination is of profound, countervailing importance in a time when we are so often the passive recipients of information and reportage. There may be more than just literary reasons for the emphasis on showing over telling in most fiction workshops. But what matters here is the recognition that, if we are to create and sustain a lively dream in the reader's imagination, then much of our revision will be about questioning our choices of narrative strategy, altering them where necessary, then fine-tuning their effects.

In practice this means hunting down those moments that unintentionally tip the reader out of the dream. They can be considered under two broad headings – problems that arise from under-writing, when the author hasn't done enough imaginative work to secure the collaboration of the reader, and those of over-writing, when the reader is crowded out by the author trying to do too much.

Merely telling the reader something that's crying out to be dramatised is a form of under-writing. William Blake once wrote that 'he who does not imagine in minute particulars does not imagine at all'; it seems clear that if we don't bring the focused energy of the imagination to bear on the scene we're writing, then we'll be unlikely to activate its full potential to excite the reader's interest. The result is inert wordage that leaves the reader cold, so it's as well to keep an eye out for the symptoms.

Prominent among them is the retreat into abstraction. Watch out for a reliance on abstract nouns in your writing, particularly those to do with states of feeling. Simply to announce that a character is 'filled with fury' or 'rotten with jealousy' is the weakest way to make your reader feel the impact of their emotions. We have your word for it, but little else. However, if you show us the children wincing as Harriet throws across the kitchen the curry she's just cooked, or we see Ken straining to overhear a telephone call through a closed door, then we draw our own conclusions. It's a useful exercise to forbid yourself the use of keynote words such as 'fury' or 'jealous' when dramatising an emotional condition. Similarly, when you find yourself writing *about* an important conversation, ask whether your readers might not prefer to hear the exchanges for themselves – particularly since characters are revealed through the different ways they use language, and dialogue can subtly move the narrative along.

This kind of dramatised showing is much harder than straight telling, and in good writing there's no distinction between language and content, so the success of a piece will depend on how skilfully your words perform the show. When you come to revise a draft, ask yourself, for instance, how many details have been blurred by the broad-brush adjectives you've used to depict a scene. Is there a more limber way of conjuring the characters into the reader's presence than merely attaching descriptive tags? Does your use of adverbs short-circuit energy out of your sentences by labelling actions that a sharper movement of the syntax might quicken into life? And when you come across a cliché, take it for what it is – a sign that you've nodded off and it's time to recharge your imagination. Somewhere behind that prefabricated block of language lies a living moment. Close your eyes, activate your inward senses, then write and rewrite till you've hit a pitch of high fidelity. After all, if you don't care enough about the characters and events of your story to do them imaginative justice, why should the reader stay inside the dream?

Over-writing indicates a failure to trust the imagination of the reader. Consider how much of the pleasure of reading comes from inferring that which has nowhere been explicitly stated. A writer who pre-empts such moments of realisation by obtrusive winks and nudges soon becomes a bore. The same is true of any lack of economy in your prose. By making a careful selection of details from a scene that you've imagined *for yourself* 'in minute particulars', you free your readers to visualise it too. But if you pile on the adjectives, or double the content of your sentences through the loose use of similes, you're more likely to crowd them out.

Often enough you'll find that less can do more. A marvellous letter written by Conrad in 1899 demonstrates what this principle means in practice. A friend had asked his opinion on some stories he had written, one of which contained these sentences: 'When the whole horror of his position forced itself with an agony of apprehension upon his frightened mind, Pa'Tua for a space lost his reason. He screamed aloud, and the hollow of the rocks took up his cries and hurled them back mockingly.' Conrad sharpened the passage to powerful effect simply by cutting out a quarter of the words. Bearing in mind his admonition that the author hadn't left enough to the reader's imagination, you might like to work out which words he cut.

Sometimes we overwrite out of the desire not so much to show as to show off; and sometimes, less exuberantly, out of anxiety to make sure that our meaning gets across. Either way we have to learn to 'murder our darlings' for the greater good of the book, and this can come hard. I was so infatuated with a sentence in one of my own novels that it passed unscathed through every draft, right through to the galley proofs, when my wife declared that she had always hated it. I woke up and saw that either the whole story dramatised what the sentence had to say – in which case it was redundant – or it didn't, in which case that sentence alone wasn't going to save the book from failure. It was an edgy moment, but I knew that in the end the finished work has to speak clearly on its own terms, uncluttered by the author's attachments. That sentence may have helped to keep me on track throughout the writing of the book, continuously reminding me what it was supposed to be about, but the reader had no use for it. So I struck it out and have long since forgotten it except as a happy reminder of the satisfactions of revision.

Alexander Solzhenitsyn celebrates the importance of such moments in his novel *The First Circle*, where one of the characters, a prisoner in the Gulag, speaks movingly of 'the rule of the last inch'. It's a rule that applies near the end of a project when you sense that, despite all your efforts, the quality you were after is not yet quite attained and there's still more to be done before the long journey of the work is over. The rule of the last inch is simply not to neglect it. It's a rule that all writers who care for their craft will strive to take to heart.

# Weaving with Light

## The Tapestries of Berit Hjelholt

This is an edited and extended version of an illustrated article originally published in *Resurgence* and subsequently featured in *Images of Earth and Spirit* edited by John Lane and Satish Kumar (Green Books, 2003).

There is a passage in Doris Lessing's novel *The Golden Notebook* where the protagonist, Anna Wulf, writes how 'I dreamed there was an enormous web of beautiful fabric stretched out ... covered all over with embroidered pictures. The pictures were illustrations of the myths of mankind but they were not just pictures, they were the myths themselves, so that the soft glittering web was alive. In my dream I handled this material, wept with joy ... it spread out ... and now I was standing in space somewhere ... time has gone and the long story of mankind is present in what I see now, and it is like a great soaring hymn of joy and triumph in which pain is a small, lively counterpoint.'

Primarily because it draws on dream imagery, there's much in this passage that excites my imagination. Because much of my work as a writer has originated in significant dreams, I'm inclined to believe that the image came from a dream with which Lessing was herself gifted. But the passage also engages me because the dream is about myths, and myths have been important to me since childhood and remain so as a further fruitful source in my work. Furthermore, it speaks about myths not as a subject of antiquarian or anthropological interest, but as animate creatures filled with light and life, envisioning them as visible motifs woven within a vast cosmic tapestry. So, for me, the essential beauty of this passage resides in the way it presents as a vital force in the imagination of a complex modern woman one of the most ancient of mythological archetypes: that of the cosmos itself as a fabric within which the history of humankind and of each life and its story are seamlessly interwoven.

That archetype still features in modern artistic consciousness. In one of his early poems W.B. Yeats famously wrote of 'the heaven's embroidered cloths', while a tapestry designed by Henry Moore illustrates with compassionate gravity the myth of the Moirae, the three Fates who measure out the span of each human life: Klotho who spins its thread; Lachesis, 'the Disposer of Lots', who gathers the pattern of the individual's fate; and Atropos, 'she who cannot be averted', who severs the life-thread with her shears. Both Yeats and Moore drew on Plato for inspiration – Moore specifically on Plato's account of the Myth of Er in *The Republic*, where we are shown how lives turn on the spindle of Necessity before the moment of birth when each is clad in the folds of its particular destiny. But the image of the cosmos itself as a woven veil is far older than Greek civilisation. The ancient Egyptians attributed the invention of weaving to the Moon goddess Neith, 'the oldest one', who was later identified with Isis; in one of her temples is the inscription, 'I am all that has been, that is, and that will be. No one has yet been able to lift the veil which covers me.' The symbol of nature as the Veil of Isis reminds us that a veil or shadow always stands between what we see and what truly is, and between reality and our understanding of it – an insight that connects with the Hindu myth of the spider spinning the illusion of time and weaving the web of Maya, but also – more provocatively – with an admission by the theoretical physicist Sir Arthur Eddington that 'we have learnt that the exploration of the external world by the methods of physical science leads not to a concrete reality but to a shadow world of symbols, beneath which those methods are unadapted for penetrating'.

That phrase, 'a shadow world of symbols', refers implicitly to Plato's metaphor of our life as a cave in which people sit with their backs to the light of Reality which throws shadows on the cave wall. It might also serve as a good translation for 'maya', a word that, like 'matter' and 'imagination', stems from the Sanskrit root 'ma', meaning 'to measure, to form, to create, construct, exhibit or display' – which brings us back to the way Doris Lessing's dream image interweaves the substance of woven fabric with emblems of myth to stimulate and enrich the imagination.

But we don't have to look to ancient philosophies or to great art for evidence of the continuing importance of images drawn from weaving in human experience. The quiet labour of spindle and loom were once so intimate a part of household life that our language remains rich in its metaphors. Yet when we speak of a high-speed train as 'a shuttle', or of telling a story as 'spinning a yarn', or talk ecologically about 'the intricate web of life', the references to weaving lack the tactile and visual actuality they once held for our ancestors. Even the common exhortation 'Let's get weaving' has largely forgotten how much of its force derives from the slow, painstaking process by which a loom must be dressed with its warp before the weaving can begin.

Few people nowadays feel the need to cultivate the patient skills that hand-weaving requires, and those with the vision to lift that craft to the level of high art are fewer still – which is only one of the many reasons why Berit Hjelholt was a person of rare value. Photographs can give only a diminished sense of the scale and texture of her tapestries, but even in reproduction you feel the impact of their emotive power in the way they excite the senses and stir the heart. A larger understanding of their imaginative reach comes with knowledge of the artist herself and of the Danish landscape where she lived and worked.

The homestead that Berit shared with her husband, the distinguished psychologist Gunnar Hjelholt, is on Thy, the wide-horizoned, airily lit island that caps the Jutland peninsula. Within walking distance of her studio are the dunes of the Vesterhavet coast overlooking Jammerbugten, the Bay of Sorrows. Here the cliff known as Bulbjerg – the Bulwark – rears above the strand to gaze out across the Skaggerak towards Norway. Fragments of Baltic amber drift in with the swell. On clear days the colours glisten with rinsed clarity in the salty light, while in the rhythmic striations of its soft limestone the cliff-face tells its own geological story.

Offshore, a solitary, cormorant-haunted stack called Skarreklit used to stand steeple-like above the foam until it collapsed during a night of violent storm in 1975. 'In the old days,' Berit old me, 'it was believed that this was earth's edge, and on the ocean side of the stack were the words "Northwest of here there is nothing." The legend has it that once a year a bird comes to sharpen its beak on the stone, and when Skarreklit is worn away the world will come to an end. There is only a little left showing above the water now.'

When I first met Berit, one frozen January several years before that ruinous storm, she was working on the vast tapestry, *Day*, which celebrates the landscape of that shore. The piece now hangs in the boardroom of the Danish National Bank, but what astonished me at the time was its intimate identity, in both material and visionary terms, with the environment within which I saw it taking shape. Berit had spun wool from the fleece of the sheep grazing the fields behind the cliff. She had grown her own flax there and coloured the yarns with vegetable dyes distilled from other local plants. By these methods she was returning what she had taken by weaving it into the landscape as known and loved in her inward vision. At the same time it was as though, through this long alchemy of patient labour, the land itself was realising something at once new and very old about its own deep nature.

So strong was the impression left on me by this powerful, tranquil process of transubstantiation that, twenty years later, those memories returned unfaded to furnish images for my own fictional weaver in the novel *Alice's Masque*. A major exhibition mounted in celebration of Berit's seventy-fifth birthday brought together the harvest of a lifetime's work. It was a life that began in the fishing community of Munsala in Finland, where in the 1920s weaving was still as much part of domestic life as mending the nets. Childhood voyages in her father's boat had taught Berit the power of natural forces together with the need to flow responsively with them. She was given her first spinning wheel by her grandmother when she was thirteen. Later, her developing skills in drawing and embroidery took her to college in Helsinki, where she studied pattern-making. From there she went on to Stockholm, where she worked for the textile artist Ann-Mari Forsberg. Marriage to Gunnar brought her to Copenhagen, and the raising of her family in the 1950s left little time for other work.

Berit's first essays in tapestry were mostly small images drawn

from memories of her childhood in coastal Finland, but then a journey to the east brought new sources of inspiration. The meditative
disciplines of Japanese aesthetics, the qualities of scattered light
through bamboo screens, the figurations of calligraphy – all influenced the focusing of her personal vision. Other inspirations would
come from her study of Neolithic cave paintings, Lappish traditions,
and the Native American medicine wheel, yet the roots of her imagination remained firmly earthed in the landscapes and seascapes of
her native Scandinavia. Berit's vision flourished to maturity when
the family moved north to Thy and the sensory impact of the natural world found a feeling answer in the symbol-making powers of
her soul.

'Nature always enters my work,' she said. 'I need that foundation
of experiences. But my beliefs, my unconscious, my soul, enter into
the tapestry as I work. It is neither "naturalistic" nor "abstract".
Fantasy and intuition go into the weaving and very often I am quite
surprised – sometimes shocked – when the tapestry is out of the
loom. Not till then do I really know what I have been doing.'

Perhaps none of the visual arts requires the maker to sustain a
single vision over as long a period of time as the weaving of a large
and complex tapestry. The wish to create the image may come swiftly enough, but how to hold the inspiration, dreams, thoughts that
started the process during the months that follow?

'Often I try to write down cue words to remind myself when I'm
stuck,' Berit said. 'The thoughts prepare and control what hands do.
It is always a building-up process, and the assurance that my safety
net – the working drawing – underlies the work on the loom allows
me to have my doubts on the way, but still to continue without un-
weaving. Once the "weave-it-over" machinery is set in motion, the
very foundations begin to break down.' The advantage of this slow
process is that 'thoughts are added which can lead to more dimensions. Light and darkness, lightness and weight – so that the spectator of the finished tapestry also gets the chance to work with it,
move into it; so the spectator's dream enters the tapestry.'

It is through this participatory nature of her art that one begins
to recognise why these images work on us with such searching power. It is as if, over the long months of marrying weft to warp, Berit

has dreamed herself so deeply into the feeling, sensuous qualities of what nature initially gave that she has broken through into that elemental ground beyond the visible – beyond the personal even – where, consciously or not, we all most deeply live. What she has accomplished there simultaneously illuminates both our outward and our inner worlds. You can sense this in the way she described the process of weaving *Night*, one of the most delicately luminous of her tapestries: 'At that time my best weaving was done between the hours of four and eight in the morning. It was the period between twilight and daybreak, which hovered in the consciousness like an infinity, a dream, transporting me into my picture-world. It was a warm summer and I slept out under the open skies, woke when the light came, and had a very strong impression of the night on its way towards light. Kristoffer, our big cat, was home from the evening's prowling and lay on my pillow. All that fresh air breathed gave me a feeling of lightness and enormous energy. I quickly began to weave while I still kept the dawn's light fresh in my memory.'

Yet the journey between conception and completion is always long and may be fraught with difficulties. The threefold tapestry *Longing for Home* dramatises something of the price its accomplishment exacted in endurance and anxiety. In a commentary on its metaphorical – one might equally well say its metaphysical – qualities, Berit explained how the left-hand panel portrays the yearning of the dark for the light; in the central panel the journeying vessel cracks in a collision of seas; yet, stricken or not, it must press on to where, in the third panel, the warmer colour-weave utters its hope for peace, for safety, for home. So the larger journey of a whole lifetime is woven through both process and theme.

Like the invisible voyagers on the recurring motif of the ship in her work, Berit's imagination travelled between darkness and light, between dream and waking, between knowledge of the world's wounds and the luminous promise of the longed-for home. The very texture of her work embraces these contraries through the technique of closely weaving the colours of rough hand-spun wool across the sheen of a linen warp to yield a breathlike transparency. It brings to mind the hazy, sometimes bitter brightness of sunlight through sea mist – the havgus that comes rolling in off the cold

177

Skaggerak to dematerialise the once solid fabric of the cliffs and dunes and fields. This effect, combined with Berit's eye for matching the design of commissioned pieces to the hang of the light in their eventual location, seems to render the world porous to its own radiance. You can see it shining down the vertical reach of *Morningsong*, through the feathery terraces of rock in *Wingspan*, and in the windjammer sails of *Homecoming*. Perhaps most movingly of all, it holds open the heart of the bounteous *Tree of Life* that hangs behind the altar of Ellabek church, its bole reaching skywards out of the streaming waters of life.

At the same time, such is the rhythmic quality of these designs that, within the stillness of the finished pieces, everything feels in motion – a constant surge of sea and contours and cloud immersed in the chromatic shifts of light and shade. It's as though we are privileged to observe at leisure a single transient moment that will never be the same again; yet this sensation of time arrested at the very instant of change has taken many months to achieve. The paradoxes are extended further in the studies Berit made of a wrecked fishing cog that was driven ashore in the Bay of Sorrows by a twelfth-century storm. Its ribbed hulk was excavated from the dunes in 1978 – a skeletal survivor of time's erosion, still redolent of human pathos before the violence of the elements. Buried in sand by the passage of the centuries, preserved and transmuted there, and exposed to the light by the kind of storm that had wrecked it long ago, the boat fetched up at last in the safe haven of Berit's loom.

Some of the pieces have abstract, almost allegorical titles – *Mercy, Forgiveness, Contact* – which set one's thoughts wondering about their non-figurative images, and reflect the compassionate preoccupations of Berit's sacred sense of life. Some, like *Morningsong* ('Tears may linger at nightfall, but joy comes in the morning'), *Forgiveness*, and *Mercy* are keyed to specific verses in the Psalms that were dear to the artist's heart. 'But if there is to be a picture which conveys more than my situation', she said, 'it needs qualities which touch parts of consciousness difficult to express in words – in the hope that the tapestries tell the spectator something about the timeless dimensions we all need to experience.'

The major exhibition to celebrate her birthday gave Berit Hjelholt the opportunity to reflect on the degree to which her beautiful work fulfils that hope. In a time when so much that passes for art is the product of left-brain ingenuity rather than of heartfelt imaginative vision; when the piece exhibited is sometimes the work of skilled artisans hired for the job rather than of the artist who conceived it; and when all too often what is on offer seems infatuated by little more than a witty sense of irony or, still worse, demands complicity in despair – in such depleted times these deeply felt, patiently fashioned tapestries draw us back, without evasion or sentimentality, on to elemental ground. By refiguring the visible so that the invisible shines through them, they affirm both the imagination's capacity for hard-earned truth and the dignity of the heart. They example us in sensitivity, vision, endurance, and compassion, and – perhaps most urgently in the environmentally unbalanced circumstances that threaten both the present and future welfare of life on this planet – they put us back in intimate touch with the sanest and most ancient myth of all – that of the primal and evolutionary bonds of kinship between the human soul and the intelligent living soul of the earth.

# Jammerbugten

*i.m. Berit Hjelholt (1920–2016)*

To the north of Jutland
off the Vesterhavet Coast
and staring over Jammerbugten,
Bay of Sorrows, stood
a cormorant-haunted stack
of rock named Skarreklit.

The old Jutes called it
Earth's Edge and believed
that on the seaward side
were carved the words:
NORTHWEST OF HERE

*IS NOTHING.*
And once a year, they said,
a bird would come to whet
its beak against that rugged
spire of stone, and when
all Skarreklit was thus worn
away, the world would end.

My friend, a weaver, told me
this, who lives nearby
and figures out that landscape
on her loom. She woke
one morning from a storm
to find the stack torn down.

So these days just a jagged
plinth of rock juts black
above the waves. Her works
have titles such as *Mercy*,
*Shadow Walk*, and *Day*.
And stones and sea are shining through
the light that's woven with each thread.

# An Interview with
# Liliana Sikorska

Liliana Sikorska is Professor of English Literature at the Adam Mickiewicz University, Poznan, Poland. The interview took place in November 2012.

*1. During the process of writing, what became* The Water Theatre *was entitled* Sun at Midnight. *What prompted you to change the title?*

During the more than twelve years it took me to complete this book another novel appeared using my planned title, *Sun at Midnight*, which I had chosen because of its association with the rites of Isis in the *Metamorphoses* of Apuleius. Somewhat regretfully, I agreed with my publisher that in order to avoid confusion it made sense to change the title of my own novel. *The Water Theatre* felt like a good alternative because it refers to the setting for the transformative climax of the book, and because water (archetypally associated with feeling) is the dominant element of this novel, as fire was of *The Chymical Wedding*.

*2. The published title refers in some way to your interests in Jungian archetypes, which were also present in* The Chymical Wedding *and* Alice's Masque. *Here, Jung works brilliantly in conjunction with the rest of the novel, making* The Water Theatre *an exquisitely rich, dense, and profound book. Was this done on purpose to show your consistent interest in psychology?*

Never having undergone analysis, I have only a layman's understanding of Jung's analytical psychology, but it seems to me that, together with the work done by the post-Jungian archetypal psychologists, his emphasis on individuation as the essential process of consciousness and his explorations of the archetypal structure of the unconscious offer a deep-searching myth of what it might mean to be more fully human and of what might be called the poetics of consciousness. Such a psychology seems to me an essential corrective to the more reductive schools of thought which have dominated recent views of human nature. Because it underpins so much of the way in which I try to understand and assimilate aspects of my own experience, it's inevitable that its modes of thought and feeling should inform my work as a novelist, though my approach to writing a novel is never schematic or formulaic. In many ways it feels more like an archaeological dig than a psychological process as I uncover a story piece by piece and eventually seek to infer the entire culture of the novel from the fragments that slowly emerge into consciousness.

*3. Yet another aspect of the novel is Martin's troubled relationship with his father. Was that part your own experience changed as necessary for the purpose of fiction? Or are the life and times of Martin pure fiction?*

Martin Crowther is a fictional creation, though, in much the same way that I have drawn on my own experience in West Africa to provide a political context for the fictional events of the novel, I have endowed him with certain aspects of my own origins in the working class of northern England. That said, I should certainly add that the whole novel is an attempt to assimilate the meaning for my own life of a dream of my dead father which first disturbed me years before I became a novelist. I gave that dream to Martin at the opening of *The Water Theatre* because it seems to me to offer a graphic image of the problems faced by masculine consciousness as it seeks to evolve beyond the limitations of an obsolete (but not defunct) paternalist culture.

*4. Martin's youth, his university years, his influences of liberalism and existentialism, are evoked to show the contrast between the two families, the Crowthers and the Brigshaws. Is liberalism the privilege of the wealthy? (This is how generations of British liberal writers are viewed in Poland.) Am I right to see his as the voice of a postwar generation, expressing both individual and more universal concerns?*

*The Water Theatre* is a bildungsroman in which I have tried to offer a picture of a man dislocated from the working-class culture of his birth through a liberal education system that shapes his awareness of the personal and sociopolitical issues of our times; so, yes, I agree with your reading. But it's hard to give a brief answer to the larger reach of your question. Liberalism seems to me to be the effort of a class privileged by both birth and education to apply Enlightenment thinking to the creation of a just and equitable society that preserves the dignity of human freedom by maintaining a stance of tolerant open-mindedness and scepticism towards the scientifically unprovable. Among its limitations, however, is a reluctance to acknowledge the power of the archetypal forces that underpin our lives and that can overwhelm them if they are nor recognised and assimilated. The insights of archetypal psychology suggest there are important values associated with those archetypal forces, which have been neglected and even demeaned by the tradition of liberal intellectual scepticism. It seems to me that an attempt to engage honestly with these values is an essential part of the evolution of consciousness which is happening in these transitional times. That effort will take us into difficult terrain, some of which will appear to defy reason as it is currently understood. Because my novel seeks to take the reader into some of those areas, it was no surprise to me that even those critics who wrote very positive reviews of the bulk of the novel were uneasy with some of the possibilities that their imagination was invited to entertain. I have no quarrel with scepticism and irony as useful defences against mystification, but I worry that their intellectual authority, in having become the default values of our confusing times, may also inhibit the creative evolution of consciousness. In this respect I stand with Yeats in what he maintained was the revolt of the soul against the intellect.

*5. As a reader I am always interested in intertexts and the stories behind them. For example, how did the Maximilian Kolbe story make its way into the novel? And how many of the Umbrian legends are real?*

The legends that appear in *The Water Theatre* are all genuine stories from the Western folk tradition, though, as I explain in the Author's

Note, for the purposes of my fiction I have transposed the legend of Fontanalba from Haute-Savoie to Umbria.

One of the themes of the novel is that of the 'proxy', which raises the question of to what degree we are all members of one another. I dramatise this issue in the way Martin and Adam seem to change each other and then begin to live out the implications of each other's original values. I have been fascinated by the brave and tragic fate of Maximilian Kolbe, the Saint of Auschwitz, since I first came across it. I wished to include it here, both as a counter to the nihilistic horror of the Dog Fox story and as a means of honouring a commitment to spiritual values different from, but related to, my own non-denominational intimations of a sacred dimension to our experience. As he went to his death in Auschwitz as a proxy for another man, Maximilian Kolbe embodied the universal value of humanity beyond the claims of the individual. His central message that 'Only love creates' carries an urgent corrective to the proliferation of material values in our time.

*6. Your African past comes alive again in the form of the fictional Equatoria. Is it true that you can leave Africa, but Africa never leaves you?*

It certainly seems to be the case as far as I'm concerned, and I'm deeply grateful for it.

*7. The motif of long-lost love, although common, is here acted out wonderfully in the conflict between friends and lover and ideas about split loyalties (which ring medieval themes again). Why is Marina blind? Such a punishment for a painter who couldn't read the reality around her when she was younger!*

Perhaps the theme of lost love and whether it can ever be recovered stirs us so deeply because it resonates not just with our outward experience of loss but also with the process by which the growth of individual consciousness can leave us feeling inwardly divided and in search of a means to become whole again. It seems that such wholeness, if it is to be found at all, emerges only through the difficult reconciliation of opposites, of which a reconciled love relationship is a potent symbol. That's what I tried to dramatise in *The Water*

*Theatre.* I agree that blindness is a cruel fate for a painter and one that I would not have wished to inflict on Marina had not some imperative of the imaginative process shocked me by demanding that I do so. I wouldn't seek to explain it as some form of punishment for her earlier failure of vision, and I would point out that the fate might have been avoided had she not persisted with her work without seeking treatment when her eyes were already warning her that something was wrong. But she is an artist and, like many artists, obsessive about her work, and also a troubled soul. Only as I pursued the implications of her blindness did I recognise that it was an essential component of the theme of darkness at the heart of this novel – darkness that is a form of blindness (i.e. unconsciousness), on the one hand, and a source of transformation (like Henry Vaughan's 'dazzling darkness' of illumination), on the other.

*8. The ultimate betrayal is again kind of Freudian – that of the father betraying the son, but perhaps also the betrayals of the mothers (both Adam's and Martin's).*

Though I admire Freud's efforts to illuminate the darkness of the unconscious mind as a titanic effort of courage, intelligence, and compassion, I find a number of his interpretations of its processes unconvincing. Jung's myth of the individuation process strikes me as more enlargingly suggestive, and I prefer to see in those rather than in Freudian terms the failures and gains, the suffering and the redemptions of the familial conflicts dramatised in this novel. The mothers are both in their different ways the victims of a paternalistic culture and both are carriers of important alternative values struggling to express themselves in a world and a time that do not know how to hear them.

# Love's Alchemy

A letter written to Professor Liliana Sikorska of Adam Mickiewicz University, Poznan, in response to issues raised by
her study of *The Chymical Wedding* in a paper titled 'The Alchemy of Love', published in *Medievalisms: The Poetics of Literary
Re-reading* edited by Liliana Sikorska (Peter Lang, 2008).

Dear Liliana,

Thank you so much for sending me your paper on 'The Alchemy
of Love'. What an extraordinary piece of work it is, impressive in the
range of its cultural, literary, and linguistic reference far beyond your
attention to my own work, and so brave in taking on themes that lie
like a hot boil of magma beneath the surface of Christianity's efforts
to resolve, order, and contain the contradictions that rack our lives.
As Fulke Greville put it in his *Mustapha* back in 1633:

> Oh wearisome Condition of Humanity!
> Borne under one Law, to another bound:
> Vainely begot, and yet forbidden vanity;
> Created sick, commanded to be sound:
> What meaneth Nature by these diverse Lawes?
> Passion and Reason, selfe-division cause.

And don't we, who strive for consciousness, all know it still?
It's so long since I wrote *The Chymical Wedding* that reading your
paper was like time- travelling back into the state of turmoil and
confusion out of which the book emerged, and of which it still ine-
radicably bears the marks. Trying to find my way through the forest
of images, sometimes luminous, sometimes bafflingly dark, that

seemed to crowd around me then, I felt as I imagine those Celtic heroes must have felt who stumbled into the otherworld of Faerie and wandered there, as one story puts it, 'in great distress of mind'. Much like Alex Darken himself!

You are correct to identify the Sheela na gig figure of Gypsy May as the key motif of the book. And not only of that book, for in one form or another she seems to haunt all my work. She is present as the outcast witch in *Sunday Whiteman*, as the bag-lady manifestation of the Loathly Lady archetype in *Alice's Masque*, as Cundrie in *Parzival*, and as Eris (modulating into the figures of Thetis, Clytaemnestra, and Circe) in the *Troy* books. (She is also the Celtic Cailleach figure in stories I retell in *Essential Celtic Mythology*.) So it seems that I'm a hag-ridden writer if ever there was one! But, for me, each of these figures is an attempt to retrieve from the shadows the demeaned, neglected, sometimes sternly repressed archetypal power of the feminine principle that has been left so disastrously out of count by our patriarchal culture, and without whose respected presence our feeling life is in deep trouble; as is our grasp of the full dimensionality of what masculinity – 'the man in man', as Nietzsche puts it – may mean. I speak personally as well as culturally, of course.

As Edwin Frere, Edward Nesbit, and Alex all find, it's a figure that seems to exercise over the male imagination a fascination that is at once exciting and terrifying. Why should this be? With his usual incisive honesty, Ted Hughes writes powerfully on the issue in *Shakespeare and the Goddess of Complete Being*:

> confronting the Goddess of Complete Being, the ego's extreme alternatives are either to reject her and attempt to live an independent, rational, secular life or to abnegate the ego and embrace her with 'total, unconditional love', which means to become a saint, a holy idiot, possessed by the Divine Love. The inevitability which Shakespeare projects with such 'divine' completeness is that there is no escape from one choice or the other. Man will always choose the former, simply because ... he wants to live his own life ... Always, one way or another, he rejects the Goddess. Then follows his correction.

One might reasonably guess that Hughes's reflections on this masculine dilemma were not solely informed by his insightful study of Shakespeare's poems and plays. I've sometimes wondered whether, when a woman like Louisa Agnew in *The Chymical Wedding* receives her lover in deep erotic encounter, she consciously or unconsciously requires him to pass beyond the limits of the divisive ego into that place where there is only body and soul in indissoluble union. But for a man who is identified with the executive ego or, like poor Frere, with a strong cultural superego, such an encounter can be experienced as the threat of engorgement, of the woman as devourer (see Edward's pathological description of Gypsy May on page 455).

Perhaps only as the centre of his consciousness shifts from ego to soul will he begin to see the ground of complete being waiting for him; for what is experienced by the well-defended ego as dissolution may be known to the soul as the indissoluble unity of being. And it may be that such a realisation can arrive through some irrevocable act of erotic transgression which propels him from a world dominated by social conventions into that impersonal space where all boundaries are transcended. Gnostic space. The psychic, perhaps sacred space where knowledge and experience are one, and communicable only to those who have been similarly initiated.

Yet the inability of such transgressive love to speak its true name more widely seems to be almost inevitable once it collides with the world whose prohibitions it violates. It may also be that, for all our yearning, the sacred marriage belongs in the archetypal realm of myth, not in the more refractory realm of fact. As Patrick Harpur suggests in his provocative book *The Philosophers' Secret Fire: A History of the Imagination*, it may be 'an image which underlies the dynamics of Imagination as it constantly shifts contradictions it cannot reconcile on to different metaphorical levels'. It's possible too that the anguish of loss that ensues from failure to live out the hope and promise carried by the image is a more reliable agent of spiritual transformation than is the love itself when it becomes confused with, and arrested by, attachment and desire.

Whatever the case, though the manner of its expression may have been literary, even ludic, in its conventions, I'm pretty sure that the tradition of amour courtois began as much more than a literary conceit. I'm inclined to believe that the most powerful of the poems and romances it inspired were the fine flower of actual, lived experiences – experiences that would have been taboo within the strict regime of the feudal order and also perilously heretical in the inquisitorial eyes of Christian orthodoxy. Hot stuff indeed, and too wild for Andreas Capellanus to tame in his prim courtly handbook *De Amore*!

Around that time, similar seismic eruptions of transgressive, erotico-spiritual experiences were recorded in the poetry of other rigidly structured societies – among the Sufis of the Near East, in the heraldic courts of Japan, and in the caste-dominated culture of Bengal. So is it possible that some vital, compensatory evolution of consciousness was beginning to take place on a planetary scale in the early Middle Ages? Is it still trying to happen?

In writing about Louisa and Frere, I had Eloise and Abelard in mind, of course, but also St Francis's struggle with his love/desire for Chiara di Offreduccio, and the way in which the Bengali Brahmin poet Chandidas was able to affirm the spiritual insights arising from his love for the low-caste washer-woman Rami only after withstanding immense, almost overwhelming pressure from his orthodox peers. More closely still, I was deeply moved by the tormented experience of a friend of mine, an Anglican priest, now long deceased, who authorised me to tell his story – which I did by attributing a version of it in disguised form to the fictional Victorian parson Edwin Frere. But this takes us some distance away from academic discourse!

Suffice it to say that the work of Margaret Anne Doody in *The True Story of the Novel* examines the possibility that such early writers of prose romances as Lucius Apuleius used fiction as an intriguing exoteric form through which the public imagination might be drawn towards the life-enlarging significance of initiatory mysteries that were otherwise available only in privately experienced, esoteric rites. Certainly, my own imagination is most excited by writing that has such an expansive effect on my perspectives.

One last thought. Back in 1990, when John Boorman was trying to make a film of *The Chymical Wedding*, he invited me to his home in

Ireland to work with him on the script. It was an exciting time – he had already cast Jodie Foster, Liam Neeson, and John Hurt in the leading roles – though sadly the project came to nothing in the end; but it did provide me with one bizarre experience. On my last morning in Ireland we went to the National Museum in Dublin to view its collection of Sheela na Gigs in order to find an authentic design for Gypsy May. One of the curators explained that the figures could not be put on public show without causing rumpuses from the puritanically minded on the one hand and militant feminists on the other, so they were all crowded together – twenty of them or more – in a small basement store-room of the museum, consigned as it were to the unconscious of history. It was one of the strangest experiences of my life to find myself surrounded by this gaggle of primitive female figures, each holding herself open, without shame or allure, for our inspection. Outnumbered this way, outstared, and perplexed beyond thought, I knew myself for sure in the presence of a mystery that would not be belittled or explained away by any interpretation that I chose to impose on it.

With all good wishes,
Lindsay

# What Mystery Pervades
# a Well!

## Wishes, Oracles, and Initiations

This talk was given at a colloquium on Sacred Waters as one of
the Mythic Imagination series of events organised by Merrily,
Patrick, and James Harpur at Cattistock in Dorset in 2017.

For sixteen years I lived in an old farmhouse standing askance its
own combe where the foothills of the Mendips roll down towards
the Somerset Levels. When my late wife and I first found the house,
a large part of its attraction lay in its secluded situation. Here was a
place where she could make pots inspired by the contours of the
landscape while I got down the writing I'd promised myself I would
do one day but had kept putting off for far too long.

Intuitively I knew that I might be helped in that work by the fact
that the house was watered from its own spring – an outlet that
broke from the limestone rock in a narrow wooded dell. Our supply
was piped underground to the house but at its source the spring
overflowed into a little rill that twisted its shine down the coombe to
pour briefly underground again beyond our garden gate. Except in
the driest days of summer, its plunge back into the underworld filled
the combe with the sound of water. Three novels found form to the
accompaniment of that sound. For me, as for countless poets and
storytellers before me, the way spring water breaks like light out of
the earth felt like a living metaphor of the way language rises – at
times, it seems, of its own volition – out of the dark places of the
unconscious mind to shape itself in images. Eventually the local
farmer retired and the fields lying above our combe were taken over

by a big commercial dairy. Unfamiliar with the land, a new farm manager pastured a large herd there and the hillside became a dumping ground for the vast swill of farmyard waste accumulated during the winter months by those patient beasts. This effluent – a mix of cowshit, hormones, bacteria, and chemicals supposed to fertilise the fields – seeped down into saturated ground and found its way, as liquid will, through the unseen limestone clefts and fissures, until we woke one morning, turned on our taps, and watched a greenish-black, malodorous slime splash down into the sink.

Weeks of decontamination would pass before the spring was deemed drinkable again. During that period our only supply of water was delivered by tankers and pumped into the house at the polluter's expense. Believe me, after such a disruptive calamity one comes to appreciate the true value of clean water. Nor is it only one's physical senses that recoil from the fouling of a spring. It feels as though some wellspring at the very heart of one's being shudders with a sense of contamination.

As a consequence of that hideous experience I came to understand with what prescience, a hundred years earlier, Marcel Duchamp had entered a urinal for an art exhibition and titled his exhibit 'Fountain'. It was a conscious act of outrage, of course, a clever, ironical move in his campaign to challenge conventional assumptions about the beliefs and values associated with the idea of art. Since then the deliberate desacralisation of both art and the world from which it arises has gathered pace and confidence. Yet for many centuries both before and after the birth of Christ, poets had celebrated the vital clarity of spring water as a sacred source both of life and of creative reverie.

The way water rises at a spring seems to mirror the mysterious inner process by which images rise into consciousness from the dark interior, and it's not surprising, therefore, that many poets like to write near to the motion and sound of water. It's as if they have never quite lost the innocent fascination with which children gaze down into wells and pools and make their wishes there without knowing that in throwing a coin into the depths they are performing the ritual of oblation by which, through thousands of years, people made prayerful sacrifices to the gods of the underworld.

Not that it is only children who are drawn to that ritual. While I was researching this talk a friend wrote to me about how she and her brother had visited a holy well at St Finbarr's sixth-century oratory on an island in the middle of a lough in County Cork. They intended to follow the age-old practice of offering coins in oblation there. But 'when we arrived at the island, with our small silver coins ready to throw in the well,' she wrote, 'we found it defaced by a bossy notice, courtesy of the Catholic Church, saying it is forbidden to throw money into the well, instead you must donate it to the church, or words to that effect. So eschewing the desecrated well, we chose a little natural, secluded spot on the far side of the island, with a view over the lake to the mountains, which seemed to us holy, and threw our coins into the lake there. But when we looked more deeply into the water where we stood, we saw hundreds of coins! Everyone else had had the same idea.'

My friend's brother is the poet James Harpur, who celebrated both the occasion and the obstinate survival of that pagan ritual in a fine poem titled 'Gougane Barra' (in *Angels and Harvesters*):

> The mist sucks in our car to a world
> That's pure except for leaves that drop
> Like bits of flame or scraps of gold.
> We arrive just as the drizzle stops;
> The lake deepens the unpeeling hills.
>
> The pilgrim hostel has no guests.
> The chapel's closed; and at the well
> We marvel at a sign's request
> To refrain from throwing in our pence –
> As if officials could outlaw
> Whistling or smiling, song and dance.
>
> We walk beside the lake, and sure
> Enough the shallows buff a mine
> Of coins, like amber eyes of fish,
> That keep lit, and hard, the faith behind
> The spinning moment of each wish.

Many poets have been inspired by the presence of water, and what I want to suggest is the possibility that, as they sit by the waterside with their thoughts and senses attuned to preverbal frequencies, such poets enter a condition very close to that of prayer – literally so in the traditional invocation of the Muses. Sometimes the response of the water can feel startlingly oracular and I shall have more to say later about the oracular function of springs and wells. For the moment, however, I want to focus on the way that, by revealing their own dark depths while at the same time mirroring the sky across the water's surface, wells and pools seem to suggest interpenetrating worlds. When the poet's own reflection – in both senses of that word – acts as a mediator between them, a poem may emerge. Perhaps it's also the case that, when staring into a pool, each of us – poet or not – recapitulates the sudden access of consciousness which must have taken place in that primordial moment when the human face first recognised its own features mirrored in the surface of water. Though it lies far beyond memory, most of us must once have experienced a similar revelatory moment with virgin senses in the early days of infancy.

The poetic sensibility seeks to preserve the freshness of such pristine vision with particular fidelity. We can feel it at work in the poem 'Shadows in the Water' by the seventeenth-century Metaphysical poet Thomas Traherne. It's a longish poem and I won't detain you with all of it, but read these opening stanzas aloud and you may note how each rhyming couplet seems to mirror in sound the visual reflection of one world in the other:

> In unexperienc'd Infancy
> Many a sweet mistake doth ly:
> Mistake, tho false, intending tru;
> A *Seeming* somwhat more than *View*;
> That doth instruct the mind
> In things that ly behind,
> And many secrets to us show
> Which afterwards we come to know.

Thus did I by the Water's brink
Another world beneath me think;
And while the lofty spacious Skies
Reversed there abus'd mine Eys,
    I fancy'd other Feet
    Came mine to touch or meet;
As by som Puddle I did play
Another world within it lay....

'Twas strange that Peeple there should walk,
And yet I could not hear them talk:
That through a little watry Chink,
Which one dry Ox or Horse might drink.
    We other worlds should see,
    Yet not admitted be;

O ye that stand upon the Brink,
Whom I so near me, through the Chink,
With Wonder see : What Faces there,
Whose Feet, whose Bodies, do ye wear?
    I my Companions see
    In You, another Me.
They seemed Others, but are We;
Our second Selvs those Shadows be.

In its final stanza the poem draws to a profoundly imagined
Christian conclusion that mirrors in the waters the movement from
Earth to Heaven:

    ... what can it mean?
But that below the purling Stream
    Some unknown Joys there be
    Laid up in Store for me;
To which I shall, when that thin Skin
Is broken, be admitted in.

The primordial bond between the power of water and the receptive human imagination was still vitally alive inside Wordsworth when, as a grown man by the banks of the River Wye, he sensed 'A motion and a spirit, that impels / All thinking things, all objects of all thought, / And rolls through all things'. But, writing only a few decades later, the highly sensitive, agoraphobic American poet Emily Dickinson would reflect on the experience of staring into the water of a well with a less majestic sense of confidence. The title of this talk is that of her poem:

What mystery pervades a well!
That water lives so far —
A neighbor from another world
Residing in a jar

Whose limit none have ever seen,
But just his lid of glass —
Like looking every time you please
In an abyss's face!

The grass does not appear afraid,
I often wonder he
Can stand so close and look so bold
At what is awe to me.

Related somehow they may be,
The sedge stands next the sea —
Where he is floorless
And does no timidity betray

But nature is a stranger yet;
The ones that cite her most
Have never passed her haunted house,
Nor simplified her ghost.

To pity those that know her not
Is helped by the regret

That those who know her, know her less
The nearer her they get.

In the figurative language of the poem, the well-water might begin as 'a neighbour from another world', yet the face that Emily makes us see on its glassy surface is not her face or our own face, but the daunting face of an abyss. And by the fifth stanza, Nature herself is felt to be a stranger, the ghostly inhabitant of a haunted house. The end of the poem presents Nature as a finally impenetrable mystery even to those who claim to know her most closely. Among the latter, one can presume to include those analytic scientists whose perception of the natural world as merely inanimate matter ripe for exploitation would eventually create circumstances in which Ted Hughes felt compelled to write a poem titled '1984 on "The Tarka Trail"'. Appearing in the collection *River*, it's a poem in which

> The river's glutted – a bloom of plenty for algae.
> A festering olla podrida, poured slowly.
> Surfactants, ammonia, phosphates – the whole banquet
> Flushed in by sporadic thunderbursts
> But never a flood enough to scour a sewer,
> Never enough to resurrect a river;

The poem tells how the wife of the polluting farmer, asked why they use these contaminating chemicals, replies, 'But the children have to be educated.'

Indeed they do, one thinks, but surely in more life-enhancing matters than the paying of private-school fees with money earned in ways that damage and contaminate the natural environment. The poem goes on to reflect how the ancient name of the river's deity was never netted by map or Latin: '*Taw* meant simply *water*.' But, now, Hughes ends,

> she truly can be called Sewer.
> (More truly: The Washer at the Ford.
> As in the old story.
> The death-rags that she washes and washes are ours).

In the rage with which it invokes a powerful motif from an all but vanished mythology, the verse trembles with an agonised sense of purity defiled. Few of us can articulate our responses with such accuracy and power, but it's not just an expedient feeling of anger and disgust which leaves us recoiling in horror from the effects of such pollution: by invoking the archetypal figure of Death, the poet insists that we feel an incipient sense of panic and mortal terror about the way a wrong-headed relationship to the natural order is threatening the primary source of life itself. In so doing he seeks to stir to more active life inside us a residual germ of feeling for that which is truly sacred.

Reflecting on the power of metaphor that Wordsworth found in water while writing his poetical autobiography, *The Prelude*, Gaston Bachelard asks in *Poetic Imagination and Reverie*, 'Could one truly describe a past without images of depth? And could one ever have an image of *full depth* if one had never meditated at the edge of a deep lake?' When he immediately goes on to assert that 'our soul's past is a deep water', Bachelard invokes an anagogical language such as Jesus Christ once used – a language in which the word 'water' speaks literally of the living liquid but also of a deeper, more fugitive meaning that it seems to carry.

On a hillside near where I live, a drinking fountain is inscribed with this utterance from Christ: 'Whosoever drinketh of this water shall thirst again; but whosoever drinketh of the water that I shall give him shall never thirst; but the water I shall give him shall be in him a well of water springing up into everlasting life.' Clearly there has been a poetical shift in the meaning of the word 'water' in this sentence, just as the word 'life' is not used in its ordinary sense. The inscription may reminds us of what Christ said to Nicodemus: 'Except a man be born of water and the spirit, he cannot enter into the kingdom of God.'

If we try to stay with the literal meaning of 'water' in either utterance we can make little sense of it. Yet if we think about water imaginatively, savouring its qualities of simple clarity and transparency, its kinship to light, and its capacity as the primary engendering medium of all life as well as the element essential for its survival, we begin to appreciate its relationship to *truth*. Not the literal truth of fact which merely tells us that water consists of hydrogen and oxygen, but spiritual or poetic truth. Truth that can irrigate our life with a vital sense of meaning. When the poet Keats spoke of this he called it the 'Truth of Imagination'.

The use of language in this esoteric way is far older than the time of Christ. There is a very ancient tradition that associates water with prophetic or oracular powers – that is with access to the kind of knowledge that is not readily available to the unassisted capacities of the reasoning intellect. Surely an intimation of those powers inspired the self-confessed sense of awe which drove Emily Dickinson to wonder, 'What mystery pervades a well?' Had she been familiar with the Chinese *Book of Changes* – the *I Ching* – she would have found in Hexagram 48 a coherent answer to her question.

That book of wisdom is at least three thousand years old and can still be profitably consulted for advice by the apparently random process of dropping three coins six times. According to the fall of the coins the person seeking guidance from the oracle builds a column of six lines corresponding to the structure of one of sixty-four possible hexagrams, each of which manifests a different, particular pattern of yin or yang energy. The book's commentaries on the indicated pattern, and the often startling relevance of the response it gives to the question asked, is experiential evidence that, far from being random, the process of consultation is governed by the principle of meaningful synchronicity. For over fifty years now I have consulted the *I Ching* at times of difficulty or uncertainty and it has proved to be a constant source of increased self-knowledge and a reliable guide to appropriate action.

The oracle can also be approached by counting yarrow stalks but I have chosen to speak about the use of dropped coins because of its close kinship to the offerings traditionally made to a well. Hexagram 48, to which I referred, is actually named Ching, which in this context means 'a well', and there is a sense in which it resumes the character of the entire book as a source of life-giving nourishment – one that makes inner truth accessible to all who draw from it.

A well is a controlled natural spring, a man-made construct to link the upper world to the underworld, which can only be built through an act of collaboration between human hands and the natural forces at work in particular places. So the hexagram states that 'the town may be changed but the well may not be changed', which is to say that, though the circumstances of human life may change over time, they remain dependent on deep unchanging sources that are not of our creation. The hexagram also warns us that if the rope lowering the jug does not reach far enough, or if the jug itself is broken, then misfortune will result. The deeper significance of what might otherwise seem a statement of the obvious becomes apparent when one recognises the well as a metaphor of the relationship between the conscious and the unconscious minds.

Whatever the particular character of the culture we inhabit, the fundamentals of human life are constant and unchanging everywhere, whether we are speaking of our common biological nature or – which is much the same thing – of the deep archetypal structure of the human mind. The town may be changed but the well may not be changed. To become more fully human and stay in creative touch with the natural order on which our lives depend, the hexagram advises us that we need to keep our inner well clear and free from mud, to make sure that it is strongly lined, and to be resolute in drawing *deeply* enough on the mysterious sources of truth and wisdom – those mysteries which, in Dickinson's words, pervade a well and are always available if we approach them in the proper spirit.

Now all of that is easily said, but not at all easily done. The commentaries on the six lines of the hexagram seem to indicate six different levels in the unconscious mind, but in only three of those lines is the enlivening and enlightening power of water available for use, and in one of them (line 3), even though the well is cleaned and clear, no one drinks from it. By and large, we live in a time when the well of sacred wisdom goes unused. Perhaps that's not surprising in a world as dizzily centrifugal as the one we have created around us, a world that has largely lost fluent contact with the intelligence of the natural world, and where the very idea of spiritual meaning is subject to sceptical interrogation, and often enough to brisk cynical dismissal.

We can see the consequences of this exposed in the contrast between ancient and modern Egypt. In ancient times, as one of the children of Geb the Earth and Nut the Sky, the goddess Isis had in her charge the rain and dew and all the wet places of the earth, and no seed could germinate or plant grow without her care. In particular, she was associated with the life-giving properties of the River Nile. The beautiful myth that tells of the loss and recovery of her brother-husband Osiris, whose inert body Isis moistened with her tears, dramatises not only the people's relationship to the seasonal ebb and flow of the Nile but also a parallel inward process of spiritual renewal.

Isis is no longer revered in Egypt and it seems she still has cause to weep. Dammed to generate hydroelectric power, the Nile no longer floods. Dense clusters of water lilies are kept in check only by the use of herbicides that have poisoned several species of fish. The crocodiles and hippos are almost gone, papyrus cannot thrive, and corrosive salt deposits are no longer washed away. Instead they blight once fertile land, while the build-up of silt on the bed of Lake Nasser impairs the efficiency of the Aswan Dam. Meanwhile nearly three-quarters of the energy the dam generates is used to produce chemical fertilisers to replace the natural sources of increase that once came free with the annual inundation.

The further irony is that the mystery rites of Isis were designed to educate the souls of initiates in ways that aligned their lives with the regenerative processes of nature. Around two thousand years ago the capacity of those rites to dissolve the ego's lust for power so that a more sensitive receptive spirit could be brought to rebirth was dramatised in entertaining ways by such prose romances as the *Metamorphoses* of Apuleius, which is a powerful work of the initiatory imagination.

In an earlier essay, 'Imagining Otherwise' (see pages 10–29), I showed how, in my writing classes, I ask my students to imagine the Imagination by visualising two overlapping circles, one representing the world around them and the other their personal inner world. I draw their attention to the almond-shaped area of overlap (the 'mandorla') as the place where the inner world negotiates with intelligence coming from the outer world about the nature of what feels true and real. For me, the place of the mandorla is the house of Imagination, and the aim is to keep the area of overlap wide enough to encompass as much as possible of the sometimes contradictory and often ambiguous intelligence beaming from both directions. The interaction between them reminds me that both I and the world are porous to the imagination, and therefore both can be transformed.

The almond-shaped space is a very ancient symbol indeed and goes by many names. Originally it spoke of the meeting between Heaven and Earth from which all life was generated, and for that reason it became the ground plan for many sacred sites. The ground plan of abbey at Glastonbury was laid to the design of the overlapping circles, and you can see the symbol elegantly cast in iron as a pattern on the lid to the Chalice Well in the garden at the foot of the Tor. The chalybeate spring that fills that well has long been one of Britain's most sacred springs, and the enclosing symbol of the mandorla seems to hold its Christian associations (as the Vesica Piscis) in creative tension with its ancient pagan origins. It is, you might say, a vivid and graphic image of the mystery that pervades the well.

Mystery rites associated with the oracular and healing powers of water were common throughout the classical world. Long before Apollo came to Delphi, the Earth Goddess Ge or Gaia had her sanctuary there; her oracle, the Pythia, was required to drink from the spring of Cassotis and to bathe in the Castalian Spring before she could make her prophetic utterances. Pausanias writes of another spring in the sanctuary of Demeter at Patras where the sick consulted the goddess. He tells how a mirror was attached to a string, then lowered so that it skimmed the surface of the water without breaking it. The oracle would be revealed by gazing into the mirror. Other ancient texts tell us how, in the temple of Apollo at Claros, the divinatory priest descended by night along a twisting path into the adyton, an underground chamber where he would drink from the spring and then deliver the oracular judgment. So, whereas the oracle at Patras read the depths in the catoptric meeting of the mirror's surface with that of the pool, the oracle at Claros seems to insist that the depths have to be *entered* for the truth to be found. That descent must hark back to the ritual descent by the earliest peoples into the underground sanctuaries formed by the passage of water in primordial times; but this mode of divination found its most complete expression in Virgil's description of the descent to the underworld of Avernus which was made by Aeneas under the guidance of the Cumaean Sibyl.

You may already be familiar with Virgil's account of that dreadful journey, and may have made the same assumption as generations of classical scholars did: that it is just an astonishing achievement of the poetic imagination. But the brave archaeological researches carried out in the 1960s by Paget and Jones along the sulphurous tunnels of the Phlegrean Fields around Cumae in Italy have shown that an actual Oracle of the Dead was located there, and that a well-established ritual process conducted pilgrims one at a time down into the underworld of Hades, where they were ferried over the River Styx by boat to consult the spirits of the ancestors as Aeneas did in Virgil's great poem of his story.

The point is that Hades existed and that it was possible to go there. Although, as the Sibyl long ago warned Aeneas, the way down into Hades may be easy – the door stands open night and day – the problem is how to find one's way back out again. Nor was the site at Cumae the only entrance. Almost as famous was the Oracle of Trophonius at Lebadeia in Greece. Both sites were characterised by the building above ground of a circular temple or 'tholos' similar to the one that once stood at the shrine of Gaia at Delphi and at the temple of Aesculapius at Epidauros. The remains of such temples are found mostly in the Eastern Mediterranean, but there is one notable exception. It once stood above the hot springs at Bath, where the geothermal waters that fell as rain on the Mendips ten thousand years ago still rise through the hot fissures of the earth deep beneath us.

We know that the site was held sacred to the goddess Sulis long before the Romans came and built their complex of temples and bathhouse buildings above and around what was once a vaporous, marshy source of water rising from the underworld. We know that the hot spring was used for divinatory purposes and that it was seen as a source of wisdom and power that might be made available for the guidance of human beings and the fulfilment of their sometimes kindly, sometimes malevolent, wishes. We know that the name of the goddess revered here was related to the word 'Suil', which in both Welsh and Old Irish means an orifice or gap, carrying the same association of meanings that cluster around the Egyptian hieroglyph 'Ru', which means 'the vulva' and 'a secret entrance to a sacred place' and is depicted in the form of a mandorla. We also know that among the monuments the Romans built above her sanctuary was a tholos. In his official guide to the Roman Baths, the archaeologist Barry Cunliffe makes an intriguing comment on this building. 'Circular temples of this kind are exceedingly rare in the western Roman provinces since the idea was originally Greek,' he says. 'Could it be that the Emperor Hadrian – who loved Greek culture – set up the *tholos* at Bath when he visited the province in the early 2nd Century? The idea is attractive,' he concludes, 'but must remain at present unproven. The *tholos* is still very much a mystery.'

My imagination is much drawn to whatever pervades such mysteries, and there is another idea too that it finds attractive. At Delphi, Lebadeia, and Epidaurus, oracular centres all, the tholos seems to mark an entrance to the underworld realm, the home of the midnight sun, and the secret source of light and wisdom. Is it possible that the tholos at Bath was built over such an entrance and that by means of it one might have made a ritual journey down to the underworld of Hades or Annwn, as the Celts called it – the nearby kingdom of the dead where one could consult the ancestors as people did at other geothermal sanctuaries? There is probably no way we will ever know, since the most likely site for the tholos has long lain beneath the west front of the abbey – intriguingly where the font stands, that symbolic sacred spring where new life is baptised into the Christian community.

I have more to say about the nature of the Hades journey in another essay (see pages 235–48); right now, it's enough to point out that its purpose was the transformation of consciousness and that water played a vital role in its rites. At Cumae they would be preceded by ritual baths, first in the Waters of Forgetfulness to cleanse the body of the world, then in the Waters of Memory so that pilgrims might recall the visions they were to be shown; and at Lebadeia water was drunk from springs with those names. Once the underworld was entered via a cleft beneath the tholos, pilgrims would be ferried across a river to the inmost sanctuary where they were sprinkled with holy water before coming into the presence of the oracular shades of the dead. As in the Christian rite of baptism, this encounter with water was a symbolic cleansing, a figurative death even, from which the initiate rose transformed and reborn. Properly conducted, the rite would have been a fearful experience, designed to induce a watery dissolution of the hardened ego so that the soul could emerge more attuned to the cycles of death and regeneration which are the mysterious ways through which life renews itself. That such rites were once powerfully effective we can gather from the high esteem in which the mysteries were held by Socrates and Cicero.

But what does all this arcane lore have to do with us today at a time when women still have to carry pans of water through the killing droughts of the Sahel and wars may soon be fought over water in the Middle East and elsewhere? Can these ancient rites possibly have any bearing on the current planetary crisis? My answer is that it very much depends how we use our imagination in relation to them. We are free to dismiss such ancient water mysteries as the deluded superstitions of a more credulous age, but a more open-minded response might be to psychologise them – to read the Hades journey as a metaphor of the arduous effort to confront the darkness of the unconscious mind and make what lies there available for greater consciousness. Then we may recall that those journeys were actually made, that the force of the word was literal as well as a symbolic, that wisdom was sought in the deeps of the earth at particular geothermal places. So it's possible that oracular insight is not the product of the human mind alone, but of its receptive relationship to the intelligence of the earth itself?

Certainly Wordsworth intuited as much. In *The Prelude* he wrote of 'unknown modes of being' in the Lakeland landscape that educated his poetic imagination. Such a vision is not so far from the ancient Sibyl's declaration that 'the great Divine commands me to speak, and my words pour out, perfect and purposeful, once they are put into my mind'. Perhaps through the fine tuning of their receptive sensibility, both poet and prophetess became instruments by which Nature could become more articulately intelligible to itself. Perhaps by responding to the natural world with the insight of the fully activated imagination they allowed its deeper reality to emerge and irrigate people's lives with meaning.

In a piece called 'Hearing the Voice' (pages 232–4), I show how the Gaia principle and the emergence of ecopsychology indicate a growing attentiveness to the earth as an intelligent, animate self-regulating system of which we humans are a part. There is a case to be made that, in our unbalanced condition, we are being called by the voice of the earth, whether we choose to heed it or not. It's a voice that can be heard most fluently in the sound of water, and our decent survival as a species may depend on our readiness to respond. Such thoughts bring the Western imagination close to the Chinese concept of Tao, which is known as the 'Way of Water'. 'Those on the Way of Tao', says Lao Tzu, 'like water need to accept where they find themselves; and that may often be where water goes – to the lowest places.' The world's dominant culture doesn't think this way. It cares more for growth than for depth; it has its mind less on origins than on the next thing. And it would be foolish to pretend that the Gaian vision is an easy stance to maintain, for it brings us up against both our individual fears and ambitions and those collective human forces which insistently push us in other directions. So it will require enormous shifts of perspective for such a vision to prevail. The stakes are already high, and it may be that such change can come about only through undergoing the ordeals of a transforming experience. But it begins in the imagination, which is the hotline of communication between the soul of the earth and the receptive human soul.

In the prose and verse I write I try to keep my imagination attuned to the sound and rhythms of water. The water's surface glitters as it passes over stones and yet draws the gaze down into the deeps beneath. My novel *The Water Theatre* was partly inspired by the Springs of Clitumnus in Umbria, which were famous for their oracular powers in ancient times. Folklore still tells us that a person who gazes into those waters will see not merely their outward appearance reflected there, but their own essential nature. When I visited the springs I found that rumour to be astonishingly true. A somewhat fictionalised account of what happened on that day can be found in *The Water Theatre*. But perhaps what they say of the Springs of Clitumnus holds true for living water everywhere, and if that is the case then we never have to look far to confront the mystery that pervades a well.

# Hermes the Disrupter

An edited version of a talk delivered at the Bath Royal and Scientific and Literary Institute in 2017 under the title 'A Dance with Hermes'. My poem sequence *A Dance with Hermes* was published by Awen in 2016.

The plan for this evening was to talk about Hermes as the archetype of the imagination and the poetic basis of mind; but life, as they say, is what happens while you're making other plans, and I've recently found myself also thinking about some surprising and convulsive events that have affected all our lives. Consider, for instance, how sudden panic on the trading floors of the world's casino shook our faith in the banks in 2008 and dragged most of us into austerity. Consider how, more recently, one prime minister, confident that the British public would share his considered opinion, submitted the country to a referendum on its future only to be ambushed by an unanticipated result, while his successor, assured by the polls that she was about to ride a landslide, found her 'strong and stable' government returned with a weakened and shaky grip on power. Not long afterwards a brash, much-bankrupted, morally dubious TV celebrity with little understanding of either world affairs or the difference between truth and narcissistic fantasy, out-trumped all the constitutional checks, balances, and presidential expectations of the USA to find himself in the White House, happily prepared to admit on Fox News that he would not be there were it not for Twitter.

In that respect he was the beneficiary of a very recent, seemingly unstoppable process of technological change so breathtakingly accelerated that it seems to demand constant updates to our brain cells. Yes, it has gifted us with new, more fluent and convenient means of communication and transformed our daily activities in helpful ways, but it is also confusing and addictive, and has opened our private affairs to the risks of hacking, leaks, cyber-theft, and scams. Moreover, alarmed by the algorithmic power of their own inventions, experts in the development of artificial intelligence now warn us that it carries a more serious threat to our future than the newly returned shadow of nuclear war.

Meanwhile, under the pressures of climate change, poverty, starvation, and conflict, much of the world is on the move, from the land into the cities, from country to country, from continent to continent. And even as we witness the largest event of migration in human history the planetary environment is itself suffering from such exploitative abuse that one of our most respected intellectuals, Stephen Hawking, recommends that, if our species is to survive at all, it's high time we make serious plans for moving house to some other world.

In such times it may seem a trivial exercise to discuss the nature and activity of an ancient, somewhat disreputable god once revered by an extinct religion. But you may already have spotted that over each of the contexts I have just outlined – trade, politics and diplomacy, messaging, technical invention, travel, theft, scams, and above all the disruption of conventional assumptions – the ancients considered Hermes to be the presiding deity. It's the contention of this talk that, behind those and other important matters, that slippery god is still alive and active among us and that if we are wise we will stay alert and respectful to what he may be saying to us through all this convulsive activity.

Let me go further and suggest that it's precisely because we have been negligent in that respect that he is now making his sometimes discomforting presence felt everywhere– in the political and technological worlds, in the news (fake or otherwise), through our social media, and perhaps also in the sudden hazards and challenges we encounter in personal life, along with occasional, equally unexpected, coincidental sources of guidance and help.

Now I'm well aware that, between the strict intellectual scepticism of materialist thought, on the one hand, and the impassioned fervour of fundamentalist religious belief, on the other, there is a widespread problem these days with the whole idea of 'gods', or even of a single 'God', so before going any further I should try to clarify my use of the word.

In doing so, I may face some difficulty because the information-based mode of education that most of us have endured leaves us more inclined to read things literally than to be open to their metaphorical significance, and such literalism is further complicated by the dogmatic assumptions of monotheistic religions of the Book. It seems to me that, in some respects, the polytheistic vision of the ancient Greek world was subtler and wider in its reach than any single god can be, and more responsive to the complexity of lived experience. While recognising the mind of Zeus as an over-arching universal godhead, that vision acknowledged a wide range of other deities that are divine and immortal because their impersonal powers are manifestly present and active in the life of every generation – though it may be more accurate to say that they are active in every generation because they are divine and immortal.

The classical world recognised such powers as Love and War and Wisdom in the form of immortal deities because they do not change over time. But what may change and – as culture evolves – *must* change is our perception of those gods and the manner in which we relate to them. Thus today, in the light of analytic psychology (which drew much of its inspiration from classical mythology), we can view the gods as aspects of the archetypal structure of the human mind. To use a contemporary metaphor, we might think of such archetypes as the software with which we all come issued at birth – that which structures the unconscious mind and may be considered instinctual; or – to put it another way – as those innate and available sources of psychic energy with which we have to make a conscious relationship if their impersonal power is not to overwhelm us.

I should add that the software metaphor feels inadequate in that it fails to do justice to what I take to be the essentially sacred dimensions of our experience, and when I speak of Hermes as a god I'm referring to a sacred, noumenal idea and energy that is irrepressibly alive in both our personal and our public worlds today, and is demanding recognition.

By now any sceptics among you may be recalling that such credentials as I have for giving this talk are those of a novelist – a writer who uses imagination to create credible fictions – and you will be aware that novelists conjure their stories into the reader's imagination by a process much akin to that of smoke and mirrors. So if what I have to offer this evening strikes you as closer to that sort of thing than to the hard coin of intellectual discourse, then it may be because there is something necessarily elusive about the duplicitous god Hermes, but it could also be because I'm hoping to speak less to your intellect than to your imagination. I shall be doing that in part by reading a few short poems from the playful, somewhat irreverent sequence called *A Dance with Hermes* which took me by surprise not very long ago; so at this point it might be helpful to describe the manner in which the god entered my own life and freed me to write verse again.

In the closing months of a terminal illness, my friend the poet, novelist, and painter John Moat completed an extraordinary memoir titled *Anyway* ... It's a moving, often funny, always beautifully worded account of a life lived in service of the Imagination, which he equated, metaphorically speaking, with the creative activity of the wing-heeled god. In one form or another, Hermes presided over much of John's life through coincidence after productive coincidence, journey after journey, improbable meeting after meeting, throughout all of his seventy-eight years – including the magically charmed set of circumstances that led to the foundation and growth of the magnificently successful Arvon writing courses, which have been and continue to be, in my opinion, one of this Britain's most liberating experiments in adult education.

As a result of those experiences, John conceived of the Imagination as a force much larger than our human share in it – a powerful, inventive life-energy with an intentionality of its own capable of shaping the lives of individuals, of communities, and even of the time itself – the zeitgeist. For John, Hermes was the archetype of the Imagination, and so engagingly was that mysterious figure conjured in his memoir that, when I wrote to him about it, I felt impelled to write a poem on the theme. I included it with the letter and John rang me shortly afterwards saying, 'Hmm, that looks like the start of something new!'

As difficult personal circumstances had blocked my own imaginative

life for a considerable time, I thought to myself, 'Hmm, if only …'
But blow me if Hermes didn't enter the house a couple of days later,
leaving another poem in his wake. Then another, and another, piling
up like stones on a cairn, until I had forty of them looking back at
me, all written in the space of as many days.

I think of them as what the Greeks called a 'hermaion', a gift
from Hermes – what we would call a 'godsend'. Here, as a general
introduction, is the first:

> The work begins and ends with him: the sly
> light-fingered god of crossways, transit,
> emails and exchange, the wing-heeled, shifty,
> wheeler-dealing go-between, who'll slip right
>
> through your fingers if you try to pin
> him down. For he is labile, street-wise
> and trans-everything. He is the one
> two-fold hermaphrodite who'll rise
>
> up sprightly from the earth and turn to air,
> and then descend into the underworld
> to point his wand at philosophic gold.
> You'll find him anywhere and nowhere,
>
> ever the unexpected messenger, who sends
> you glimpses of the wet fire and the lit dark
> in the loded stone. With him the magic work,
> of which one may not speak, begins and ends.

Any of you familiar with alchemy will have noted how the poem
conflates attributes of the Greek Hermes with those of Mercurius
Duplex, the spirit presiding over the alchemical operation that rec-
onciles and transforms conflicting elements into the Stone of the
Philosophers. In that spirit the poem also employs anachronistic
references and colloquialisms. It's composed in four quatrains held
together by the regular use of half-rhymes to suggest the elusive nature of the god – something almost grasped but not quite – with

occasional full rhymes echoing on his presence. The format of that poem recurred in those which followed hot on its winged heels almost by dictation.

As I've already indicated, those poems came thick and fast, trotting out what they had to say with a kind of nonchalant jollity and verve that felt different from the characteristically earnest and sober note of almost all my previous writing. So breezily did they tip me out of what had been a gloomy state of creative arrest that the experience of finding myself appointed as midwife for their delivery left me convinced that, for all our attempts to understand the process of creativity, it remains deeply mysterious. I sensed immediately that it had something to do with the unpredictable nature of Hermes himself – the god whom Jung had identified as the archetype of the unconscious mind, and whom John Moat regarded as the inventive spirit of the Imagination. So the fact that Hermes was speaking to me through the medium of verse – a form to which I had lost hope of ever finding fluent access – left me thinking about the god in relation to poetry and language and to the nature of mind itself.

Those themes are brought together in a phrase that had already intrigued me for some time – 'the poetic basis of mind'. The phrase is not mine, of course. In a manner typical of Hermes, it's a theft, lifted from the archetypal psychologist James Hillman, whose wise post-Jungian imagination insisted on the primacy of images over concepts as a means of relating to the operations of the soul, and on mythology and the arts as the primary guides to those operations. He used the word 'mind' because it encompasses both waking consciousness and the work of the unconscious, which is structured around those archetypes which we can only perceive as images – such as those which appear in our dreams, and in the myths of the Olympian gods and similar figures who display their powers through the colourful stories told about them as the imaginative basis of culture worldwide. Hermes, for instance, has close relations in the Yoruba trickster god Eshu, in the Navajo figure of Coyote, in the Chinese Monkey King, in the daimonic Papa Legba of Voodoo culture, and in the disruptive figure of Loki in Norse mythology.

But what about consciousness? We all have a sense of what it means to be conscious, and yet consciousness is notoriously difficult to define. So difficult that in the *Macmillan Dictionary of Psychology*, Stuart Sutherland wrote, 'Consciousness is a fascinating but elusive phenomenon. It is impossible to specify what it is, what it does, or why it has evolved. Nothing worth reading has been written about it.' I'm inclined to agree with that blithe assessment, perhaps because whenever I try to read the work of such formidable thinking types as Daniel Dennett and Stephen Pinker on the subject, I'm left feeling that I'm drowning in my own shallows. After a time I begin to sense Hermes behind me whispering that the efforts of a mind consciously seeking to describe the nature of consciousness much resemble those of a man trying to examine the back of his own head by turning it round to look in a mirror.

Yet doesn't Sutherland's phrase 'fascinating but elusive phenomenon' have more than a hint of Hermes about it? If I use my imagination I can begin to see the cranium as a kind of crystal ball inside which a whole galaxy of neurons ceaselessly flash and sparkle as they transmit messages across the synapses at quantum speed, constantly trading images, energy, and information over the porous boundary between the conscious and unconscious minds. And then I think of Hermes, the messenger god of thresholds and trade, travelling about his business of negotiation and exchange between our human world and the world of the gods, the upper world and the underworld. Hermes – a god with so many attributes and functions that he incarnates in his own polytropic character the subtle polytheistic nature of the whole archetypal pantheon that the Greeks placed on Mount Olympus but that we have come to see are deities who, as William Blake once put it, 'reside in the human breast'.

Such changes of perspective seem to reflect evolutionary shifts in the inflections of our consciousness and we can see them already happening in the way that the ancient perception of the god Hermes evolved and changed over the course of hundreds of years. So let's take a closer look at him.

We might start by considering a few of his many splendid praise names.

Among a thesaurus of other titles, he was known to the ancient Greeks as Angelos Athanaton, messenger of the deathless gods; as Diaktoros, a guide; as Agathopoios, he who makes good, meaning 'fertile'; as Khrysorrhapis, the golden-wanded one, referring to his staff, the kerykeion or caduceus, which brings about magical transformations and is thus a powerful emblem of the imagination. He was Psithyristis, the whisperer, referring to the inwardly mentoring voice of the daimon. He was Eriounes, bringer of luck, and as Psychopompos he was present at every death, ready to lead the soul across the asphodel fields into the underworld kingdom of Hades.

These are all attributes of the Hermes who was, among all the gods, the friendliest to men. But the Greeks were also well aware of his untrustworthy shadow side. To address him as Mekhaniotes, the contriver, was to praise his ingenuity, but it also carried a wary recognition of his trickster cunning; so he was also known as Polytropos, meaning 'shifty', and as Pheletes – a thief – and Klepsiphron, a trickster and deceiver. Despite all these disreputable tendencies, perhaps even because of them, he occupied a special place in the hearts of the Greeks, who also knew him affectionately as Koinos Hermes, the ordinary or commonplace god, the god who was to be found everywhere.

Etymologically, the name Hermes has been translated as 'the god of the stone pile', and among the most ancient images of him was the herma – a heap of stones placed as a boundary marker, or as a way-sign indicating a nearby spring, or at a crossroads, where, as many stories tell us, strange, life-altering events are prone to happen. Hikers and climbers still add herm-stones to cairns, but there is an essential ambiguity in the nature of this god of the stone pile. He may be there as a guide across difficult terrain but he may also, for reasons of his own, choose to lead us astray. Some of you may already have taken a wrong turn on a journey only for something to happen which turned out to be more interesting and engaging than the route you had planned.

In ancient times, as the image of Hermes evolved, instead of a stone pile a monolith stood in some terminal places, and eventually a bearded head was added to the standing stone, and out of its limbless pillar was thrust a vigorously erect penis. Here was Hermes demonstrating his power as a god of fertility, an ithyphallic alpha male, formidably guarding his flocks and herds beside the life-giving feminine presence of a spring. In places where the herma marked that liminal space which is a boundary between territories, people would have made a market for the exchange of goods, either using the silent trade or through interpreted languages. Human nature being what it is, this custom would have supplied ample scope for theft and swindling, and, along with the ability to cross marked boundaries, the business of trade and exchange, the complexities of language and the need for go-betweens, and a talent for opportunist sexuality, many other aspects of the god would have manifested there. As they still do, of course, on a larger scale in the busy marketplaces and international trade fairs of the commercial world.

Writing on the theme in his *Cratylus* dialogue, Plato said, 'I should imagine that the name *Hermes* has to do with speech, and signifies that he is the interpreter or messenger, or thief, or liar, or bargainer: all of that sort of thing has a great deal to do with language.' The etymology is dubious but the myths credit Hermes with the invention of language and we know what that led to. Here's a poem called 'He Giveth Tongue':

> Surely it takes a god this versatile
> to dream up language? He must have watched
> dumb mortals grunt and point before he matched
> their daily needs with eloquence and style
>
> by putting words into their mouths. And then
> all babel was let loose. Once taught to speak
> the glib ones found innumerable ways to tweak
> the truth of things, as poets and liars, admen,
>
> lawyers, politicians, journos, novelists.
> And just to complicate the case, Hermes
> invented polyglottal possibilities to tease
> the world into confusion. Still he broadcasts
>
> means of fabulation: he's the SIM card in your phone,
> your satnav's voice, your texts and Twitter, webcam,
> broadband fount of knowledge and the source of spam …
> and he'll still be laughing when all's said and done.

I'll say more about his relation to language later, but for the moment the point I want to make is that Hermes entered the Homeric world of the Olympian gods – the world in which he is most familiar to us – bringing with him deep-rooted associations and attributes from a far earlier age.

The story of his debut among the Olympian gods is beautifully told in the Homeric Hymn to Hermes, which was composed not by Homer but by the Boeotian school of peasant poets around the seventh century B.C.E. The *Iliad* and the *Odyssey*, both featuring Hermes, were composed around a hundred years before that, and the first surviving mention of him can be traced right back to the Linear B tablets scribed about 1000 B.C.E. Yet Hermes appears in the hymn to his name not as a wise old man of great age, but as a newborn babe, a love child sired by Sky-Father Zeus on the shy nymph Maia where she lived in seclusion from the world in a cave on Mount Kyllene in Arcadia. So Hermes arrives as something new – a baby, yes, but a baby who lay in his mother's womb for ten months and emerged with extraordinary powers.

We know that the Hymn to Hermes was composed at a time of rapid social change when the power of the age-old agrarian regime of tribal kingdoms was weakening and a new urban merchant class was on the rise with ambitions to institute a more democratic form of government. So, it's as if in the Hymn's retelling of the story of Hermes an urgently felt need for a new perspective on the god had burst through into the Greek imagination and found expression. What it celebrates is a disruptive rebirth of his subversive energy in more nuanced form. If you wish to pursue the theme, Jules Cashford gives us a graceful translation of the Hymn to Hermes in *The Homeric Hymns*, published by Penguin Classics. I try to explore that radical impulse of renewal in a sequence of short narrative poems that are somewhat coarser. They begin with an account of his conception and birth, and of his precocious first flight across Arcadia when he discovers a tortoise:

> A light-bulb moment this! He picks it up,
> admires the polished pattern on its shell,

then scoops the creature out. This will
become his Stratocaster once he's cut

some strings and tuned them with a pick.
A bit more work. He plucks a note and likes
the sound. The tortoise sings. He strikes
a chord, sets generations dancing at the trick.

The moment related in those stanzas dramatises a primary creative gesture of the Imagination. Where others may have seen only
the shell of a tortoise, Hermes has seen the shape of a lyre and the
thought resonates in his mind as the possibility of music. It is a fine
example of that 'double vision' – the simultaneous apprehension of
both literal fact and transformative insight – which William Blake
saw as the essence of imaginative energy. Having invented the lyre,
Hermes immediately goes on to sing a song in praise of his father,
his mother, and his home. He does it, says the Hymn, in the same
way that 'a quick thought darts through the heart of man'. We have
already seen that this extraordinary, ordinary god was credited with
inventing language; now we hear him singing the very first song,
which means that in the same creative moment he invented poetry
too.

The lyre and poetry are often associated with Phoebus Apollo,
the god who was Hermes' elder brother, but the Hymn to Hermes
assures us that their origin does not lie with the Apollonian archetype. According to the vision from which the Hymn springs, music
and song, language and poetry were all primary acts of the *Hermetic*
imagination.

Language is the means by which we human beings are able to
create the rich variety of cultural worlds that are distinct from, if
finally dependent upon, the received world of the natural order. It's
the means by which we name our feelings and, by articulating our
thoughts, ascribe meaning and value to them. So if the myth of
Hermes offers a metaphorical truth, and this ability can be traced
back to his gift of poetry, then might we possibly learn something by
looking to the figure of Hermes for illumination of what could be
meant by the poetic basis of mind?

Let's try for a moment to consider the nature of poetry and what it does. Following the thoughts of Ingmar Bergman, the best definition I've been able to come up with is that poetry is a musical form of language which speaks in images *from* the soul *to* the soul through the senses, and it does so  in a manner that subtly resists the ego's intellectual efforts to remain in control. John Middleton Murray, a friend of D.H. Lawrence, once suggested that a poem communicates a truth so mysterious that it can only be uttered in that precise pattern of words. Poetry cannot be paraphrased or explained without loss of that truth because images, music, and experience are inseparable there. Something powerful, something with the transformative effect of a magical spell, is happening as we write a true poem or read one aloud. There is a kind of virginity to the openness of that experience which makes me wonder whether we might be most conscious when we are least *self*-conscious. It leaves me pondering the impact of what Emerson might have meant when he said that 'language is fossil poetry' – a metaphor implying that poetry is prior to the prosaic use of language.

Thoughts related to that idea were explored in Owen Barfield's remarkable book *Poetic Diction*. Barfield was one of the Oxford Inklings group along with Tolkien, C.S. Lewis, and Charles Williams, and he's a philosopher who should be better known for his use of linguistic and mythographic evidence to advance an evolutionary theory of consciousness. He suggests that consciousness began in the age of what he called 'Original Participation' – that time when human beings had no sense of their separate existence outside what was experienced as the seamless unity of being which is the Soul of the World. We entered the state of Withdrawn Participation once self-consciousness emerged and, with it, the capacity to objectify the world outside ourselves. Our power over what was now viewed merely as inanimate matter swiftly expanded through the application of rational analysis. In consequence we found ourselves estranged in a universe devoid of meaning because meaning was now confined inside our clever heads. Barfield believed that the next stage – and it may be one we are already entering – is that of Final Participation, in which a new relationship opens up between the evolved human soul and the Soul of the World, and the analytic powers derived from separated consciousness are reunited with the sense of our inseparable involvement in the entirety of being.

Barfield traced the origins of language to the era of Original Participation, the mythological age in which, as Blake declared, 'The ancient Poets animated all sensible objects with Gods or geniuses, calling them by the names and adorning them with the properties of woods, rivers, mountains, lakes … and whatever their enlarged and numerous senses could perceive' – senses that, he says in another context, 'discover'd the infinite in everything'.

In thinking about language, Barfield explored the evolution of certain words by tracing their roots into that mythic sensibility of our early ancestors. He showed for instance, how the words 'breath', 'wind', and 'spirit', which belong for us to separate categories were all, for the ancient Greeks, expressed by the single unifying word 'pneuma', which acknowledges no distinction between them. This was not a matter of analogy, but of identity, and so the word, by holding together what we have come to consider as separate referents, enacts in microcosm what was originally experienced as the primordial unity of things.

For me such a unified sensibility is beautifully illustrated in that moment of the Hymn when infant Hermes breaks into song as quickly as 'a swift thought darts through the heart of man'. Language has sprung to life in him, flowing from the immediacy of his fresh experience. When sensitively read aloud, the Hymn can work on us today with the same poetic force.

Why does any of this matter? Perhaps because it suggests that the poetic basis of mind, as dramatised by the Hermes archetype, has a significant bearing on our efforts, in these transitional times, to evolve a fresh mode of consciousness – a *trans*rational mode that, without demeaning all the knowledge that has been gained through the rational intellect, puts the human soul into closer, more responsive relationship to the living Soul of the World.

Yet we should remember too that the figure of Hermes is subversive, and we should certainly be wary of thinking about him in monotheistic terms. He is just one among the gods, and maybe his unruly impudence as a liar and thief was the most effective way to make his presence felt in their divine company. So we might consider his arrival among the gods to be a witty, corrective challenge to the dignified Olympian pantheon in much the same way that a provocative impulse of the unconscious mind can subvert what might have grown too rational and authoritative, perhaps even boring, in the prevailing conscious order. Consider, for instance, his dealings with his brother Apollo.

His first big escapade is to steal Apollo's cattle. It's a caper that he pulls off with characteristic ingenuity by driving the herd backwards to confuse the trail and wearing sandals that reverse his own footprints. Far-seeing Apollo is not deceived for long, but Hermes is not at all intimidated by the anger of the god who is, as another son of Zeus, his elder half-brother. Having denied all knowledge of the crime and broken wind in Apollo's face, he is brought for trial before the court of Zeus, where the Lord of Olympus is charmed by his son's insouciance. Even the outraged Apollo is enchanted by the sound of the music that Hermes proceeds to make on his lyre. So Hermes cuts a deal. He reveals the whereabouts of the hidden cows and then gives Apollo the lyre he desires. His generosity of heart dispels all hostile feelings and the half-brothers make a vow of friendship. Apollo swears he will never love any of the immortals more than Hermes, and Hermes promises never to steal from his brother again.

So out of a story that begins with theft and is compounded by lies, two different but related modes of consciousness begin a new relationship. The light of rational discrimination – the hallmark of solar intelligence – is modified by the mercurial power of lunar intuition. The order of divine harmony is enlivened and enlarged. And it's the music of poetry which generates the transforming power by which this new gain is made for consciousness.

I believe that the story has particular relevance to our contemporary condition because for a long time now Apollo has dominated Western consciousness in a manner that has left it seriously unbalanced and may have brought it to a potentially disastrous pass. Iain McGilchrist's book *The Master and His Emissary* comprehensively illustrates how corrosive on sensibility and culture are the effects of our over-reliance on the analytic, conceptualising powers of the left brain at the expense of the right brain, which, as the source of meaning and value, provides a larger, coherent context to our experience.

We can hear this process of deterioration at work in the kind of language we have been increasingly pressured to speak these days if we wish to be taken seriously, particularly in our intellectual and professional lives. I mean that drift into abstraction that employs phrases from which our senses instinctively recoil, phrases such as 'engineering deliverable outcomes' in management-speak, and in military parlance the talk of 'degrading enemy assets'. The point is strongly made in David Lodge's *Consciousness and the Novel*, in which he wrote (with a measure of satirical intent) that 'There is a certain affinity between the poststructuralist literary theory that maintains that the human subject is entirely constructed by the discourses in which it is situated, and the cognitive science view that regards human self-consciousness as an epiphenomenon of brain activity'.

To me such language feels symptomatic of what Barfield called 'Withdrawn Participation'. The words are stacked like breeze blocks, almost as if designed to obscure experience rather than reveal it. It's a way of wielding language which gives its users a heady sense of power and leaves those who don't share its codes feeling impotent and confused. In recent times other professions than that of literary criticism have begun to write and speak in jargon so abstract that it's largely impenetrable to those uninitiated in its obfuscating rhetoric. The rage for it has become so contagious that even in common usage people frequently utter such clumsy abstractions as 'on a daily basis' where our parents simply said 'daily' or 'every day'.

Hermes prefers poetry because it has the feel and taste of language alive. This is language that may be in love with metaphor but also likes to call a spade a spade. Because it wants to excite the imagination and strike an echo in the heart, it has small use for the left-brain abstractions that so appeal to the clever mind and now oppress so much of our thought and speech. This matters because, as Wittgenstein said, 'Our language is our world.' If we are to change our world in a way that makes it more responsive to the living quick of the natural order on which our existence depends, as well as to the deep needs of our own bewildered souls, then don't we need a language that speaks through the compassionate imagination with a more sensitive voice? To learn that kind of language we must listen to our poets – those among us who, like Hermes, are most closely in touch with the poetic basis of mind.

Poetry is powerful in the way that it touches and shakes the heart, but, as Shelley insisted in his *Defence* of the art, it can also be subversive of oppressive authority. Here too Hermes has a significant role. As trickster, he is always ready to pull the rug from under the self-important. By tricking them and us he reminds us that we are only human and, being suspicious of all grand narratives, he will find ways to disturb our complacency by stage-managing anomalous events that question our assumptions and make us think again. Hence, in a world inclined to insist that only that which is measurable, quantifiable, and demonstrable by repeated experiment can be firmly classified as real, he throws up crop circles and accounts of abduction by aliens, conspiracy theories and other puzzling phenomena from the daimonic realm. Here's a poem called 'He Considers Grand Unified Theories and Such':

> He likes it when we hanker after truth
> in things, yet smiles to see how serious
> we are in postulating theories
> of everything (e.g. the thoughts of Alan Guth
>
> on quantum fluctuations in the vacuum,
> Dawkins on genes, Karl Marx on history,
> and imams or the Pope on God). For mystery
> abides whatever postures we assume,
>
> and Hermes knows the universe expands
> each time we think we've got the explanation.
> Not this, not that, but both, or maybe none
> of the above, his tricksy wisdom understands
>
> what unassisted reason often fails to see:
> the tongue can't taste its buds; the only snake
> to swallow its own tail does not mistake
> itself as literally true ... and nor, he thinks, should we.

However seriously we take our private and professional lives, isn't it salutary to remember that the incorrigible impudence of the hermetic spirit can keep us on our toes by prodding us into greater tolerance of ambiguity and alerting us to the dangers of complacency? If we impose dogmatic theories and standard practices on the quick of lived experience without regard to immediate needs and circumstances, shouldn't we be grateful when he finds ways to deflate us? If he steals from us, might it make us wonder whether we were too attached to whatever he took? If he dupes us, might it be to show how easily we're fooled? If he tells us lies, might it lead us to question more closely what is real and true? And doesn't his talent for crossing boundaries provide valuable guidance out of the ego-managed control of our lives into the fertile deeps of the unconscious?

He does that perhaps most provocatively through our dreams. So maybe it's his liminal figure who ushers us through that evanescent moment when the waking mind vanishes into sleep. But the archetype of Hermes can lead us deeper still. According to the myths he is our guide into what has become the last great obscenity of our materialist age, the one that some people are seeking to make optional rather than accepting it as an inevitable and finally desirable destination. I mean, of course, the shadowlands of death. Perhaps all we living can ever know of death is myth, and myth is an act of the poetic imagination. So maybe it's there, where language is silenced at last, that we re-enter that poetic sense of the seamless unity of being from which we and words first sprang. Who knows? But the Greek myths tell us that, alone among the gods, Hermes is able to travel between the heights of Olympus and the lower depths of the underworld which are the kingdom of his uncle Hades. He is perhaps never more our friend than when he comes to lead us down that dark way.

Our lives are sometimes haunted by the fear of change and of the loss of ego control, but death presents an inescapable challenge to the sense of order and security on which we seek to build our lives. It is, so to speak, the final and complete disrupter; but nothing in the mortal realm lasts for ever, and in that context let me refer you back to the unexpectedly disruptive events with which this talk began.

Like the ancient Greeks of the time when the Hymn to Hermes was composed, we find ourselves in uncertain times of rapid social change; but also in a time for which our expectations and sense of entitlement have left us ill-prepared. As the gap between rich and poor grows ever wider, so too does the gap between centralised government and the daily reality of those who have to endure the consequences of its policies. Faith in long-established institutions dwindles, voices are raised that have too long gone unheard, and affirming echoes resound along the channels of social media. When those who feel unrepresented are given the chance to act, surprises get sprung, and those who believed that their control of affairs was strong and stable, rational and orderly, find themselves shaken awake as though from a bad dream. Behind all such events the archetype of Hermes is at work – that sometimes troubling, certainly unpredictable god who is ever ready to disrupt any social or psychological system that is becoming complacent and sclerotic.

Maybe he does it so that ground can be cleared for something new and fresh to happen? Perhaps in times such as these he rises up from the depths of the unconscious as an impersonal, countervailing power looking to correct that which has drifted seriously out of balance? Yes, his actions may appear capricious and irresponsible to our limited vision, but, as the ancient Greeks remind us, Koinos Hermes, the common or everyday god, is also the friendliest to human beings, and his heraldic emblem is the caduceus, his wand that symbolises the transforming power of imagination.

A fine engraving by the seventeenth-century sculptor Andraes de Vries depicts Mercury and Psyche closely intertwined in an erotic dance, their bodies twisting around a centre of gravity like the serpents on the caduceus or the double helix of our DNA. Mercury and Psyche, Hermes and the Soul, in mutual embrace – the image depicts how intimate is our psychological involvement with the archetype of Hermes. So there's much more to say about the tricky fellow. In *A Dance with Hermes* I have poems that reflect on his relations with the feminine and the natural world, on dreams, on our disastrous recourse to warfare and his care for refugees and lost children, on alchemy and the reconciliation of opposites, and other themes suggested by his versatile nature. Yet for me he remains above all the god and archetype of the Imagination, and as such he is

> The god in the louche hat, the liminal,
> crepuscular and volatile grand master
> of quick whispers and shady deals, can pull
> deft tricks and optical illusions faster
>
> than the pixels shift in CGI. He seduces us
> and mystifies our senses with his wand,
> the Kerykeion or (latinate) Caduceus –
> that snake-twined staff he carries in his hand
>
> to work such vivid magic as draws doves
> from darkness or releases some poor captive
> from a cabinet of knives. What he loves
> best is to astound the mind with such deceptive
>
> art as brings about true transformation,
> and it's the virtue of his wand to wide-awaken
> into lucid dreams of the Imagination
> those who don't yet see we are myth-taken.

So could that be why he is provoking us in these turbulent times? Could he be pointing out that the conventions, assumptions, and myths by which we are living our lives may have grown threadbare and obsolete, and so no longer answer vitally either to our social needs or to the deep needs of the soul? Could what he is asking of us now be a larger, stronger, more athletic exercise of the imagination in response to the potentially disastrous problems that have arisen as the unintended consequences of our intended actions? For in both its poetic, inventive aspect, and in the empathic power through which we reach a compassionate understanding of lives other than our own, the Imagination is the always available agent of renewal – so long as we stay open to its claims.

John Moat's marvellously insightful memoir begins with these words: 'I see now what I must always have known, that even if *we* are not, our lives certainly *are* in the play of Imagination.' Even as he was dying he affirmed it as the power that gives life its shape and meaning. Where others might see only coincidence, or luck, or random chance thrown up by an absurd universe, John discerned an unfolding order and intentionality that was essentially poetic. It was, for him, as it has become for me, a matter of lived experience, and we both saw its often elusive but always enlarging nature most vividly characterised in the enduring mythological figure of Hermes.

# Ghost Dancers

A review of *Mystic Warriors of the Plains* by Thomas E. Mails (Council Oak Books, 1995), originally published in *Resurgence*.

So dreadful are the many crimes that have been committed in the name of progress during the past two centuries that to dwell on them too closely can break the heart. Yet dwell on them we must, and perhaps for the very reason that in the sclerotic state of Western culture wholehearted renewal may come only on the far side of the broken heart.

Surely among the greatest of these crimes was the brutal, faith-breaking, and staggeringly brief effort of genocide through which the white immigrants of North America acted out what they saw as their manifest destiny by seeking to exterminate the aboriginal peoples of that continent, most famously the diverse cultures of the many nations of the Great Plains. More than a century of worldwide atrocity has passed since the last of the massacres, yet the imagination of the Western world is still haunted by those ruthless acts of genocide. The ghost dance that was stamped out at Wounded Knee goes on, though the ghost dancers are inside us now.

The guilt is such that as soon as we come to speak of those people we find ourselves in difficulties. What are we to call them even? The old term 'Red Indian' insults them with inaccuracy on both counts. The currently preferred description, 'Native American', contaminates their culture by its irrelevant reference to an obscure Italian navigator of the late Middle Ages whose surname few remember. The profuse names those nations had for themselves (which often translate simply as 'The People' or 'The Human Beings') refuse a single collective noun and constitute both a telling reminder of what has been destroyed and a devastating criticism of the reductive

227

classifications of monocultural perspectives.

By the 1890s there remained in North America only around 250,000 survivors of the people who had once freely roamed the fenceless spaces of an unsullied continental land mass only a couple of lifetimes ago. What most of us think we know about them is what Hollywood has chosen to tell. In its fictions they were diminished to the less coherent if more colourful part of the archetypal split between 'Cowboys and Indians' which magnetised and disfigured the imaginations of generations of children. Assigned the ambiguously glamorous role of savages, their job was simply to drum, whoop, and die through film after film. Though a later, more sensitive school of directors tried to give them larger dignity, even in such sympathetic films as *Little Big Man* and *Dances with Wolves* the centre of consciousness remains persistently 'white'; and the prejudiced assumption that an honest and unflinching account of death on the plains would mean death at the box office prevented Marlon Brando from making a more deeply serious film. Meanwhile, as fortunes are made in the film industry, the remnant of these once noble peoples live out demoralised and impoverished lives in Midwestern shanty towns or fight as best they can for their rights.

At one level the issues are legal. In a country that prides itself on freedom guaranteed under law, they are the victims in continent-wide cases of robbery with genocidal violence and of fraudulent dispossession. But the culpable defendant is the government itself, so the issues are political too; and if the political health of a nation is evidenced by its treatment of minorities then the body politic of the USA is terminally sick. But we know that already; know too the difficulties of doing anything significant about it. So once again we are brought up against the destructively problematic nature of colonialist Western consciousness which underlies this as it does so many soul-racking issues.

The issue is agonisingly resumed in Jung's account of his meeting with the Pueblo shaman Ochwiay Bieno in *Memories, Dreams and Reflections*. Both men are dreamers, healers, and psychologists. They meet in good faith and mutual recognition. Then the shaman describes the restless, greedy appetite he sees in white faces (the raptorial eagle as totem bird) and says he considers it to be symptomatic of the madness that comes from thinking with the head. But 'What do you think with?' asks Jung in surprise.

'We think here,' Ochwiay Bieno answers, and indicates his heart.

'Of course,' we may think at once, 'how true, how wise!' But which of us can honestly say we fully understand what was meant by that simple gesture? We can reflect on it, as Jung himself does. We can think such enlarging thoughts as this: if thought is located in the heart then it must circulate through the whole body in the blood-stream, and thus there can be no actual split between body and mind, and the body must be consciousness incarnate. We can take it further and think: but if that is the case then it can't stop at the boundary of the body, there can be no split between mind and matter, and matter at large must also be consciousness incarnate. Then we might begin to see how such an experienced mode of embodied thought opens reverentially on a world that is a sacred, undivided whole within which human life becomes sane again – that is, whole; that is, holy. But which of us truly understands what that might mean as we suspect Ochwiay Bieno understood it? And unless we do, what hope is there for a unified vision of life?

Of course thousands of decent Americans are now working conscientiously at this problem, as are people right across the planet. On that difficult vision-quest they have come to recognise the dispossessed indigenous peoples of North America as their teachers; and it is probably there, rather than in the dreams of blood and guilt, that the ghost dance is at its most potent and vital, for it nourishes all that is most fruitful and transformative in American poetry, thought, and ecological practice.

The book under review has played an important role in educating our understanding of what has been lost with the destruction of the traditional cultures of the plains, and in striving to keep their spirit alive. Thomas Mails has attempted a comprehensive portrait of the life of the plains nations at the moment of their undisrupted liberty around the turn of the nineteenth century. His sources are rare books, ancient pictures, private and public collections of artefacts, the work of living scholars, and, wherever possible, the accounts provided by the people whose way of life he celebrates. His chapters cover their origins, customs, personal and domestic life, their mode of government, religious beliefs and practices, their arts and crafts, their weaponry and warrior culture. The lore made available through this book is vast, intricate, fascinating, and lovingly assembled. It is, above all, a very beautiful book. Rather than relying on photography, Mails generously illustrates his text with his own paintings and drawings, which seem, by a curious trick of the imagination, more faithful to the vividly heraldic spirit of these peoples than the grainy, monochromatic texture of the famous old photographic plates. The limber pencil-line of the drawings quivers with life; the colours of the paintings are (as Mails admits) sometimes astonishingly vivid. Though enormous care has been taken to keep these images accurate in every detail, the effect is to activate the imagination through evoked archetypes rather than through the narrower perspectives of journalistic realism. So the book itself becomes a kind of vision-quest.

The text is lucidly written, making available to a lay readership much information that might otherwise be found only in less accessible anthropological studies. The author's passionate attachment to the material about which he writes comes through clearly; but Mails is a retired Lutheran minister and, though his Christian charity is generously ecumenical, it somewhat colours his perspectives in a reductive manner. He is less strong, for instance, on the ecstatic aspects of vision-quest culture than a more thorough description might be, and the catlinite pipes that he draws so beautifully seem to burn nothing stronger than tobacco. Nevertheless, his section on the visionary practices of these peoples is a powerful reminder that reality is not simply a matter of agreed externals and that the deepest tutelary wisdom arises from a generative encounter between the natural environment and the activated imagination of the unconscious mind.

Such visionaries as Henry David Thoreau recognised the true stature of America's indigenous population and the abiding value of their wisdom, but the dominant white culture of his day sought to exterminate the peoples of the plains as it sought to rob tribal people worldwide of the dignity of their languages, myths, and lives. In a time when the destructive consequences of such colonial and industrial history become ever more apparent, so too does the need for a greater understanding of the traditional patterns of wisdom which underpinned the lives of those people. In that respect this book does valuable service.

The wonder and generosity of those traditions is that the spirit of their wisdom still abides, but active understanding and assimilation of it will come only at a cost. The courage, grandeur, nobility, and passionate commitment to life of the peoples celebrated in this book are reminders that a life lived in avoidance of necessary sacrifice may be less than half a life; and that, as Ochwiay Bieno reminded Jung, a life passed in the prayerful spirit of those nations is a life lived not for the self alone, but for the enduring benefit of the wider world.

# Hearing the Voice

This review of *The Voice of the Earth: Explorations in Ecopsychology* by Theodore Roszak (Phanes Press, 2001) was first published in *Resurgence*.

Theodore Roszak came to Schumacher College in the summer of 1991 to lead a course on the themes of 'Earth, Soul and Imagination'. He brought with him the keen intellectual skills, the interdisciplinary range of vision, the passionate sense of justice, and the lively eloquent voice that have made him a key figure in radical thought since the 1960s. The insights he shared there with a small group drawn from many nations are now publicly available in this important book.

*The Voice of the Earth* seeks to extend the study of human psychology into an area astonishingly neglected hitherto – its vital continuity with the natural order from which it arises; but its aims reach far beyond the theoretical. 'My purpose here', Roszak says, 'is quite frankly to span the gap between the personal and the planetary in a way that suggests political alternatives.' Though the ambition may sound high-flown, it is governed throughout by a just sense of proportion, and its aim is to leave us more deeply earthed.

At the heart of the argument lies the conviction that the human psyche is linked to the natural environment through 'the ecological unconscious'. Roszak suggests that repression of this fundamental relation lies at the root of our ills in industrial society and the harm we do to the world around us. A critical survey of the development of modern psychology from Freud onwards reveals it to be a largely urban phenomenon, one that defines the environment only in familial and social terms, making scant reference to the natural order that sustains our life. In contrast to the healing rites of traditional cultures which require a transactional relationship with nature, modern Western psychiatry 'has split the inner life from the outer world – as if what was inside us was not also inside the universe'. But if we have lost touch with that aboriginal quality of experience, as with the animistic enchantments of childhood, how are the values associated with them to be recovered? Not, Roszak insists, regressively, but only 'as a project that will have to integrate with the kind of consciousness that has evolved modern science'.

His review of the development of the scientific attitude examines the historical and temperamental factors that have contaminated much of its programme and that have tended, reductively, towards a picture of life as a random accident in a universe without significance. Over against this dismal cosmology he sets the insights arising from recent scientific endeavours. He shows how the evolution of the anthropic principle and the more expansive reach of systems theory seem to have put life and mind 'back at the centre of cosmology as matters to be accounted for and reckoned with'; his thesis of an ecological unconscious as the ground of our psychic being draws strength from possible implications of James Lovelock's Gaia hypothesis.

While respectful of Lovelock's efforts to dissociate himself from teleological interpretations of his theory, Roszak explores crucial issues arising from the view of the planet as a self-regulating system. Where do we fit inside that system? How are we implicated in its regulatory functions? In what ways are we regulated?

In trying to answer such questions he extends the Gaia hypothesis into a psychological dimension. Is it not possible, he asks, that the recent emergence of the hypothesis itself, together with the increasing pressure of ecological activism which has evolved around it, may be evidence of that regulating system at work inside our own unbalanced species? Or, to put it another way, that the environmental crisis we have precipitated by our unseemly patterns of production and consumption may be urging on us a necessary evolution in the nature of our consciousness? The earth's voice is speaking to us; are we prepared to hear?

The re-emergence of the goddess archetype in popular consciousness and the work of the deep ecologists and the ecofeminists may be further signs of such a change. So too may the unprecedentedly widespread urge towards greater self-knowledge and the methods of groupwork through which efforts to raise consciousness are made. Some critics have dismissed these as evidence of a culture of narcissism, but Roszak reads them as aspects of a hopeful search for the bright, relating spirit that resides, however deeply occluded, in each one of us.

Such seekers will find confirmation and clarification in the principles of the ecopsychology that he adduces from his insights and observations. Here is a psychology that seeks to heal the split between mind and nature by reviving the innately animistic experience of childhood in the creation of a mature adult ego responsibly related to the environment as a whole. It requires a revaluation of our concepts of masculinity and of the real needs concealed beneath our addictive appetites and drives. Roszak is frank too about the wider ethical and political changes demanded by a view of the world in which 'the needs of the planet are the needs of the person, and the rights of the person are the rights of the planet'. These are the challenges put to us by the unsentimental voice of the earth. Our survival may depend on our capacity to respond.

No doubt specialists in a number of fields will find things to quarrel with in this book. I'm not convinced that Roszak does full justice to the breadth of Jung's vision, nor can I share his faith in the development of science as the best chance of 'uniting us as one human family'. I'm a storyteller, and my own (perhaps still more tenuous) faith lies in the universal power of story to exercise the ethical imagination in its reach for wider horizons. But Ted Roszak is a storyteller too and, whatever the validity or otherwise of the various scientific models on which he rests parts of his case, my sense of the world is enlivened and enlarged by the poetry of his vision and by the story he has to tell of the way the voice of the earth is speaking to us now; and that story, in an age when so much conspires to diminish and demean it, is a precious gift.

# The Hades Journey

An extended version of a previously unpublished talk originally delivered as a C.G. Jung Public Lecture in Bristol.

Let's begin by acknowledging that we are complicated creatures inhabiting a mysterious world whose nature we do not fully understand and where, if we are honest, we will admit that there is little we know for certain. Not one of us here can even be sure that we will return safely to our home when this talk is done; still less can we know what will happen to us tomorrow or the next day. Nor can any of us yet know whether something might be said during this brief time together which will alter the course and compass of our life for ever. I would go further and suggest that, despite our best convictions, we don't fully comprehend who we are, we don't know for sure why we are here, and we don't know what will become of us.

This is, and has always been, the essential uncertainty of the human condition; but how many of us are at ease with it? And isn't it out of that inescapable existential uncertainty that arise all the stories and stratagems by which we strive as best we can to shape life to our purposes, to seek to make a go of things, to try to become what we believe ourselves to be while trying at the same time to make sense of all the others around us who are caught up in the same marvellous and fateful dance?

But if our lives are rounded by such radical uncertainty and ignorance, then how confidently can any of us answer John Cowper Powys when he remarks in his *Autobiography* how 'the look from the eyes of a living being is a strange and terrible look, not easy to be discounted', and asks, 'What is it that gazes forth, so grim, so furtive from the eye of a man?' Perhaps most of us at some point in our encounters with others have been confronted by the imponderable wonder and mystery of their being there at all, and by the unique, inimitable manner in which they present themselves.

Certainly, I feel I am standing before you today as an object lesson in such a state of perplexity, wondering who I am, and what I'm doing here, and having the same sort of questions about you. Some of you may have read my books or heard me speak before and will have a sense of what kind of creature it is who's addressing you right now. You will know that my principal interests are not psychotherapeutic in any professional sense of the word, and you may recall that they are not even strictly literary. I write novels because imaginative fiction is the best way I've found of making sense of certain formative experiences in my life, and – as my particular contribution to a general evolution of consciousness which is happening in our time – I try to do it in a way that will engage others.

I expect that most of you share my anxious concerns about the future of our species, and some of you may also share such tentative hopes as I have about it. Those hopes arise from two significant factors: the recent development of our ecological understanding, on the one hand, and the astonishing growth in the number of individuals seriously engaged in the search for greater self-knowledge, on the other. But neither development is widely and strongly enough established to ensure a happy outcome to the gathering crisis of our time, and I suspect that the latter development is less common than it might be were it not for an evasive aspect of human nature which was identified by Jung in paragraph 439 of *Psychology and Alchemy*. He declares that 'the dread and resistance which every natural human being experiences when it comes to delving too deeply into himself is, at bottom, the fear of the journey to Hades'.

The question I want us to think about is just *why* we should be afflicted by such a profound resistance to knowing more about ourselves, and I hope to encourage you to reflect, both conceptually and imaginatively, on what has been meant by the Hades journey in the past and on what powerful resonances it may still have for us today.

Hades, you will remember, was the name given to the Greek god of the underworld, the realm of the dead. According to Plato, the name derives from a Greek root meaning 'unseen' or 'hidden', though linguists also suggest a connection with a Semitic root that alludes to waters that rise from the deeps of the underworld. If that is the case, then somewhere at its root the idea of Hades is connected not only with death but also with the source of life.

Either way, the Lord of the Dead was held in such exceptional awe by the ancient Greeks that they created no statues of him, raised no temples to him, and his name was rarely spoken. As the dark brother and underworld counterpart of Zeus, he remained an invisible presence, usually referred to only by one or other of his attributes, such as Pluto, which means 'wealth' or 'riches', or Trophonius, which means 'nourishing'. The name Hades also came to refer to the underworld itself, the place where the god ruled with his bride Persephone, and to which human souls were consigned after death. But the Greek myths insist it was also a place that might be visited by those who had not yet died; they tell of the differing journeys made to Hades by Orpheus, Heracles, and Theseus, among other legendary figures.

One would expect that an image of such archetypal power would be found in other cultures than those of the Greeks and that is, of course, the case. An important book is waiting to be written by someone with the scholarship and patience to trace its worldwide resonance; but suffice it for the moment to mention a few examples. An early Sanskrit text, the *Kathopanishad*, tells how Nachiketas won the reward of immortality by making the journey down to Yama, Lord of Death, in full consciousness; the litanies and rituals recounted in the Egyptian *Book of the Dead* describe changes in consciousness undergone by the soul on its descent; a Sumerian poem tells of Inanna's descent; the Akkadians tell how Ishtar descends to Aralu, and similar stories are also to be found in the Book of Enoch, in the folktales of Europe, in the Japanese myth of Izanami, and among the traditions of the Aztecs and Amerindians.

So powerfully was the hold of this archetype on the Western imagination, as evidenced by the Mysteries of Eleusis and the Orphic rites, that the early Church Fathers found it necessary to include it as an article of faith in the Christian creed even though no canonical evidence for Christ's descent into Hell is to be found in the Gospels. Much later, inspired by his reading of Virgil, Dante would structure the *Inferno* cantos of his great cosmic poem of judgement and redemption, *The Divine Comedy*, around a Christian form of the mythologem. In one version or another the story of the descent into the underworld is present everywhere in human culture, and it is always a journey filled with dread and danger, a matter of life and death to be undertaken only by a person ready to undergo the transforming ordeals of initiation into the deepest mysteries.

In speaking of the initiatory rites of Isis in his *Metamorphoses*, Lucius Apuleius declares that 'the delivery of her mysteries is celebrated as a thing resembling a voluntary death'. Plutarch offers a complementary insight when he claims that, 'at the time of death, the soul has an experience like that of men who are undergoing initiation into great mysteries'. So it seems to be the case that the journey to Hades involves a willingness to become one among the dead before one has actually died; or, as Apuleius puts it, to undergo an experience akin to voluntary death. What we fear, therefore, when we contemplate the Hades journey is the stark black fact that haunts our days – the inevitability of death itself.

All mortal creatures, including, as Jung says, 'every natural human being', seem to be imbued with an instinctive fear of death. In a culture such as the modern West, where it has become the last and greatest obscenity, and where some technocratic optimists would have us believe it might eventually become optional, a lot of energy gets consumed in postponing that encounter for as long as possible. By way of contrast, however, we have both literary and archaeological evidence that, in the ancient world, important cult centres were designed to serve the specific purpose of satisfying in ritualised form the desire to make, at considerable personal expense, the risky journey into Hades' kingdom of the dead during one's lifetime.

From an account by the initiate Pausanias we know, for example, of the dramatic rites performed at the Oracle of Trophonius at Lebadeia, where, having been ritually cleansed and made the appropriate sacrifices, the seeker descended by ladder into a cave, crawled feet foremost into a narrow hole, and was sucked downwards as if by a whirlpool into the deranging realm of the dead. Once there, if he was fortunate, he would receive the revelatory oracle he sought, though it was said that some seekers never returned.

More famously, we know from Virgil's *Aeneid* of similar necromantic rites that were practised under the aegis of the Sybil at Cumae in southern Italy – where the hero Aeneas makes his descent into Hades, encounters the shade of his dead father, and is given an inspiring vision of the future course of Roman history. Archaeological research has uncovered the existence of an underground cult centre in the seismic landscape of the Phlegrean Fields near Cumae; its layout corresponds so closely to the place described by Virgil that it is now accepted to be the site of the Oracle of the Dead.

It seems probable that this was also the cult centre in which, during the prolonged course of his journey home to Ithaca after the fall of Troy, Odysseus undergoes his encounter with the dead in Homer's *Odyssey*. That particular context brought the nature of the Hades journey sharply into focus for me when I was writing my novel *The Return from Troy*.

My previous novel, *The War at Troy*, had followed a narrative trajectory from the realm of the gods down into the hot broil of erotic passion and violent conflict in what I hoped could be read as a credible human story – one set in the late Bronze Age yet with clear reference to contemporary passions and conflicts in a war-torn world where we seem to have learned very little in the past three thousand years. This approach presented me with tricky problems when I came to write the sequel because many of the best-loved parts of the *Odyssey* involve encounters with mythical creatures such as the Cyclops and the Sirens. Nor did I want merely to write a prose version of an incomparable poem; so it seemed to me that if I was going to tell the stories of the aftermath of the Trojan War I would have to find a way to do it in a new way for our own time.

The process began with a revisioning of the complex figure of Odysseus. In the *Occidental Mythology* volume of *The Masks of God*, Joseph Campbell offers a Jungian view of him as a man who undergoes 'psychological adventures in the mythic realm of the archetypes of the soul, where the male must *experience* the import of the female before he can meet her perfectly in life'. Anyone familiar with my novels will know that I'm more than sympathetic to such a vision, but I find it hard to square Campbell's picture of a hero who undergoes an ego-transforming sequence of psychological ordeals with the vainglorious character in Homer's poem who cruelly taunts the blinded Polyphemus, draws a sword on Circe, and eventually returns to Ithaca to butcher all his wife's suitors and watch in approval as his son strings up all the young women who have dallied with them. Indeed, there is a case to be made that Homer's Odysseus learns nothing very much from all his travails, and I suspect that Campbell's initiatory reading of the poem tells us rather more about Campbell himself and the needs of modern times than it does about either Homer or his portrayal of Odysseus.

On rereading the *Odyssey* I was struck by the dread of the feminine which seems to haunt its majestic lines. True, they do contain remarkable portraits of women, but almost every danger that besets the life of Odysseus and his crew seems menacingly female – Circe turning his men to swine, the Siren-song luring him to destruction, the engulfing monsters Scylla and Charybdis, and the sensual Calypso who uses her magical powers of enchantment to detain him for many years. Meanwhile, though the goddess Athena is celebrated throughout as the presiding deity of the poem, whenever she manifests among mortals it is almost invariably in masculine form. This is unsurprising if one recalls that the earliest recitations of the *Odyssey* were performed for the entertainment of a warrior aristocracy and spoke to the culture of a phallocentric society that preferred to see Athena as the daughter of Zeus, sprung directly out of his head, rather than as the archaic snake-wreathed deity who once bore her name. But the longer I looked at the poem the more I thought I saw the lineaments of another story concealed inside it – a story that might have made good sense to an earlier goddess-worshipping culture, and that might speak more urgently to our time.

It was a story that turned some of the events of the *Odyssey* inside out and brought a more feminine perspective out of the shadows to reimagine the tale from its point of view. A clue to this approach was provided by those lines from Homer's poem in which Odysseus weeps at the court of King Alcinous as he listens to the blind bard Demodocus singing of the fall of Troy. The grief in those lines is conveyed by a powerful but somewhat surprising image. In the translation by Richmond Lattimore, Homer sings that Odysseus wept –

As a woman weeps, lying over the body
Of her dear husband, who fell fighting for her city and her people
As he tried to beat off the pitiless day from city and children;
She sees him dying and gasping for breath, and winding her body
About him she cries high and shrill, while the men behind her,
Hitting her with their spear butts on the back and the shoulders,
Force her up and lead her away into slavery, to have
Hard work and sorrow, and her cheeks are wracked with pitiful
    weeping.
Such were the pitiful tears Odysseus shed from under his brows.

These moving lines are offered in description of a man who only a hundred or so lines later is coolly telling the Phaeacian court how, in the country of the Cicones after the fall of Troy, he 'sacked their city and killed their people, and out of their city taking their wives and many possessions, we shared them out, so none might go cheated of his proper portion'. Such a casual account of a merciless atrocity is in stark contrast with the description of Odysseus as a man overwhelmed by grief at the thought of the terrible things that were done at Troy. The latter was more of an Odysseus with whom I could empathise.

In my telling of his story, Odysseus is already sickened by the war long before its end. He had never wanted to go to Troy and was drawn there only by the same sort of pressure that he himself later exerted on Achilles to bring him to the fight. Both men are victims of what the novel calls 'the dreadful patrimony of war' and both become exponents of it. Achilles dies in the struggle, while Odysseus longs to return to his wife on Ithaca. He conceives the stratagem of the wooden horse as a way of ending the siege and secures the collaboration of Trojan defectors to get the horse into the city by vowing that all who lay down their arms will be spared. But Agamemnon has other ideas, and Odysseus soon discovers that his ingenuity is responsible for what becomes a horrific atrocity.

In a dream after the fall of Troy, he sees his wife running to meet him, but as he hurries to embrace her Penelope's face falls in dismay. Perplexed, he looks down and sees that he is still covered in blood. He has become a man of blood, a man no longer fit for decent company, a man who, like some veterans of the wars in Vietnam and elsewhere, avoids going home because, in the increasingly familiar psychological jargon of our time, he is suffering from severe post-traumatic stress disorder.

Having once prided himself on his fame, wit, intelligence, and valour, he must now undergo a sequence of ordeals by which he will be transformed before emerging anew to return to Ithaca and his wife in search of reconciliation. The creative aspect of those ordeals begins at the court of Circe, who conducts him through a deranging process of breakdown and recovery before – and here is the point of this digression – she sends him on the revelatory journey to Hades by way of the Oracle of the Dead at Cumae. The account given in *The Return from Troy* of the journey he makes from breakdown to breakthrough was an effort of the imagination intended to take both me and, I hoped, the reader along with him as he makes his descent into the underworld.

Having read both Homer and Virgil, I considered there were four key factors to such an experience. Firstly, it involved a movement away from the norms and values of the upper world and an actual descent into the body of the earth – and descent, as the archetypal psychologist James Hillman reminds us, implies a movement down into the realm of soul. Secondly, the journey could not be undertaken without ritual cleansing and the voluntary sacrifice of things of personal value – acts that symbolise the more radical self-divestiture that is to come. Thirdly, it was clear that the primary encounter had to be with a *female* figure, for Hades remains invisible and it's through the voice of the Sybil as representative of Persephone, daughter of Ge (or, more familiarly, Gaia) and wife of Hades, that the oracular wisdom is conveyed. And, fourthly, such wisdom was in the gift of the dead ancestors – a gift that can be received only through a temporary evacuation of the ego and a new openness to a mode of understanding which is a matter not of the conceptualising intellect but of lived experience.

It's my belief that those ancients who were seriously in search of wisdom and self-knowledge had a deep intuitive awareness of the relevance of such interrelated factors to their well-being. From their surviving accounts, it seems that their readiness to undergo the ordeals of such mystery rites deepened their consciousness of their own true nature and its relationship to the wider cosmos in ways that can make our own objectively analytic grasp of the world feel relatively impoverished.

We no longer live in a culture where this kind of rite is commonly available, though the intensive process of psychoanalysis may deliver a comparable experience. But it was my conviction that, as was the case with the ancient epic poems and prose romances, a seriously conceived attempt to retell the story of Odysseus might also offer the reader a correlative of such a rite through the work of the imagination. In my attempt to accomplish this I was aided by R.F. Paget's detailed account of his exploration of the remains of the Oracle of the Dead at Cumae, *In the Footsteps of Orpheus*. Yet works of art are made by nursing obsessions, and the presiding myth behind all my work is that the route into the deeps of life lies through the effort to shift the centre of consciousness from ego to soul. So, however fictional the final form it took, the principal authority on which my account of the descent of Odysseus was based would have to be, to some degree, that of examined subjective experience.

Many years ago a major transforming experience in my own life had something of the deranging quality of a Hades journey. It happened with the simultaneous collapse of my first marriage and my hitherto well-defended masculine ego. At that time, driven by a devastating sense of betrayal that left me reeling in a convulsive fit of shock, fury, and despair, I dropped out of normal consciousness for a time into what felt like a different realm populated by some fearsome inward figures, each of which I had to recognise and confront before a way could open through.

Still blazed most fiercely on my mind is the memory of gazing into a mirror and seeing a vile, malevolent face stare back at me. Unquestionably my own face, it was disfigured by the sneer of what felt like a truly diabolical sense of power – the power to punish the world which had hurt me by plunging irretrievably further into madness or, better still, by killing myself and so destroying that world with me.

In that malignant moment I heard myself saying aloud, 'I feel evil.' My voice sounded fiendishly cold, and the feeling behind it was utterly alien to anything I had ever previously known; but it seems that something was literally *expressed* by those three dark words – something that might have proved utterly destructive had they remained locked away in silence inside me. When I looked back at the face again, all the malevolent power seemed to have shrivelled from it. What I saw in its place was merely defeated and so pathetic that I heard the phrase 'poor devil, poor devil' echoing in my mind.

When I think back on that moment now, Prospero's deep-reaching admission about 'the beast Caliban' in the final act of *The Tempest* resonates through my imagination with familiar force: 'This thing of darkness I acknowledge mine.' My own words may have lacked such force of conscious acknowledgement, but something in the structure of my consciousness had shifted and I was through into the next transformative phase of an ordeal that would end only many hours later when I woke and stepped out into the dawn light of a bright spring day and knew that everything around me had changed.

What had changed, of course, was me. The best way I can describe how that felt is to say that the false self I had constructed in seeking to manage the stresses of my previous life had fallen away and I was open to a new, almost virginal mode of perception – that of life unfolding in its own all-embracing flow; but I now sensed myself a part *of* it, not apart *from* it.

Let me quickly add two further thoughts. Firstly, that my ego built back quickly enough, though that critical encounter with a deeper self – with the soul, if you prefer – had irreversibly altered the cardinal orientation of my life, and I now knew that any recusal from its directives would be an act of self-betrayal. Secondly, that I'm quite sure I'm only one of many people the world over who have experienced a similar change and renewal as a result of what felt like a catastrophic moment of breakdown in their lives.

In one way or another, I've been engaged with the personal import of that experience ever since. In trying to make imaginative sense of it, it helps to work with it in much the same way that the evolutionary psychoanalyst Anthony Stevens encourages us to work with our dreams. Each time we fall asleep at night, he says, we 'visit, on a purely transitory basis, the kingdom of death'. By honouring this tie to the mythology of Hades when we work with the dreams that come, and thereby linking our personal story to one of the great transpersonal stories of humanity, it may also prove possible to forge a deeper sense of connectedness to the cosmos and further the work of the soul in advancing the art of consciousness.

It will be obvious that, for me personally, the mythologem of the Hades journey is packed with a powerful charge of meaning. It furnishes a graphic and often much-needed reminder that where I am most fully alive is not among the devices and desires of my restless mind, or in the relative security of established theories and systems of thought, but in that uncolonised space where I'm most open to what the flow of being makes available through each present moment. In that respect, it's also a valuable reminder that, at its deepest level, self-knowledge is very different from ego-knowledge.

The ego – that occupant of the penthouse flat on the executive floor where control is kept over our affairs and our managerial decisions are made – may have a necessary role in helping us to deal with the vicissitudes of the world, but it also keeps a confining, sometimes reassuringly comfortable, grip on us. As the agent of our worldly power and the jealous guardian of our reputation, it seeks to mask our vulnerabilities, while its clever mind is firmly set against anything that might threaten it with transformation. Yet what do such anxiously maintained efforts of control have to do with who we deeply are?

The ancient wisdom traditions of the world suggest that, far from furthering and protecting our real interests, the managerial devices of an ego-centred mode of consciousness are obstinate defences raised against the claims of a richer, more soulful sense of what is durable and real. But how are we to attain and *inhabit* such an understanding?

Perhaps one way is when all the stratagems and defences fail and we find ourselves ravished by Hades in the form of some grave disappointment or defeat, a failed ambition, an illness or accident, a grievous bereavement. Perhaps it's there, when we are drawn down into some divesting encounter so distressing that there is no denying it, perhaps it's there, at the point of utter helplessness, that the soul can find space to emerge most clearly from its dark confinement.

Might this be the place where Hades Trophonius manifests as the nourishing source of unexpected abundance and we receive a richer understanding of who we truly are? For what the ego fears as dissolution and death may then be welcomed by the soul as a newly creative participation in the indissoluable unity of life.

Whatever their role in strengthening social cohesion, the rigorous initiatory rites of the ancient world and those traditional cultures which struggle to survive in these global times must also have helped individuals to prepare for, and deal with, the severe involuntary, unexpected, stresses that life can bring to bear. Writing about the Eleusinian Mysteries in *De legibus*, Cicero said, 'Just as they are called initiations, so in actual fact we have learned from them the fundamentals of life, and have grasped the basis not only for living with joy but also for dying with a better hope.' One wonders what aspects of our own social structures and systems of education could confidently make such claims.

I have also begun to wonder whether, beyond its personal relevance, the mythologem of the Hades journey may speak to much wider concerns, for, just as we are all headed, like it or not, towards the eventual fact of our death, so the whole powerful culture of our time seems far advanced on a Hades journey of its own. As the human population increases exponentially while other species are extinguished, as the air we breathe turns dirtier, as ancient forests are felled and the seas are fouled with plastic, and as atrocities we once though unrepeatable return to darken the day's news, it can feel in our more desperate moments as though it's all drifting to Hell in a bucket! Yet as long as we locate the blame, and delegate the suffering, out there, and seek solutions to the multiplying problems only through amelioration of the misguided attitudes that have produced them, we are merely falling asleep in our own shadows. In this context it strikes me that the image of the *completed* Hades journey may have something to teach us.

In Holocaust theology a word has been coined to convey the gravity of what is required by a consciousness engaged in the effort to comprehend the full import of what was done in the Nazi death camps. It's a word that presented itself out of the recognition that the atrocious reality of the camps cannot ever be transcended, for as

Arthur A. Cohen says in *The Tremendum: A Theological Interpretation of the Holocaust*, 'there is no way of obliterating their historicity by over-leaping them. Quite the contrary. If there is no transcendence be-yond the abyss, the abyss must be inspected further … In a word, the abyss must be *sub-scended*, penetrated to its perceivable depths.'

Perhaps such a tremendous act of imaginative *subscendence* is the deep significance of the Hades journey – that willingness to go down into shadowland darkness, to endure in the deeps of one's imagina-tion the terror and dread daily inflicted on the world by short-term greed and the abuse of power; to begin to own one's complicity, as a fallible human being, in their destructive effects; and then to push on through to larger understanding and deeper compassion without falling asleep or into despair.

As Thomas Hardy once put it, 'If way to the better there be, it exacts a full look at the worst.' When I think about what might be demanded by the implications of his words, I wonder whether some of the values that might guide us may already be present in the my-thologem of the Hades journey.

As I suggested earlier, the ancient rites made four key demands on the participants in its mystery: sacrifice of something valuable, a courageous descent into the underworld, a revelatory encounter with the feminine power, and open responsiveness to the dead ancestors. Translated into contemporary terms, this is what those factors might require of us:

- a willingness to sacrifice those of our many privileges shown to be unjust by a comprehensive system of ac-countancy which recognises their harmful impact and costs on other people and other species;
- a need to explore and develop a creative relationship with the impersonal archetypal powers resident in the under-world of the unconscious mind;
- a recognition that such a descent into the unconscious re-gions of the soul will involve (for both men and women) a transforming encounter with those life-affirming values of the feminine principle which have been neglected and de-meaned in our paternalist culture;

- a revaluation of the wisdom of the ancestors, not only as it remains available in surviving texts but as an intrinsic part of the lively intelligence of our own genetic structure – the dead ancestors alive inside each one of us and speaking to us, if we will listen, through our dreams and genes;

- additionally, in relation to each of the above, we will need to develop a due responsiveness to the comprehensive intelligence of the earth, since each of us, however clever or powerful, is only a single filament in the planet's evolving consciousness.

These are severe and difficult demands; each of them runs counter to the practices and priorities of powerful forces – both outward and inward – that show limited interest in answering them and have a strong interest in resisting their claims. Yet if we engage with them courageously and to the best of our ability, we may find that we emerge from the ordeals of the Hades journey with a deeper understanding of ourselves and with greater strength to address the challenges pressing in upon our lives from the world around us. As far as those challenges are concerned, the odds against enough of us recognising the full gravity of our present situation, and taking the action needed to answer the formidable, planet-wide demands it presents, can feel insuperable. So, it may be helpful to remember the single-word injunction frequently uttered in the initiatory prose romances of the ancient Hellenic world: 'Tharsei.' It means 'Take heart, be of good cheer,' since that way, in company with others, one may retain the hope and trust that a deeper insight into how things are can be achieved, and with it a more benign access of power and energy for a truly creative life.

# The Peach Blossom Cave

## A Novelist's Take on Myth, Vision, Synchronicity, and Consciousness

This a much modified version of a talk given at a conference on Metaphysical Art at the University of Sussex and later published in *The Review*, Vol. 4.

Where am I? Who am I? How did I come to be here? What is this thing called the world? How did I come in to the world? Why was I not consulted? And if I am compelled to take part in it, where is the director? I want to see him.

Such were the anguished questions with which the Danish philosopher Søren Kierkegaard addressed the metaphysical problem of our existence. They raise philosophical issues by which most of us have been troubled at some point. I suppose that, in its attempt to shape a more or less orderly picture of the world and of human relations within it, every novel is implicitly philosophical. Some novelists – Iris Murdoch was a good example – are also practising philosophers, but I'm no such animal. I have no particular talent for the abstract analyses and speculations of formal philosophy, and when confronted by the word 'metaphysical' I tend to think of the capacious way it is used to characterise the Metaphysical poets of the seventeenth century, those ardent, amorous, and pious spirits whose imaginations worked with centripetal power to summon many aspects of their experience – erotic, scientific, theological, and philosophical – into the embrace of the poem, and thereby related intelligence derived from their feelings, thoughts, and animal senses to larger orders of meaning.

So, for me, what is most engaging in metaphysics must be close kin to what could broadly be called a *religious* feeling for life – the continuing quest for meaning in our experience, which I take to be a fundamental human need. The words are vague, I know, but such a quest seriously undertaken requires us, again and again, to contend with the claims of reason and the limits of language. 'At the maximum of our imagination,' said D.H. Lawrence, 'we are religious'; and perhaps for that reason I am more at ease with the imaginative story-time emblems of mythological thinking than with the conceptual abstractions of philosophical thought.

Myth is best understood less as a pre-rational mode of thought than as an expression of the archetypal content of the poetic basis of mind, and what most impresses me about myths is the way that they take the big questions of our lives – where do we come from? which gods shall we serve? where are we going? – and dramatise them in the form of imaginatively engaging, symbolic narratives that refuse to be pinned down with literal interpretation. I think of the knowledge offered by myths as 'metabolic' or 'erotic' knowledge, because the contrary tensions evident in our lived experience of those questions feel embodied there and reconciled through an irreducibly dramatic form that is accessible at a variety of levels, both conscious and unconscious

Anthropologists have shown us how the public world we inhabit is sanctioned by a story, or collection of stories, which as long as it remains vital in the imagination of its hearers will be experienced not merely as fiction but as the very fabric of reality. The same is true for our personal lives. So, it is by and through such mythic stories that we live. What matters is the breadth of their embrace and how dynamically they bring into creative relation those opposing powers which often threaten to tear us apart and thereby open up opportunities for personal and cultural renewal. It was through great cycles of myth that the ancestral world addressed the mysteries that attend our lives, and their enchanted narratives still engage us because they place human life within a larger cosmic order of meaning by illuminating correspondences between the structure of the human psyche and its observations of the outside world. Which is a way of saying that they are convincing acts of the initiatory imagination.

For that reason, both the ethical force and the transforming power of story rightly told were well recognised by ancient and traditional peoples. The myths of ancient Greece, as dramatised by the great poets, worked on the imaginative capacity for pity, fear, and awe in ways that wrought cathartic change in those who attended to them. But the modern world, divested of the sacred authority celebrated by such mythological traditions, tells itself a different kind of story. In the literary circles of the mid twentieth century, such books as Erich Auerbach's *Mimesis*, Ian Watt's *The Rise of The Novel*, and Frank Kermode's *The Sense of an Ending* were based on the assumption that, in Western cultural history, myth has been replaced as a valid means of making sense of our experience by a more mature, accurate, and rational instrument of consciousness – the novel.

*Don Quixote* is usually cited as the turning point, and the rational tide seems to have been well up by the time Samuel Richardson's Pamela complained that the romances she read 'gave me no great pleasure; for either they dealt so much in the *marvellous* and *improbable*, or were so unnaturally *inflaming* to the *passions*, and so full of *love* and *intrigue*, that most of them seemed calculated to *fire* the *imagination* than to *inform* the *judgment* … And what', she demands, 'is the instruction that can be gathered from such pieces, for the conduct of common life?'

The critics I mentioned have larger demands to make, but they seem to imply that, by putting aside its infatuation with the stuff of marvels and taking a focused interest in the daily life of the world, prose fiction comes to maturity. Both theme and genre have passed through critical changes. The mythic imagination is consigned to the nursery, and a new adult form – the naturalistic novel – gets down to the serious business of examining the social, marital, and monetary preoccupations of the merchant class, along with the fascinating shadows they cast in the adventures of whores, rogues, and rascals.

Or so the mainstream myth of the novel would have us believe. There's no doubt that enormous gains were made for consciousness through the sensibilities of the great eighteenth- and nineteenth-century novelists who worked in that spirit; but some of those gains were made at the cost of serious exclusions. Thus, aspects of our experience which are illuminated only by penetrating the veil of naturalism into more visionary realms, are usually ignored in such stories

(*Wuthering Heights* is a magnificent exception) or admitted only in the acceptably 'realistic' form of dreams and madness, which may therefore be given disproportionately representative importance.

Nevertheless, such wondrous things were accomplished in this new mode of prose fiction that Thomas Carlyle elevated novelists to the rank of social prophets and moral teachers. For whole generations they were the supreme arbiters of consciousness. And still, as we watch Dorothea Brooke or Julien Sorel live out their fictional destinies on our behalf within the constraints of their particular social, cultural, and historical situations, we are privileged to observe both their outward behaviour and the secrets of their hearts; the perspectives of our own moral world are widened as we are drawn into imaginative engagement with their dilemmas; and our awareness is thrown open to the eternal questions and longings that attend our mortal lives.

But in these fragmented times novelists no longer hold sway over the public with the moral authority they once exerted, and the shadow cast by their predecessors' impressive achievements can seem as dauntingly deep as our debt to them. What's more, we now live in times when the often phantasmagorical aspects of what passes for reality can out-trump fiction at every turn. In such a world, asks J.G. Ballard in the preface to his novel *Crash* (1973), can the writer 'any longer make use of the techniques and perspectives of the 19th Century novel, with its linear narrative, its measured chronology, its consular characters grandly inhabiting their domains with an ample time and space? Has the writer still the moral authority to preside over his characters like an examiner knowing all the answers in advance?' Ballard goes on to admit that 'in a sense the writer knows nothing any longer. He has no moral stance. He offers the reader the contents of his own head, a set of options and imaginative alternatives. All he can do is to devise various hypotheses and test them against the facts.'

This diminished version of the novelist was prefigured in the 1960s by an American writer, Ronald Sucenick, who, in a story called *The Death of the Novel*, offered us a kind of extinction myth. 'The contemporary writer is forced to start from scratch,' he declares. 'Reality doesn't exist, time doesn't exist, personality doesn't exist. God was

the omniscient author, but he died; now no-one knows the plot …
In view of these annihilations it should be no surprise that literature,
also, does not exist – how could it? There is only reading and writing
… ways of maintaining a considered boredom in the face of the
abyss.'

You may recognise the cadences of the postmodern voice: dry,
disenchanted, ironically feigning an objectivity it knows to be impossible, and incredulous even of its own negations. Deconstructive
modes of thought have accelerated since then and those of us still
trying to write fiction do so in a climate that has witnessed a collapse
of faith in almost everything, including even the ascendancy of the
critical intellect. With the absolutes gone, we are left mapping a dar-
kling landscape of moral relativities while passing-bells toll not only
for God and the novel but for just about every major aspect of the
Western cultural project – the end of theology, philosophy, art, history, the possibility of objectivity in science as it was once understood, and even of truth itself. Since the 1960s when Sucenick's fictional writer began considering his boredom, the world has moved
on in alarming ways. In an uncertain culture still in shock from the
holocausts of two world wars and their consequences, the planetary
scale of the problems that now demand the best of our consciousness is oppressive enough to daunt the most magisterial imagination.
If in these circumstances writers wish neither to defect from responsibility to this dismal predicament nor to settle for complicity with
its counsellors of despair, in which direction should they turn?

We might start by taking seriously both the possibilities and the
difficulties raised in the postmodern insight (long foreseen by William Blake) that makes the fictional nature of our world transparent
to us. We now recognise ourselves as creatures of story, and if the
reality we inhabit is largely porous to the imagination, then it very
much matters what kind of stories we tell; for, as James Hillman
suggests, 'the manner in which we tell ourselves about what is going
on is the genre through which events become experiences'.

What might happen, then, if we widen our gaze beyond the
mesmerising black holes of the post-postmodern condition to take
in its more positive aspects? Paradoxically, although there may be no
consensus on the nature of reality to guide us through the early

decades of a new millennium, we are endowed with an unprecedentedly wide array of perspectives with which to take our bearings on the issues confronting us.

A walk along the shelves of any good bookshop shows how every important element of the intellectual past is now available to us. What's more, many perspectives that were neglected or demeaned by mainstream Western thought have emerged from the shadows with new relevance. I would cite the revival of interest in pre-Socratic and Neoplatonic philosophers, in mythology, mystery religions, Gnosticism, scholarly astrological perspectives, the hermetic tradition and other intriguing heresies. Wide access is now available to spiritual practices across a broad spectrum: Buddhism, Sufism, Hinduism, Taoism; Native American, Aboriginal, and other shamanic cultures. Meanwhile, science has moved beyond hard-nosed reductionism to offer holistic visions of planetary life which view the material world as intelligent, unfolding, and responsive to our approaches.

Such a plethora of perspectives can easily lead to a sort of pick-and-mix supermarket of consumer beliefs, but another version of the postmodern condition is feasible: that plurality need not be pandemonium. It can offer unprecedented opportunities for imaginative conversation between differing religious, scientific, and philosophical perspectives in all their ambiguity, complexity, and contradictions. Such conversations can open fruitful ground for renewal. It may also be the case that in this centrifugal era of deconstruction and unmasking, of systematic profanation of all the mysteries, a countervailing, centripetal move towards integration is also at work.

Amid all the chaos and confusion of this turbulent world, countless people are on a quest for greater self-knowledge. Stricter minds than mine might consider this to be little more than symptomatic of 'me generation' narcissism. More charitably, such widespread preoccupations could be read as evidence that, consciously or otherwise, renewed attempts are being made to seek the transforming ground of reconciliation between humanity and nature, between subject and object, between the conscious and unconscious minds, between spirit and matter, between intellect and soul.

This is a phenomenon that demands to be taken seriously, a

marvel of our time, and anyone concerned with the writer's role as agent of awareness should, I believe, find much to engage them in developments that presage an evolutionary shift in consciousness. The difficulty is that any writer who attempts to use serious fiction as a credible means of undertaking this task is likely to come up against the resistance of an intellectual mainstream still in thrall to positivist assumptions about what can and cannot be taken seriously as a realistic version of the world.

I have certainly encountered this problem in my own career. Even those reviewers who responded enthusiastically to *The Chymical Wedding* and *The Water Theatre* tended to shift uneasily in their seats when they came across those climactic implications of the narratives which seek to draw the reader's imagination into terrain other than that of conventional social and psychological 'realism' while also refusing to take cover behind the ingenious literary conceits of so-called 'magic realism'. Nor am I alone in this respect.

Much interesting writing of this exploratory order is available only in the virtually samizdat form of publication by small independent houses that have limited resources and therefore limited circulation for the work they sponsor. This is because the commercial preoccupations of what is now aptly termed the 'book industry' keep a tight corporate hold on mainstream publication – and therefore, to a large extent, on the public imagination. My late friend John Moat who, in addition to co-founding the Arvon writing courses, was himself a fine novelist and poet, once said to me, 'Each time I send off a manuscript to a London publishing house, I do so untroubled by hope, and with the feeling that I'm committing the grotesque social gaffe of trying to talk about a big dream at a cocktail party.'

Because compelling dreams have been the source of much of my own writing, and because John's work, like my own, was shaped by the imaginative vision arising from the transformative power of early breakdown, I find his picturesque utterance apposite; and each time I think about it I recall the story of the Peach Blossom Cave.

It's a story that has the virtue of being very ancient, and, though the glamour of fairy tale shimmers over its events, I take it to be a true story too – not least because it's told in a variety of ways across many parts of the world. In the version told by the fourth-century

Chinese poet T'ao Ch'ien, it goes something like this …

In despair at the wretched state of a world riven by violence and oppression, a fisherman allowed his boat to drift into a previously unexplored tributary of a great river. Eventually he came to a stream down which floated a long trail of peach-blossom petals. Made curious by the discovery, he followed the trail upstream to where dense groves of peach trees blossomed on either bank. Deep within the groves he saw the headwaters pouring from the dark mouth of a cave just wide enough for a person to pass through. Deciding to explore further, he tied up his boat and entered the cave. It proved to be a long tunnel that opened at its end on to a bright, fertile land abundant with mulberry trees and bamboo, where people were working happily in the fields. Though surprised to see him, they graciously welcomed him into an arcadian world where they lived in peace and harmony with one another, ignorant of all the evils of war, famine, and injustice which, for five hundred years, had been the dire history of his own country the other side of the Peach Blossom Cave.

The fisherman, it was clear, had stumbled into paradise, and would happily have remained there had not yearning for his family and friends eventually drawn him away. On his departure, the people, whose ancestors had retreated from the misery of the world centuries earlier and had lived apart from it ever since, asked him to keep to himself the secret of their blissful existence. The fisherman promised to do so, but once outside the cave he left markers that would help him to find his way back and then hurried homewards with the belief that the news of his discovery might persuade his people that a happier way of life was possible in their own world too.

Sceptical of his enthusiastic account, the elders of his village demanded that he give them proof of his story by leading them through into the peace and plenty of the other world. But, search as he might, the fisherman could find no trace of the markers he had left. He was never able to find his way back to the stream that led to the land of the Peach Blossom Cave.

The events recounted in that story are not as unusual as they may sound. Doesn't something of the sort happen to those of us who try to argue for a more peaceful and equitable way of managing the world, only to be told by the 'realists' around us that we are deluded, bleeding-heart idealists? And doesn't something of the sort happen when you try to engage another person's reluctant interest in an important dream from which you've just woken?

The difficulty with all such privately initiatory experiences is that, as far as anyone else is concerned, the only sign that something unusual has come to pass is to be seen in its effects on the person to whom it happened. The rest remains (in the dismissive phrase often found on the lips of positivists) merely anecdotal. Yet a life may turn on such a dream or similar visionary experience.

Once the transformative experience is over, there you are, alone with it. You know that something important has happened, something that may have felt so charged with meaning that you know your life can never be quite the same again. Perhaps anticipating that only immediate memoranda would help you recapture its distinctive quality, you kept your wits about you as the experience unfolded and made careful notes afterwards; but it turns out that all sensory evidence of its actuality vanishes at the exit, and you arrive back in the shared world empty-handed. Yet ever afterwards, if you stay true to the claims of the vision, you are, like the fisherman in the story, a denizen of two worlds and must somehow strive to reconcile them.

The world that has not shared the experience will find ways of accounting for it, not least a more or less sympathetic reminder that in all such matters there is (and I don't deny this) much scope for self-delusion. Those around you may be unsettled by the changes it has worked on you, but chances are they will accommodate them on their own terms or give the implications of those changes little serious consideration. You are then left with such knowledge as lodges in the memory and with the story you have tried to tell. Behind both lies the irrecusable authority of the experience itself, but that has now receded out of reach of everything except the imagination and the will. So what matters is what you make of it.

My own solution has been to write novels that have their origins in meaningful personal experience but offer fictional correlatives to that experience in a manner designed both to entertain and to engage the reader's imagination with greater energy than a raw, uncontrived admission of the facts of my own case would achieve. Which means, to be blunt, that my novels have designs on the reader.

In the purist world of the contemporary literary intellect – a world that otherwise seems to be increasingly chary of making value judgements – this is largely regarded as a shameful thing to confess and a disreputable thing to do. For that reason, I think of myself less as a 'novelist', in the way that the term is conventionally understood, than as an activist of the imagination who uses fiction to explore currently unfashionable but potentially fruitful perspectives on experience. Primary among them is a serious insistence on the role of the unconscious mind as a wellspring of the creative process.

Ours is a time pathologically obsessed with conscious control. Think about targeted management systems and scientific experiments, for example; also about the collection and manipulation of data, surveillance techniques, even domestic squabbles over the TV remote, which might be considered a talisman of the age. But beneath this vigilant surface the unconscious abides, beyond control, healthily dissident, quietly performing essential metabolic chores with no conscious effort on our part and sometimes, if we are not careful, running amok with our lives ('Whatever possessed me to do that!?'). Meanwhile, each night it patiently takes over as the ringmaster of our dreams.

In that last respect the unconscious has provided for me a principal source of inspiration. Many years ago, I was summoned out of teaching by a dream in which I was volubly lecturing a group of students when I noticed a newcomer at the back of the class regarding me with a wry expression that seemed to say, 'How much longer do we have to listen to this tosh?' In that shocked moment I recognised him as the poet W.B. Yeats. When he got up and walked out of the room, indicating that I should follow him, I was led into a luminously green garden where he squatted like an Indian yogi, holding a snake in his hands. As bidden, I sat across from him. Not a word was spoken, but it instantly became clear that the question was whether or not I would let his snake bite me.

I sensed what a delirious loss of control it would mean for the venom to swirl through me, and I knew that no antidote was available. I also sensed that to refuse the challenge might be a moral disaster. Before any decision was taken, I woke, sweating, from the tension of the dream. But somewhere I knew that my days as a full-time teacher might be numbered and the time would come when I would either address the long-evaded central challenge of my life – to find the courage to write – or live a frustrated half-life for the rest of my days.

The deeps of the unconscious had shown me both the opportunity and the urgent need to change, and dreams would become the portal of my writing life. Anyone reading *The Chymical Wedding* will see how important dreams are to the narrative, but what may be less apparent is the fact that the novel was written as a way of opening for public consideration a particular dream that had come to me years earlier. In 1980, at a perilous moment in the Cold War, my inability to allay a child's fears of imminent thermonuclear disaster led to a restless night during which came the dream of the Keepers of the Keys – a dream I eventually gave to the narrator of the novel.

Like the potent images of the alchemical opus (see pages 125–44), that dream's archetypal concern with the critical problem of the resolution of opposing forces arose from those unconscious levels of our being which underpin all our lives and which we ignore at our peril. Whatever the dream might have meant for me personally, I was convinced it had wider value. That feeling was affirmed much later by responses to the novel and by the words of the Nobel Prize winning physicist, Wolfgang Pauli, who declared in his lecture on 'Science and Western Thought' that he considered 'the ambition of overcoming opposites, including a synthesis embracing both rational understanding and the mystical experience of unity, to be the mythos, spoken or unspoken, of our present day and age'.

Yet we live in a time when violent conflicts continue to spread the seeds of further violence to come, and when the fissive, exterminating power of nuclear weaponry still hangs over us all. Such are the perilous consequences of our failure to meet Pauli's stated ambition for us, and it is clear that an adequate response to the problem it poses must surely lie beyond the reach of unassisted reason, otherwise it would have been accomplished long ago. Perhaps we will find such a response only by opening ourselves to areas of experience and insight that are not entirely subject to conscious control. Doing so may engage us with matters not considered worthy of serious scientific interest. In this pursuit, novels that make initiatory demands on the active imagination of the reader may have a part to play.

My novel *The Water Theatre* seeks to make such demands. It has its origins in a dream of my dead father which deeply disturbed me at a critical moment in my life and which I later recorded in this previously unpublished 'Dream Poem':

Long after I had thought you safely dead
    you came to me in sleep, where we two
walked together, side by side,
    trying the beer in certain pubs you knew.
I was a man by then and we were friends
at last: you proud of me, and I grown
    tolerant, and glad to be beyond
the years of silent rancour. All the town

lay still around us. I could smell heat
steaming in the kitchens that we passed,
    and knew it Sunday noon and that
our wives were waiting now to lift the roast;
but on we walked on from pub to pub. And it
felt good to shrug and humour you this way,
    to listen to your bar-room wit
and laugh amid the rough complicity

of men, their talk of politics and sport,
their jibes at the expense of women,
    stories of the war they'd fought,
their rants, the dirty jokes they told. But then
the scene had quickly shifted; we were gone,
beer bitter on our breath, to stride out now
    along the quarry-rim alone.
You called to me. Surprised, I turned and saw

you fall, and held you lax and naked at my side,
all strength drained from your limbs, your head

hung slack, the open bedsores red
and weeping at your back as on the day you died.
I jumped awake at that, appalled to know
you dead again with no one standing by
    to help or carry you away, and I
stunned, shaking in my sweat, unable still to let you go.

I gave the dream to the narrator of *The Water Theatre*, the war re-
porter Martin Crowther, but what I did not include in his narrative
was an account of the immediate aftermath of my dream. I decided
to omit it, not out of any sense of personal embarrassment, but because I thought it would too heavily tax that willing credulity of the
reader on which serious novels depend. I have, however, decided to
speak of it here because of the evidence (albeit anecdotal) that it offers of the wider creative reach of the unconscious mind.

Waking in shock from the dream, I did what I often do when I
feel in need of wiser guidance than my native wit can provide: I
turned to the *I Ching*, hoping it would help me understand the import of the most deranging dream I had experienced in a long time.
Hurriedly, without any meditative preparation, I cast the coins six
times, building a hexagram of six lines according to their apparently
random fall. The pattern they formed pointed me to Hexagram 18,
Ku / 'Work on What Has Been Spoiled (Decay)'. The first line of
the hexagram had been determined by the fall of the coins as three
tails, which meant that it was charged with particular significance for
my situation. Eager to find out what that was, I reached for the Wil-
helm translation of the *I Ching*, but in my haste I opened the book
not on the principal Text of the hexagrams in Book One, but on the
Later Commentaries which are recorded in Book Three. Turning
there to Hexagram 18, my eyes fell immediately on the commentary
on that first line. It had this to say:

> 'Setting right what has been spoiled by the father.'
> He receives in his thoughts the deceased father.

Later, calmer reflection on the meaning of the entire hexagram
made it clear that the dream had reached me because at that stage of

my life I was still lamentably prone to the kind of male chauvinist behaviour that may have been socially acceptable among the northern working men of my father's day but was deeply questionable in mine. Metaphorically speaking, I was carrying my dead father around with me, and what the *I Ching* called 'rigid adherence to tradition' had resulted in decay. If I were to correct that behaviour, the hexagram instructed, I would not only improve my own moral welfare, I would relieve my dead father of any blame for the decay in human relations which he and his generation had, in the words of the book, 'allowed to creep in'.

However, the immediate point of this story is less to advertise my own (belated) moral development than to draw attention to the acausal manner in which the activity of the unconscious not only prompted awareness of a serious problem through vivid dream imagery, but also directed attention to a three-thousand-years-old oracular text that spoke to my situation with startling precision. I had indeed received in my thoughts the deceased father.

As evidence that subtle forces other than the normal laws of causality are powerfully active in our affairs, this event is entirely anecdotal, unquantifiable, and not replicable on its own specific terms. To a positivist mindset. the symmetry between the images of my dream and the text of the hexagram might be dismissible as either coincidence or delusive claptrap. But, like the fisherman in the Peach Blossom Cave, I know that something remarkable happened, and I know that my life is richer for its openness to wonder in such matters than it was when I lived within the confines of a narrow, controlling rationalism that seeks to legislate about what is acceptably real.

If I had included in my novel an account of this synchronistic aftermath to the dream, I would have been accused of a shameless authorial fix. Such meaningful coincidences are not acceptable in contemporary fiction – except perhaps as an ironical gesture of the ludic imagination. In any case, the need to challenge that judgement did not arise because the mental state of my narrator, Martin Crowther, was not, at that moment of his career, that of a man inclined to consult an ancient oracle for advice. Yet the point I'm trying to make still holds. As things stand, anyone wishing to be taken seriously as a novelist has to be aware that, however true such an event might be to one's experience, an account of it can have no respectable place in literary fiction.

This has not always been the case. Ancient romances and early modern novels are packed with coincidences. Strip even one of the greatest novels ever written down to its narrative structure (as happened for TV adaptation) and *War and Peace* is revealed as riddled with chance meetings and coincidences. Meanwhile, now as ever, countless people are occasionally wonderstruck by such events in their lived experience, and often in such life-altering ways that mere coincidence seems an inadequate explanation for their occurrence.

Why should this present a problem for contemporary fiction? Can a brand of scientific materialism, with its claims to strict objectivity and its roots in a well-founded mistrust of the abuse of power by organised religion, have instituted among the intellectual mainstream a form of intellectual censorship which seeks to rule out of court the authority of the individual soul's unprovable experience? And, if so, are subtle dimensions of existence, which have been indispensable features of a meaningful life throughout generations of our history, also being jammed from serious consideration, if not actually erased, by that school of secular fundamentalism?

I am thinking, for instance, of the wisdom tradition associated with divination, which is an active and open form of prayer. In their attempts to align human purposes with their understanding of sacred order, highly intelligent people of the ancient world (as of traditional cultures everywhere) were wise enough to trust that sources of guidance lying beyond the range of human ingenuity could be made available through consultation with oracles. In one form or another, all such divinatory practices seem to demonstrate the activity of what Jung called the acausal connecting principle of synchronicity. They rely on the belief that whatever happens in any given moment possesses the quality peculiar to that moment, and that all its relations are charged with meaning that is legible and comprehensible if one is appropriately attentive.

Nor does access to such guidance require a solemn ritual process. In what the Greeks called a 'cledon', for example, the words of a voice randomly overheard in the street can spark a creative thought or a sudden moment of decision. Many writers, not all of them with a taste for the mystical, will confess to a grateful fondness for the timely manner in which the invisible Library Angel answers their need by bringing exactly the right book to hand at the perfect moment.

In certain gifted individuals – mediums, clairvoyants, shamans, poets – such synchronistic divinatory powers may be more keenly attuned to unusual frequencies of intelligence than is the case for most of us. Yet, because those faculties arise from the shared depths of the unconscious, we all have a degree of access to them, and if taken seriously they can be trained and developed. That being the case, their effective performance must surely raise thought-provoking questions about our standard perceptions of time, space, causality, and the structural order of the world around us and within.

As the pioneering depth psychologist Gerhard Adler once asked, 'Are the experiences we encounter predestined, or do we feel them so intensely and remember them so well because of inner need? Or is there a coincidence of inner needs and outer events, an intercon-nectedness of within and without, which makes this division into two spheres irrelevant and even misleading?' 'As above, so below,' the old alchemists insisted, and the comprehensive statistical studies conducted at the Sorbonne by Michel Gauquelin have demonstrated that there is a significant correlation between the position of the planets at the moment of birth and the course of an individual life. Practitioners of astrology encounter many striking examples of syn-chronicity in their work, perhaps because, as Liz Greene suggests in *The Astrology of Fate*, 'once one enters this archetypal "field" one rap-idly becomes exposed to the strange way in which it seems to "or-der" both outer and inner events'. Something similar might be said of practising psychoanalysts, and of clairvoyants whose capacity to 'see' future events seems to belie the serial nature of time. Nor does this capacity belong only to those engaged in depth psychology or the psychically gifted. In her memoir *Unremarried Widow*, Artis Hen-derson records how her husband, the pilot of an Apache helicopter gunship, told her of a dream in which he witnessed, as he rose above burning wreckage, what proved months later to be the exact circum-stances of his death in the course of the war in Iraq.

That dream arose from the unconscious that exists, Jung be-lieved, in an 'irrepresentable space-time continuum' in which past, present, and future are an indivisible field. Perhaps in such a field every moment is unbounded, timeless, and eternal, and synchronicity and continuity thus elide. If that possibility is true of time, then might space also be a related seamless field – not merely the vacant emptiness for which we take it, but an active medium vibrant with its own subtle conduits of intelligence?

Who knows? But the questions have consequences for the way in which we see the world and the way in which we understand the dimensionality of our human nature within it. I should say too that, though I have been critical of the more reductive tendencies of the scientific attitude, I also recognise that scientists working at the cutting edge – particularly the quantum physicists and the deep ecologists– are well aware of the issues and have greatly contributed to a fuller appreciation of the subtle psychophysical fabric that holds the world together, as they have also enhanced our sense of wonder.

Here too, to return to my own central concern, fascinating prospects have been opened up for imaginative work in fiction. In the 1950s Lawrence Durrell's *Alexandria Quartet* attempted a quasi-cubist narrative form that dramatised the space-time relativities of Einstein's universe, intercalating sexuality and spirituality, politics and art, against a background of world war. Later, the ambiguities in the behaviour of quantum particles engaged Ian McEwan's imagination in his novel *A Child in Time*, and in *The Medusa Factor* Russell Hoban wrote, 'what passes for reality seems to me mostly a load of old rubbish invented by not very inventive minds. The reality that interests me is strange and flickering and haunting.' More recently, a heightened ecological awareness has required some writers – Alan Garner and Paul Kingsnorth are good examples – to follow the earlier explorations of John Cowper Powys into the role of landscape in human drama.

As for my own work, *The Chymical Wedding* was a pioneering attempt to pursue the implications of a dual narrative set in two different but interpenetrating time zones. Shortly after it was published I came across a reference to a paper on quantum correlations at subatomic levels which describes how 'two events happening at different times influence each other in such a way that they seem to be happening at the same time. In fact, they manage to reach across time in some synchronized dance that defies all our common-sense bound imagination.' This paper describing the behaviour of particles felt like an accurate, if somewhat abstract, synopsis of my novel.

It appears that the world is always stranger than we think and we are always living on the edge of the unknown. But the novel, as an imaginative instrument of metaphysical enquiry, offers an engaging means to explore whatever might be out there in the darkness, or here, in the darkness inside. I often regret that the name we use for that darkness – the 'unconscious' – is posed as a negative term – that which is not conscious – rather than affirming it as an autonomous life-force in its own right. Yes, as psychoanalysis has shown us, its impersonal, archetypal powers can certainly trip us up, even swallow us up, if we fail to establish good relations with them, and it's certainly the lair of our repressed emotions and unacknowledged shadow side; yet, as an aspect of the soul, it is also a marvellous reservoir of wisdom and sustenance, which generously makes itself available through our dreams, through our activated imagination and calmer meditative states, and through oracular, synchronistic, or otherwise daimonic events that alert our lives to a larger order of being.

This is far from a comprehensive account of its mysterious nature. I can offer no adequate account of the source of its intelligence or of its astonishing range of reference, and I have no explanation of the means by which it works on us. Nor do I even know whether it's inside us or outside us or both simultaneously. What I remain convinced of, however, is that the more deeply we relate to the unconscious, and diligently work to assimilate the significance of its archetypal imagery for the way we live our lives, the more fully conscious we become.

Such deep engagement is an initiatory process through which we undertake the rites of individuation. By intimately acquainting ourselves with the impersonal ground – the fluid magma, if you prefer – that underpins all of our lives, and by building a conscious relationship with its formative energies, we may enhance the possibility of our evolution into the unique self whom we were always meant to be, and without which the total scheme of things could never be complete. If at the same time, we remain open to the frequencies of intelligence which reach us from the animate world around us, we may attain a still more comprehensive perspective that recognises the nature of consciousness, not as a mere epiphenomenon of neural activity – a property tightly confined inside the human brain – but as an intrinsic quality of the manifest cosmic order, from which the star-stuff of life emerged and to which we deeply belong.

It would be foolish to believe that such initiations are ever easy. We may be given glimpses of the land beyond the Peach Blossom Cave but we have to return again and again to the troubled world where our present loyalties lie. Yet we shouldn't let ourselves be discouraged from sharing the traveller's tales we have to tell, however dubious their reception; rather we should hold on to the courage to stand inside our own truth while keeping the imagination wisely open to the possibility of truth in what other earnest explorers tell of their discoveries – however strange and improbable their stories may seem to be.

# Haiku

Observe with wonder.
Penetrate this present depth.
Life is not elsewhere.

# Acknowledgements

The author wishes to express his gratitude to the Royal Literary Fund for its generous assistance during recent years. He also wishes to thank the editors of the books and magazines in which some of these essays were originally published, and the organisers of those events in which the talks were delivered. A particular debt of thanks is owed to Adam Thorpe's Grand Phoenix Press, through which some of the poems first appeared, and to Anthony Nanson of Awen Publications, whose enthusiasm prompted the compilation of this book and who went on to edit its pages with a keen mind and an acutely scrupulous eye.

# Bibliography

Ackroyd, Peter, *Blake*, Sinclair Stevenson, 1995

Anderson, William, *Green Man: The Archetype of Our Oneness with the Earth*, HarperCollins, 1990

Bachelard, Gaston, *On Poetic Imagination and Reverie*, Spring, 1987

Barfield, Owen *Poetic Diction*, McGraw-Hill, 1964

Baring, Anne and Jules Cashford, *The Myth of the Goddess: Evolution of an Image*, Viking, 1991

Barker, George, *In Memory of David Archer*, Faber & Faber, 1973

Beer, Gillian, *The Romance*, Methuen, 1970

Booth, Wayne C., *The Company We Keep*, University of California Press, 1988

Booth, Wayne C., *The Rhetoric of Fiction*, University of Chicago Press, 1961

Broch, Hermann, *The Style of the Mythical*, Bollingen Foundation, 1975

Brook, Peter, *The Empty Space*, Avon, 1968

Campbell, Joseph, *The Masks of God: Occidental Mythology*, Viking Penguin, 1964

Cashford, Jules (trans.), *The Homeric Hymns*, Penguin, 2003

Cashford, Jules, *The Moon: Myth and Image*, Cassell, 2003

Coen, Arthur A., *Tremendum: A Theological Interpretation of the Holocaust*, Crossroad, 1988

Collingwood, R.G., *The Principles of Art*, Clarendon Press, 1938

Doody, Margaret Anne, *The True Story of the Novel*, HarperCollins, 1997

Fowles, John, *Wormholes: Essays and Occasional Writings*, edited by Jan Relf, Jonathan Cape, 1998

Fraser, Robert, *The Chameleon Poet: A Life of George Barker*, Jonathan Cape, 2001

Greene, Liz, *The Astrology of Fate*, Weiser Books, 1984

Harpur, James, *Angels and Harvesters*, Anvil, 2012

Harpur, Patrick, *A Complete Guide to the Soul*, Rider, 2010

Harpur, Patrick, *The Philosopher's Secret Fire: A History of the Imagination*, Blue Angel, 2002

Hillman, James, *Healing Fiction*, Station Hill Press, 1983

Hillman, James, *The Soul's Code*, Random House, 1996

Hooker, Jermey, *Imagining Wales*, University of Wales Press, 2001

Hughes, Ted, *The Hawk in the Rain*, Faber & Faber, 1957

Hughes, Ted, *River*, Faber & Faber, 1983

Hughes, Ted, *Shakespeare and the Goddess of Complete Being*, Faber & Faber, 1992

Hughes, Ted, *Winter Pollen*, Faber & Faber, 1995

Jung, C.G., *Answer to Job: Researches into the Relation between Psychology and Religion*, Routledge, 1984

Jung, C.G., *Memories, Dreams and Reflections*, Routledge & Kegan Paul, 1963

Jung, C.G., *Mysterium Coniunctionis*, Routledge & Kegan Paul, 1963

Jung, C.G., *Psychology and Alchemy*, Routledge & Kegan Paul, 1953

Lodge, David, *Consciousness and the Novel*, Secker &Warburg, 2002

Loveday, Simon, *The Romances of John Fowles*, Palgrave Macmillan, 1986

Lubbock, Percy, *The Craft of Fiction*, Jonathan Cape, 1921

Mails, Thomas E., *Mystic Warriors of the Plains*, Council Oak Books, 1995

McGilchrist, Iain, *The Master and His Emissary*, Yale University Press, 2012

Moore, Thomas (ed.), *The Essential James Hillman: A Blue Fire*, Routledge, 1990

Oswald, Alice, *Memorial*, Faber & Faber, 2011

Paget, R.F., *In the Footsteps of Orpheus*, Scientific Book Club, 1967

Peltier, Jacqueline, *Proteus and the Magician*, Powys Society, 2014

Powys, John Cowper, *Autobiography*, Macdonald, 1967

Powys, John Cowper, *A Glastonbury Romance*, Macdonald, 1933

Powys, John Cowper, *The Pleasures of Literature*, Cassell, 1938

Powys, John Cowper, *Porius*, Overlook Duckworth, 2007

Powys, John Cowper, *Visions and Revisions*, G. Arnold Shaw, 1915

Rees, Alwyn and Brinley Rees, *Celtic Heritage: Ancient Tradition in Ireland and Wales*, Thames & Hudson, 1961

Roszak, Theodore, *The Voice of the Earth: Explorations in Ecopsychology*, Phanes Press, 2001

Sagar, Keith, *The Laughter of Foxes*, Liverpool University Press, 2000

Stevens, Anthony, *Private Myths: Dreams and Dreaming*, Hamish Hamilton, 1995

Tarnas, Richad, *The Passion of the Western Mind*, Harmony Books, 1991

Yeats, W.B., *Mythologies*, Macmillan, 1959

*Also available from Awen Publications:*

# A Dance with Hermes
## Lindsay Clarke

In a verse sequence that swoops between wit and ancient wisdom, between the mystical and the mischievous, award-winning novelist Lindsay Clarke elucidates the trickster nature of Hermes, the messenger god of imagination, language, dreams, travel, theft, tweets, and trading floors, who is also the presiding deity of alchemy and the guide of souls into the otherworld. Taking a fresh look at some classical myths, this vivacious dance with Hermes choreographs ways in which, as an archetype of the poetic basis of mind, the sometimes disreputable god remains as provocative as ever in a world that worries – among other things – about losing its iPhone, what happens after death, online scams, and the perplexing condition of its soul.

Poetry/Mythology ISBN 978-1906900-43-4 £9.99

# Soul of the Earth: the Awen anthology of eco-spiritual poetry
## edited by Jay Ramsay

Beautifully crafted, yet challenging received wisdom and pushing boundaries, these are cutting-edge poems from a new generation of writers who share a love of the Earth and haven't given up on humans either. In poems as light as a butterfly and as wild as a storm you'll find vivid, contemporary voices that dare to explore a spiritual dimension to life on Earth and, in doing so, imply that a way out of our global crisis of ecological catastrophe, financial meltdown, and bankruptcy of the spirit is to look beyond the impasse of materialism. With contributions from poets in the USA, Canada, UK, Australia, and New Zealand, this anthology reaches out across the planet to embrace the challenges and blessings of being alive on the Earth in the twenty-first century.

'All real poetry seeks to "renew the face of the earth" – and so to resist the exploiting, banalization or defacing of what lies around us. I hope this collection will serve the renewal of vision we so badly need.'
*Most Revd Dr Rowan Williams*

Poetry/Spirituality ISBN 978-1-906900-17-5 £12.00

# Ditch Vision:
## essays on poetry, nature, and place
### Jeremy Hooker

*Ditch Vision* is a book of essays on poetry, nature, and place that extends Jeremy Hooker's thinking on subjects that, as a distinguished critic and poet, he has made his life's work. The writers he considers include Edward Thomas, Robert Frost, Robinson Jeffers, Richard Jefferies, John Cowper Powys, Mary Butts, and Frances Bellerby. Through sensitive readings of these and other writers, he discusses differences between British and American writers concerned with nature and spirit of place. The book also includes essays in which he reflects upon the making of his own work as a lyric poet. Written throughout with a poet's feeling for language, *Ditch Vision* is the work of an exploratory writer who seeks to understand the writings he discusses in depth, and to illuminate them for other readers. Hooker explores the 'ground' of poetic vision with reference to its historical and mythological contexts, and in this connection *Ditch Vision* constitutes also a spiritual quest.

Literary Criticism  ISBN 978-1906900-51-9  £14.00

# Words of Re-enchantment: writings on
## storytelling, myth, and ecological desire
### Anthony Nanson

The time-honoured art of storytelling – ancestor of all narrative media – is finding new pathways of relevance in education, consciousness-raising, and the journey of transformation. Storytellers are reinterpreting ancient myths and communicating the new stories we need in our challenging times. This book brings together the best of Anthony Nanson's incisive writings about the ways that story can re-enchant our lives and the world we live in. Grounded in his practice as a storyteller, the essays range from the myths of Arthur, Arcadia, and the voyage west, to true tales of the past, science-fiction visions of the future, and the big questions of politics and spirituality such stories raise. The book contains full texts of exemplar stories and will stimulate the thinking of anyone interested in storytelling or in the use of myth in fiction and film.

'This excellent book is written with a storyteller's cadence and understanding of language. Passionate, fascinating and wise.' *Hamish Fyfe*

Storytelling/Mythology/Environment  ISBN 978-1-906900-15-1  £9.99

# Exotic Excursions
## Anthony Nanson

In these stories Anthony Nanson charts the territory between travel writing and magic realism to confront the exotic and the enigmatic. Here are epiphanies of solitude, twilight and initiation. A lover's true self unveiled by a mountain mist ... a memory of the lost land in the western sea ... a traveller's surrender to the allure of ancient gods ... a quest for primeval beings on the edge of extinction. In transcending the line between the written and the spoken word, between the familiar and the unfamiliar, between the actual and the imagined, these tales send sparks across the gap of desire.

Fiction/Travel  ISBN 987-0-9546137-7-8  £7.99

# Iona
## Mary Palmer

What do you do when you are torn apart by your 'selves'? The pilgrim poet, rebel Mordec and tweedy Aelia set sail for Iona – a thin place, an island on the edge. It's a journey between worlds, back to the roots of their culture. On the Height of Storm they relive a Viking massacre, at Port of the Coracle encounter vipers. They meet Morrighan, a bloodthirsty goddess, and Abbot Dominic with his concubine nuns. There are omens, chants, curses ... During her stay Mordec learns that words can heal or destroy, and the poet writes her way out of darkness. A powerful story, celebrating a journey to wholeness, from an accomplished poet.

Poetry  ISBN 978-0-9546137-8-5  £6.99  Spirit of Place Volume 1

# Mysteries
## Chrissy Derbyshire

This enchanting and exquisitely crafted collection by Chrissy Derbyshire will whet your appetite for more from this superbly talented wordsmith. Her short stories interlaced with poems depict chimeras, femmes fatales, mountebanks, absinthe addicts, changelings, derelict warlocks, and persons foolhardy enough to stray into the beguiling world of Faerie. Let the sirens' song seduce you into the Underworld ...

Fiction/Poetry  ISBN 978-1-906900-45-8  £8.99

# The Firekeeper's Daughter
## Karola Renard

From the vastness of Stone Age Siberia to a minefield in today's Angola, from the black beaches of Iceland to the African savannah and a Jewish-German cemetery, Karola Renard tells thirteen mythic stories of initiation featuring twenty-first-century kelpies, sirens, and holy fools, a river of tears and a girl who dances on fire, a maiden shaman of ice, a witch in a secret garden, Queen Guinevere's mirror, and a woman who swallows the moon. The red thread running through them all is a deep faith in life and the need to find truth and meaning even in the greatest of ordeals.

Fiction  ISBN 978-1-906900-46-5  £9.99

# The Long Woman
## Kevan Manwaring

An antiquarian's widow discovers her husband's lost journals and sets out on a journey of remembrance across 1920s England and France, retracing his steps in search of healing and independence. Along alignments of place and memory she meets mystic Dion Fortune, ley-line pioneer Alfred Watkins, and a Sir Arthur Conan Doyle obsessed with the Cottingley Fairies. From Glastonbury to Carnac, she visits the ancient sites that obsessed her husband and, tested by both earthly and unearthly forces, she discovers a power within herself.

Fiction  ISBN 978-1-906900-44-1  £9.99  The Windsmith Elegy Volume 1

# The Fifth Quarter
## Richard Selby

The Fifth Quarter is Romney Marsh, as defined by the Revd Richard Harris Barham in *The Ingoldsby Legends*: 'The World, according to the best geographers, is divided into Europe, Asia, Africa, America and Romney Marsh.' It is a place apart, almost another world. This collection of stories and poems explores its ancient and modern landscapes, wonders at its past, and reflects upon its present. Richard Selby has known Romney Marsh all his life. His writing reflects the uniqueness of The Marsh through prose, poetry, and written versions of stories he performs as a storyteller.

Fiction/Poetry  ISBN 978-0-9546137-9-2  £9.99  Sprit of Place Volume 2

# Glossing the Spoils
## Charlotte Hussey

Each poem in *Glossing the Spoils* works like an intricate time-travel machine, carrying the reader back to the beginnings of Western European literature. Like an ancient clapper bridge with its unmortared slabs of flat sandstone, these poems step us across the choppy currents of the past 1500 years. Anchored at one end in the deep past and at the other in the turbulent present, they explore interconnections between historical, personal, psychological, and mythic states. Plundering their opening passages from such early texts as *Beowulf*, *The Mabinogion*, and *The Tain*, these glosas address eternal themes of love and war and give voice to the surreal potency of the Western European imagination.

'I would highly recommend *Glossing the Spoils* … as exemplary in re-envisioning the oldest myths of Western European tradition with formal mastery.' *Lorna Smithers*

Poetry ISBN 978-1-906900-52-6 £8.99

# Pilgrimage:
## a journey to Love Island
## Jay Ramsay

In the summer of 1990 Jay Ramsay set out on pilgrimage with an interfaith group from London to Iona. The result is his most ambitious book-length poem, an astonishing tour de force in the tradition of Wordsworth and Chaucer. Epiphanic, conversational, meditational, psychological, political, it divines 'the cross' of spiritual and ecological being in Britain's radical tradition, as symbolised by Iona as the crown of the Celtic church and the direction that Christianity lost. Constructed as a series of 25 'days', the narrative builds symphonically like waves of the sea up to its visionary climax. Full of stories, reflections, memories, and images, Pilgrimage is above all a love poem, an invitation into the greater love that is our true becoming where we can find the God most personal to all of us – alive in the heart of Life.

'It is strange and beautiful how everything he passes comes into colour, into focus – is born. And I ran along after him and listened as he changed the colour of the sea and broke down doors.' *Peter Owwn Jones*

Poetry/Spirituality ISBN 978-1906900-54-0 £15.00

# By the Edge of the Sea:
## short stories
### Nicolas Kurtovitch

Nicolas Kurtovitch is one of the leading literary figures in the French-speaking country of New Caledonia in the South Pacific. The twelve short stories in *By the Edge of the Sea* are written with a poet's sensitivity to style and the significance of what's left unsaid. They convey an enchantment of place in their evocation of physical settings; an enchantment too of the conscious moment; a big-hearted engagement with indigenous cultures and perspectives; and arising from all these a sense of possibility permeating beyond what the eye can see. This seminal first collection of Kurtovitch's stories appears here in English for the first time, together with an introduction to the author's work and New Caledonian background.

'This collection of stories retains its appeal and importance, its freshness, a quarter-century after it first appeared, and that can now be appreciated for the first time by an English-speaking public thanks to Anthony Nanson's careful and sensitive translation.' *Peter Brown*

Fiction  ISBN 978-1-906900-53-3  £9.99

# The Tragicall History of
# Campbell McCluskie
### Alistair McNaught

The question that haunts Ian Alexander MacDuffy is why the playwright Campbell McCluskie was murdered at 10.30 p.m. on Wednesday 16 June 1954, for that was the very moment that Ian's mother died giving birth to him. The coincidence suggests that some universal meaning may lie behind that gratuitous and painful event. Ian tries to uncover every detail of Campbell's short but eventful life: the guilt-ridden hypocrisy of his grandfather; his father's success as a shoe manufacturer; his childhood in Clydebank; the death of his favourite aunt; his bewildering role in the D-Day landings; his post-war success as a playwright; his passionate and colourful love life; his ambiguous relations with the criminal underworld; his violent death – because as Campbell himself wrote, in his inimitable style, 'It's all down tae patterns and figures; if you can decipher them, then Auld Nickie-Ben'll dance tae your tune.'

Fiction  ISBN 978-1-906900-55-7  £10.99

# Dancing with Dark Goddesses:
## movements in poetry
### Irina Kuzminsky

The dance is life – life is the dance – in all its manifestations, in all its sorrow and joy, cruelty and beauty. And the faces of the Dark Goddesses are many – some are dark with veiling and unknowing, some are dark with sorrow, some are dark with mystery and a light so great that it paradoxically shades them from sight. The poems in this collection are an encounter with many of these faces, in words marked with feminine energy and a belief in the transformative power of the poetic word. Spiritual and sexual, earthy and refined, a woman's voice speaks to women and to the feminine in women and men – of an openness to life, a surrender to the workings of love, and a trust in the Dark Goddesses and their ways of leading us through the dance.

'A mythological journey of archetypes.' *Richard McKane*

Poetry/Dance ISBN 978-1906900-12-0 £9.99

# Silver Branch:
## bardic poems and letters to a young bard
### Kevan Manwaring

What does it mean to write and perform bardic poetry in the twenty-first century? This monumental collection, from the author of *The Bardic Handbook* and *The Way of Awen*, brings together 25 years of selected verse to explore that challenge. The diverse range of poems can be enjoyed for their own sake and will also inspire others to craft and voice their own creative responses to identity, ecology, and community, grounded in the body, the land, and conviction. *Silver Branch* includes an introduction to the author's practice as a performance poet, originally published as *Speak Like Rain*, along with the Bardic-Chair-winning poem *Spring Fall*; *Bio\*Wolf*; *Green Fire*; *Dragon Dance*; *The Taliesin Soliloquies*; *Thirteen Treasures*; poems from the stage shows *Arthur's Dream*, *Robin of the Wildwood*, *Return to Arcadia*, and *Song of the Windsmith*; plus more recent bardic poems and songs.

'Within *Silver Branch*, the ancient and modern worlds are woven together in the remaking with which we have to engage at every moment, perceiving the ancient and allowing its currency to irrigate our time and deepen our, often, surface culture.' *Caitlín Matthews*

Poetry/Mythology ISBN 978-1-906900-42-7 £16.00